To Ron—

In the magic of His love—

Rudi Nelson

Matt. 25: 35-40

# DOIN' TIME

## AN IN-DEPTH LOOK AT LIFE BEHIND BARS THROUGH A WINDOW OF HOPE

# RICK NIELSEN with RON KUNTZ

DOIN' TIME

Rick Nielsen, Doin' Time

ISBN 1-887002-31-6

**Cross Training Publishing**
**1604 S. Harrison St.**
**Grand Island, NE 68803**
**(308) 384-5762**

This book is manufactured in the United States of America.

Library of Congress Cataloging in Publication Data in Progress.

Published by Cross Training Publishing,
1604 S. Harrison St.
Grand Island, NE 68803

# DEDICATIONS

**Rick Nielsen–**

I'd like to dedicate *Doin' Time* to Bunny Martin and also to the entire family of counselors on the Bill Glass team. *Bunny, you have been my mentor and friend. Thanks for breaking me into magic and for initiating my involvement with the Weekends of Champions. I cherish all the great memories we've shared–in and out of prison–and especially our friendship. You have inspired me spiritually and professionally.*

And counselors, you truly are the unsung heroes of the Bill Glass Prison Ministry. Dr. Joseph R. Sizoo best describes you:

## Unsung Heroes

Let it never be forgotten that glamour is not greatness; applause is not fame; prominence is not eminence. The man of the hour is not apt to be the man of the ages. A stone may sparkle, but that does not make it a diamond; a man may have money, but that does not make him a success. It is what the unimportant do that really counts and determines the course of history. The greatest forces in the universe are never spectacular. Summer showers are more effective than hurricanes, but they get no publicity. The world would soon die but for the fidelity, loyalty and consecration of those whose names are unhonored and unsung.

**Ron Kuntz–**

I'd like to dedicate this book to my wife, Nancy, and all of my family who have permitted me to visit hundreds of prisons across the country over the past twenty-five years, and also to the thousands of men and women who faithfully serve in prison ministries in the United States, entering Satan's stronghold with the good news of the Gospel of Jesus Christ. I count it all joy that God has allowed me to be a part of this great adventure, sharing the love of our Lord with inmates.

# CONTENTS

Foreword    7

About the Authors    9

Acknowledgments    13

Introducing . . . Bill Glass    17

Art and Thoughts From Charlie's Cell    19

Introduction    21

1. *What is a Weekend of Champions?*    *23*

2. *Ron's First Prison Weekend*    *37*

3. *Rick's First Weekend of Champions*    *41*

4. *Platform Guests – Past and Present*    *67*

5. *Counselors, Coordinators, & Prison Ministry Directors*    *81*

6. *Prison Staff – Officers and Chaplains*    *115*

7. *Ex-Offenders Involved*    *129*

8. *Death Row Experiences*    *147*

9. *Divine Appointments*    *179*

10. *Personal Encounters*    *201*

11. *Can You Keep a Secret?*    *241*

# FOREWORD

*Doin' Time* is an intriguing title because all of us are "doing time." The only difference between the people doing time in Rick Nielsen's book and the rest of us is that they are people who are doing their time behind bars, many on "death row."

For the casual reader or those who simply glance at the title or read the dust jacket, it might be difficult to believe this is an inspiring book. However, if victory is inspiring, then *Doin' Time* is an inspiring book. Rick shares his heartwarming experiences behind prison walls and steel bars. In vivid detail he describes the fears, doubts, anger, hatred, loneliness, despair, depression, paranoia and every negative human emotion imaginable that inmates, particularly those on death row, experience. The inspiration comes when these men and women, with tear-filled eyes, express in childlike gratitude the peace which comes with the ultimate victory, the committing of their lives to Christ. Their victory over sin and death, with the assurance that their sins are forgiven, helps them know that their time in prison was more than worthwhile.

Rick Nielsen gives you a different perspective as you learn about some of these hardened criminals who had lived lives of crime and the changes that take place in their lives when they commit themselves to Christ. It makes you realize that they, too, are human beings and that Christ died for them, just as He did for you and me. You also get a different perspective about the difference it can make when someone is treated with respect. I was particularly moved as Rick shared the story of his experience with an inmate named Ken. After a shaky beginning, Rick got his attention with card tricks. Then Ken opened up, began to talk, and Rick was able, through the grace of God, to lead him to Christ. Ken expressed his gratitude by sharing his meager resources in a unique way, which was to prepare Rick a cup of coffee using a very unusual method.

The other part of the story is what made the first part possible. Captain Bill Treadwell was the officer in charge of "H-Block," and Rick was fascinated by the fact that as Treadwell took him around he assured him that all of these men had some good qualities. One was a poet, one an artist, another loved his family, etc. As Captain Treadwell introduced

Rick to each inmate, he had something good to say about him. He called the men by name, shook their hands and treated them with respect.

Not long after that memorable experience, Rick learned that Treadwell had required heart surgery and had retired. On his last day on the job many of these "hardened" criminals were heard weeping. Captain Bill Treadwell had sown the seeds and God had used Rick Nielsen to reap the harvest. Message: regardless of who you are and what you do, you, too, can touch lives with words of hope, encouragement and respect. And God can use you to claim souls for the Kingdom.

As part of the Bill Glass ministry, Rick Nielsen volunteers as many as one hundred days each year to go into prisons and help his fellow-man. Nationally, there are several thousand men and women who regularly volunteer and, of the dozens I have talked with, without exception, they always say they are the ones who are the big winners. If you're a person who really believes it is better to give than to receive and that "he who would be the greatest among you must first become a servant of all," you will find *Doin' Time* a valuable investment to read and share with friends.

Zig Ziglar
Author
*Over The Top*

# ABOUT THE AUTHORS

## Rick Nielsen

Rick Nielsen is the founder of Blueprint For Life, Inc. As president of this nonprofit corporation, he speaks and entertains for a wide variety of audiences including corporations, schools, churches, and athletic teams. He consistently demonstrates a unique ability to relate to audiences of all ages and occupations. Not only a dynamic speaker, he is also a magician, juggler, and humorist. The combination of these talents provides a motivational, inspirational, and entertaining program. He is a member of the National Speakers Association and has been a keynote speaker from coast to coast, sharing the platform with many successful people.

After graduating from the University of Northern Iowa, Rick was a teacher and a coach. He then became Iowa's first State Director for the Fellowship of Christian Athletes, coordinating the growth of the program into one of the strongest in the nation.

With messages and programs that address the needs of today's students, he has become one of the most popular and requested speakers on high school and college campuses nationwide. Leading business professionals have all agreed that Rick's program is a sound investment in the success of their companies. Within the framework of the church, his presentations provide a strong spiritual challenge, and many congregations have been encouraged in their faith through his inspirational outreach. Having been an outstanding high school and college athlete and a coach, Rick is right at home in the sports world, frequently speaking to high school, college, and professional sports teams. He has been involved in numerous videotape projects including tapes on goal setting and self-image in the Survival Guide for Teenagers series, and has served as host on two 5-tape video series on parenting and marriage.

Since 1985, Rick has volunteered a great deal of his time serving in every position with the Bill Glass Prison Ministry's Weekends of Champions as counselor, coordinator, platform guest, and weekend director, and has participated in over one hundred weekends through a decade of active participation. His work includes frequent visits to death rows, segregation lockdowns, AIDS wards, and hospital units, and he has been in over three hundred of America's toughest prisons.

Rick and his wife, Jan, have two daughters, Jennie and Julie, and make their home in Des Moines, Iowa.

### Ron Kuntz

A natural progression from his high school interest in photography led Ron to his current status as one of the most renowned photographers in the world. He started his illustrious career with United Press International (UPI) in 1953. During forty years behind the camera, he has literally been around the world.

As a photographer in the Army, Ron was assigned to a ship that traveled above the Arctic Circle to shoot pictures of the resupplying of the DEW (Distant Early Warning System) line. The following year he spent four months on Greenland's ice cap, six hundred miles from the North Pole, taking pictures of Camp Century, a camp that would later be operated by atomic power underneath the ice.

While with UPI, Ron covered the Olympic Games in Munich, Montreal, Moscow, Los Angeles, Seoul, and Barcelona. In 1972 one of his pictures was judged the best of the Munich Olympic Games. He has also covered the Winter Olympics in Lake Placid and Calgary.

Other overseas assignments included the Ali-Foreman fight in Zaire in 1974, the World Cup soccer championship in Argentina in 1978, and the Pan Am Games in Caracas, Venezuela in 1983. Ron was also one of only four media persons to visit the South Pole in 1986.

He has regularly covered sports teams in the Cleveland, Ohio area, but has also traveled coast to coast photographing all kinds of major sports competitions including the World Series, Super Bowls, NBA Finals, major golf tournaments, the Davis Cup, and thirty consecutive Kentucky Derby events.

In addition to extensive work in the world of sports, Ron has covered every United States president since Eisenhower, the Sam Sheppard murder trial, major disasters, plane crashes, and hundreds of other special interest stories.

Having won many national and international awards, and being nominated for four Pulitzer prizes, Ron was inducted into his high school Hall of Fame in 1987 and given the Distinguished Service Award from the Society of Professional Journalists. His pictures hang in the Pro Baseball and Football Halls of Fame.

With over two decades of service as a photographer with the Bill Glass Prison Ministry, Ron has participated on 150 weekends and has been in over five hundred prisons.

Ron and his wife, Nancy, have five children, Ronald, John, Stephen, Rebecca, and Joshua, and reside in North Olmsted, Ohio.

# ACKNOWLEDGMENTS

I'd like to give a big high five and a pat on the back to some very special people who have helped make this dream of writing my first book come true.

My wife, Jan, who serves as the Blueprint For Life secretary, labored at the keyboard many hours to produce the final manuscript for *Doin' Time.* In addition to all of the typing, she spent a great deal of time working to bring the copy to life. *Thanks for your never-ending support on this project and with all of my work.* And I couldn't ask for two greater daughters, Jennie and Julie. *Girls, I love you and am proud of you. Thanks for the encouragement and support you give me. I am thankful for your commitment to the Lord and pray you will remain faithful to Him the rest of your lives.* Thanks also to my parents, Fritz and Sandy Nielsen . . . *You are simply the best.*

One of the best teachers in America works at Central Minnesota Christian School in Prinsburg, Minnesota. Irma Beekman, or "Mrs. B" to her students, has gone the second mile on helping with this book–proofreading all of the copy and providing invaluable suggestions and revisions to produce an error-free manuscript. In addition to her editing skills, she has provided large doses of encouragement that have kept me moving forward and inspired to complete *Doin' Time.* I'll never forget a quote in one of Irma's letters that helped me keep writing at times when I didn't feel like it. *Irma, thanks for pointing out that "a drop of ink can make thousands think." Because of your help, thousands will now have that opportunity. Shortly after you shared this bit of wisdom with me, I ran across this quote from Julian Huxley which takes your "drop of ink" idea a step further:*

> By speech first, but far more by writing, man has been able to put something of himself beyond death. In tradition and in books an integral part of the individual persists, for it can influence the minds and actions of other people in different places and at different times: a row of black marks on a page can move a man to tears, though the bones of him that wrote it are long ago crumbled to dust.

*Thank you, Irma, for helping Ron and me convey our legacy through years of involvement with prison ministry.*

I know Ron feels the same way I do about Bill Glass and the thousands of counselors who have faithfully served on prison ministry weekends over the years. *Bill, thanks for building such an outstanding prison ministry. And counselors, I've always said, "You are the real heroes of the Weekends of Champions."*

What a thrill it has been for me to share the platform with many of America's greatest Christian athletes and entertainers. *Thanks for your time, commitment, and encouragement that have helped me grow spiritually. I'm thankful for the friendships we've formed serving together.*

I'd be remiss to not extend my admiration and respect for correctional officials and officers in institutions all over the country. These brave men and women lay their lives on the line every day. *Thanks for your help and cooperation, and for your watch care on the weekends we've spent in your facilities.*

I also tip my hat to Zig Ziglar. I'll always remember a meeting we had the morning following one of his seminars in Des Moines. We visited at length about my work, and he kept stressing the importance of writing a book that would share the incredible story of the Glass prison ministry. *Thanks, Zig, for the initial inspiration and nudge, and for endorsing my work by writing a foreword. Your vote of confidence will certainly add credibility and exposure to the book. I appreciate all you've done to help me in our profession of public speaking, and admire all that you've accomplished throughout your career. Thanks for the many lives you've touched and inspired, including mine.*

There's no way I could have given so much time to prison ministry without the generous contributions of donors who have provided financial support to Blueprint For Life for over a decade. *Your commitment has enabled me to share my faith on over one hundred prison ministry weekends with thousands of lost and hurting inmates. Together, we are making a positive difference!*

I promised myself if I ever wrote a book, I'd be sure to thank many of my close friends who have indirectly contributed to it through our relationships over the course of my life. Ray Hildebrand and Max Stratton, two of the Fellowship of Christian Athletes' finest staff members of all time, helped me build a solid spiritual foundation in my life while I was in high school and college. And it was through the ministry of a Fellowship of Christian Athletes camp in Estes Park, Colorado in 1968 that I, as a high school sophomore, trusted Jesus

Christ as Lord and Savior in my life. This ministry helped shape me spiritually. Also, Father Verne Stapenhorst and my high school football coach, Keith Christie, were great Christian role models for me, and provided so many wonderful opportunities to strengthen my relationship with the Lord through our involvement in FCA. Ed and Sharon McNeil and Jay and Annette Cookman, also active in FCA, provided continued spiritual encouragement through my years at the University of Northern Iowa, and during my teaching and coaching career in West Des Moines, as well as while serving as Iowa's first FCA State Director.

During over a decade of service as the president of Blueprint For Life, a number of other individuals have made contributions toward the completion of *Doin' Time*. Special thanks to Dave Nielsen, an attorney friend from Nebraska; Andy Hickman, my magician friend from Texas; Keith Province, a businessman from Missouri; and Doug Sellner, a businessman from Iowa. These men were board members of Blueprint when the book was completed, and I couldn't ask for four better friends.

Flying all over the country to the prison weekends and to all of my engagements, I've come to depend on the friendly folks at Northwest Airlines. My sincere thanks to Kris Parlee and the rest of the Des Moines-based crew who have provided top-notch service through the years. Also, the wonderful women who work in the Minneapolis World Club deserve special mention. During my many layovers in the Twin Cities, they have helped make my travels much easier and have become good friends and comrades in my work. "Some people just know how to fly," and I'm one of them.

Thanks also to Steve and Tanya Alford and Trent and Cassandra Dilfer. *I admire your athletic achievements, but I am most impressed that you have used the platform of success to share your Christian witness with others. I am grateful to be "more than a spectator" through your continued athletic involvement, and I am overwhelmed by your generosity toward this project.*

And finally, let me pay a special tribute to Ron Kuntz. Everyone needs a friend like Ron. I haven't met many people who are the best in the world at their profession, and yet have been able to tame their egos and exhibit humility. That's what I admire the most about Ron. Although there's no end to his list of accomplishments and achievements, he's down to earth and easy to get to know. Ron can strike up a conversation and friendship with a stranger quicker than anyone I've ever met. He has an incredible desire to share his faith with others and puts "shoe leather" to his faith on a daily basis. *Ron, thanks for being my friend, my partner in the prison ministry, and a brother in Christ. I hope our book will encourage many others in the faith.*

# INTRODUCING . . . BILL GLASS

A former All-American football player at Baylor University and an All-Pro Defensive End with the Cleveland Browns, Bill Glass left the National Football League in 1969, after a twelve-year career, in order to devote his time solely to evangelistic activities he had begun during off-seasons with the Browns. After completing seminary, Billy Graham invited him to speak at a crusade. He encouraged Bill to follow the call he felt to be an evangelist, and Bill launched out in full-time evangelism. In those initial years of city-wide crusades, people from all walks of life responded to the Gospel as this young evangelist traveled back and forth across the nation preaching to grassroots America. At this point in his life, however, Bill had no idea God was preparing him for an added challenge–perhaps the biggest of his life.

Having enjoyed success as a full-time evangelist for three years, Bill received a call to speak at a prison in Marion, Ohio. He reluctantly accepted the invitation, but as he spoke and looked into the faces of hundreds of attentive inmates, he saw the tragedy of the 60's in their wasted lives. His heart went out to those young men who were already serving prison sentences, many of them in their early twenties. Suddenly, he knew this was an outreach God had prepared for him. Bill said,

> I would have never chosen prison ministry. But I chose to follow the humble Galilean and instinctively knew that my ministry wouldn't continue in the flamboyant way that it began in pro sports. I never really planned anything as humbling as a prison ministry. It was somehow beneath me. But as time went on, it was obvious that it was of God. It kept me up in the face of the worst of Satan's castoffs. It made my preaching ever so gut level. It regularly purged me of any phony trappings of the clergy.

And twenty-five years after a friend bullied Bill into his first visit behind bars, this graduate of Fort Worth's Southwestern Theological Seminary and member of the College Football Hall of Fame has visited more than one thousand correctional institutions and continues to lead the nation's largest evangelical prison ministry. He still conducts his city-wide crusades, but since 1972 he has never reduced his pace in prisons, which balances his crusade preaching. As he says,

Going into prisons has always brought me back down to earth. I find myself trudging through three to seven prisons (each month) ten months of the year watching hurt and emptiness, smelling the stink and rottenness, hearing the noises of a dying, sick society.

The effectiveness of Bill's prison ministry is found in his unique approach of combining celebrity athletes and entertainers with volunteer lay counselors who share their Christian faith in the guts of the prison complex over the course of three days. This strategy commands the attention of even the most hardened criminals. Through the programs and one on one witnessing, lives are transformed for eternity.

A prison chaplain at McNeil Island Correction Center in Washington perhaps best described the impact of this approach after Bill brought the Weekend of Champions program to his facility:

The staff has been real impressed by what they have seen. You have chosen to walk where Jesus has walked, among tax collectors, prostitutes, and sinners, and you make our work a lot easier. These men are waiting for hope, and you have brought it to them.

This type of response has been typical of chaplains and correctional officials throughout prisons across America over the years.

In addition to his extensive involvement with the prison ministry Weekends of Champions and city-wide crusades, Bill is in great demand as a nationally known motivational speaker for banquets and conventions. He is the author of nine books including *Get in the Game, Stand Tall and Straight, Free At Last, Don't Blame the Game, Expect To Win, and How To Win When the Roof Caves In*. Bill and his wife, the former Mavis Irene Knapp, are the parents of three children–Billy, Bobby, and Mindy.

# ART AND THOUGHTS
# FROM CHARLIE'S CELL

This unique picture of Rick and Ron on a prison yard was drawn by Charlie Norman, an artist, writer, and Christian who has served over seventeen years in Florida prisons after being convicted of murder. He maintains his innocence. Charlie has won several national writing awards for his plays, articles, stories, and poems about prison. He is an accomplished self-taught artist whose sculpture of "Young Thurgood Marshall" won a state award, and is on display in a museum. He paints watercolor portraits, and is working on a series of pen-and-ink drawings of leopards, tigers, and lions that he hopes to have published as prints and cards.

Rick and Charlie have corresponded for years. Charlie loves art, and in one of his recent letters he explained how it has helped him survive so many years in prison:

Being in prison, where we have virtually no control over anything, when I can isolate myself from the surroundings and work on a drawing, what I make the pen do is one of the few times I have any control over anything. It's also a place where the guards can't intrude or dictate, and I can escape from the confines of these fences for a little while, forgetting the shotguns and razor wire. I push my abilities to the limit, see how far I can go with it, try to do each drawing a little better than the last one, and squeeze every bit of talent and observational skill I can out of that little pen tip.

A friend recently commissioned me to draw a rough sketch of something for an illustration for an article he was printing. He told me what he wanted, I got a piece of paper, scribbled and scratched on it for five minutes, and although I wasn't that impressed with it (it looked like something little Johnny scribbled at the day care center), the man was thrilled, thought it looked great, and published it in a magazine. However, sometimes even five minutes at the drawing board could bring a big pay off. Whenever I draw for even a very short period of time, I always remember an interesting story about the great artist, Pablo Picasso.

Picasso lived in a castle in Spain, and every few days he walked down to the village to take his dirty clothes to the cleaner and pick up the clean laundry. He never carried any money; instead, the launderer tore off a sheet of wrapping paper, handed Picasso a pencil, and he whipped out a drawing right there on the counter to pay for his laundry. This went on for many years, and eventually the fellow had one of the largest collections of original signed Picasso drawings, and became a wealthy man. So maybe those little five-minute drawings will pay off.

After years of praying for a miracle, a major law firm has taken on Charlie's case "in the interest of justice," turning up newly-discovered evidence, perjury by state witnesses at his trial, and misconduct by the police and prosecutors. One of his judges went to prison for bribery and corruption. Lawyers are seeking a new trial and clemency for Charlie.

# INTRODUCTION

While working with the Bill Glass Prison Ministry, Ron Kuntz and I have had some incredible experiences, many of which Ron has captured on film while serving as the official photographer since 1973. I've been involved since 1986 and have developed a close friendship with Ron since we met on my first Weekend of Champions in Indiana. We've spent a lot of time together behind the razor wire and bars of prisons all over America. Needless to say, it has been quite an adventure–one certainly worth sharing.

You don't have to be around Ron or me very long before the conversation turns to prisons and prison ministry. Unfortunately, there never seems to be enough time to answer everyone's questions or share all our stories and pictures. Hopefully, *Doin' Time* will serve that purpose.

But there is more to this book than that. It is a tribute to the Bill Glass Prison Ministry–a unique approach to prison ministry. The ministry is a combination of guest celebrity athletes and entertainers, teamed with lay counselors, who spend three-day weekends in the prison environment to present the Gospel of Jesus Christ to inmates and officers. For nearly twenty-five years, Bill and thousands of faithful volunteers have brought the Weekend of Champions program into hundreds of prisons. As you will discover, this is no small undertaking and has been a labor of love and sacrifice by countless individuals who have volunteered their time and energy to these incredible events. Through this book Ron and I have done our best to give a "high five" and a pat on the back to many of these Christian "warriors" who deserve credit for their generous commitment. It is impossible to include everyone, so we apologize to our friends whose names aren't included. But in no way are we minimizing anyone's importance. Any person who has ever participated on one of these life-changing weekends is a hero. *Doin' Time* also pays tribute to those who serve in various capacities in corrections and outlines their specific roles.

Many of Ron's photographs relate directly to our stories, while other pictures tell their own tales. I carry a large stack of these photos with me to share when I'm speaking, and they are always intriguing to my audiences. I often receive requests for copies, and this book will now allow Ron and me to grant those requests. But also, as people show the photos to their friends, others we'll never meet personally can enjoy them as well.

Ron and I also tell the stories of amazing experiences we've had. We introduce you to some remarkable people, both in and out of prison, and we take you on a journey behind prison walls and into prison yards and cell blocks across the United States.

When you finish reading this book, you'll understand why the Bill Glass Prison Ministry has had such a positive effect in prisons all over America for over two decades, and why Ron and I have been involved consistently through the years.

We're also hopeful that the book will motivate you to join us someday to serve as a counselor on one of these exciting weekends. You'll be surprised at how much you have to offer and how much joy you experience in serving. This unforgettable adventure will also provide a real spiritual boost in your life. For further information on how you can join the Bill Glass team, contact: Bill Glass Ministries, P.O. Box 9000, Cedar Hill, TX 75104, phone (214) 291-7895. They will be happy to visit with you about participating on a Weekend of Champions.

And if someday you find yourself in a prison somewhere in America, involved for the first time in a Weekend of Champions, be sure to introduce yourself to Ron and me. We'd love to shake your hand, thank you for coming, and enjoy doin' time with you.

# CHAPTER 1

# WHAT IS A WEEKEND
# OF CHAMPIONS?

$B$ill Glass, a Cleveland Browns' all-pro football player, was studying to be an evangelist at a seminary in the off-season, and dreamed of preaching at large crusades in cities across America. During that time he was approached by a local banker friend about speaking in a nearby prison. Bill was very reluctant, and he really wasn't sure inmates would be interested in listening to an evangelist. He was skeptical that they might show up just to hear and meet a professional football player.

But all of that changed after Bill agreed to do a brief program at a correctional institution in Marion, Ohio, which launched the Bill Glass Prison Ministry. A large crowd of inmates turned out, and not only did they respond with great enthusiasm when Bill talked football, but they hung on every word he spoke with spiritual connotations. Once Bill finished the program, his greatest disappointment was that he didn't have time to personally visit with each inmate who responded to the invitation to receive Christ at the conclusion of his message. He immediately realized he would need to bring some Christian teammates with him who could deal with the spiritual needs of inmates on an individual basis. Thus, through the combination of an athletic celebrity, and a one on one witness with a lay counselor in the confines of a prison, the Bill Glass Prison Ministry began in 1972.

Later that year, after the Marion experience, Bill Glass and other program people teamed up with counselors to share their faith during three days in a Tahachape, California prison. This mission was considered a huge undertaking, even though the team spent their whole weekend in just one prison.

Eventually, however, as the word spread about this outstanding program, more weekends were scheduled annually, and the next big step was to work in more than one prison on the same weekend. Obviously, this required a greater number of counselors, as well as more platform guests. Because the Weekend of Champions required no expense to the prison, many facilities began putting out the welcome mat. Each year since 1972, Glass has added more weekends and worked in areas of the country where there are large clusters of prisons, sometimes scheduling programs in as many as thirteen to fourteen units at a time. In 1995, the Bill Glass Prison Ministry conducted twenty-four Weekends of Champions, including the largest weekend in the history of the ministry which occurred March 23-26 in Huntsville, Texas. The team worked in twelve facilities, with one thousand counselors and forty platform celebrities. It was a massive project and there was an incredible response.

## The Making of a Weekend of Champions

A Weekend of Champions begins when prison officials extend an invitation to Glass to bring the event to their area. If the institutions give Bill a green light by meeting the ministry's needs to effectively implement the program, a date is established.

The time of year is very important. Because the platform guests usually speak outdoors, most of the northern states book the summer months, while Florida, California, and other warm climate states are scheduled for December through February. Usually the goal is to schedule an area during their ideal weather months.

Also, it is necessary to alternate the weekends in such a way that the entire country is covered at regular intervals, giving counselors from each geographic area a chance to be involved when the program is close to their homes.

There are a number of states which Glass tends to be in several times a year. Texas, California, and Florida have the largest number of total prisons, and their institutions are usually built in clusters, which provides an ideal set-up for a Weekend of Champions. Consequently, a lot of weekends are scheduled in those states.

Months before the actual weekend, the prison ministry director goes to the site to meet with prison officials to plan the specifics for the team's upcoming visit. This is a time-consuming process, especially if a large number of units are involved. Prison officials are very busy, so a specific time is set for the meeting, and wardens are encouraged to bring as many key people as possible to the meeting, specifically the chaplain and security chief. The goal is to supply the most effective program possible, yet keep the prison officials totally comfortable with security, schedules, etc. Obviously, every prison is different, so the program must fit into the particular institution's unique characteristics. Two critical factors are the number of inmates in the facility, and whether it is a maximum, medium, or minimum security unit. Beyond that we must build our program around counts, meals, and other security details.

A good program site in the institution must be established. Most of the time we end up in the yard or a large gym. We tend to stay out of the chapel, if possible, since many inmates will not go to a program if it's in the chapel, and those are usually the inmates we are the most concerned about reaching. It would be nice if every prison had a large, comfortable auditorium, but unfortunately, most of the time we operate off a big hay rack set up in the yard and cross our fingers for a decent P.A. system. Needless to say, there is an extensive checklist that is used to prepare the specific weekend schedule for each institution, and most officials are very accommodating, allowing us to present the most effective weekend possible.

Two other significant factors that must be addressed at this preliminary meeting are the maximum number of counselors the officials will allow us to bring into the prison, and whether we'll be permitted to visit inside the cell blocks and dormitories. We know from experience that the more counselors we can bring in, the greater the number of decisions that will be made. Also, when we have total access to every inmate, we can do a better job of helping them. Most of the time, our team is allowed inside the housing areas, we are permitted to eat with the inmates, and we can send counselors to share in heavy security areas like lockdowns and death rows. This is one of the unique aspects of this ministry and is also why a Weekend of Champions has such a positive effect on so many lives.

Another essential task on this preliminary check-out is to secure a headquarters hotel that will accommodate the entire team and be somewhat centrally located to all of the prisons in which we are working. Every effort is made to secure a good rate since the counselors are paying their own expenses, and most share rooms in order to split the cost. After the institutions give us the maximum number of counselors we can bring, an appropriate number of motel rooms are blocked off. This search for hotels can often take a great deal of time and effort, especially in larger cities. It's nice to be able to put everyone in the same hotel, but on some of the larger weekends, a second or third hotel must be used. For the huge weekend in Huntsville, Texas in 1995, eight hotels were booked to capacity.

Once the prisons have been covered and the hotel is booked, the director will begin looking for area volunteer churches to host the team for banquets on Friday and Saturday nights after the counselors return from the units. Once again, this can be quite a job on larger weekends. It has been amazing, however, over all the years to watch God's people provide in this way.

When the weekend director returns to the Glass office, the entire schedule and all the agreed-upon arrangements are confirmed in writing and sent to each institution. The information and application forms are sent to the entire counselor mailing list, with a strict deadline for their return in order for participants to attend the weekend. The deadline is normally determined by how much lead time the institutions need to run a record check on each counselor who has completed an application and is planning to attend. If for some reason a red flag comes up on an application, the Glass office is notified and efforts are made to clear up the problem. The office will either reassign the counselor to a different institution or notify the counselor that he or she won't be permitted to come. The latter would usually occur with ex-offenders trying to return to an institution or state in which they previously did time.

As completed counselor application forms are received, the Glass office continues to communicate with prison officials, finalizing any last-minute details, and making sure everyone is on the same page prior to the weekend. A lot can occur in a prison between the time of the pre-check and the weekend, and flexibility becomes the name of the game if a prison has had an incident that leaves the institution in a less-than-secure position. Frequently adjustments must be made during the actual weekend if there is a riot, fight, escape, etc.

## The Weekend Begins

Most of the leadership team for a Weekend of Champions arrive

Wednesday evening to receive their particular prison assignments and meet with the prison ministry director. These team leaders are called coordinators, and their job is to direct the weekend program in their assigned prisons. The coordinators work directly with the prison officials and the counselors to ensure that everything runs smoothly, and they meet with all of the prison officials Thursday to review the final schedule and go through an extensive checklist similar to the one used on the initial check-out. Occasionally minor adjustments are needed, but before the coordinator leaves the institution, everyone will be comfortable with the schedule, and the officials and the coordinator will have established a working relationship prior to bringing in the counselors and the platform guests. The coordinator will also now be able to provide his or her team all of the necessary information about the prison they'll be working in together, plus the names of key people in leadership positions at the facility. One of the most important aspects of the coordinator's meeting with the prison officials is to help them to see we are there to work with them and hopefully make their jobs a little easier, not to tell them how to do their jobs and create security problems. We are their guests, and our total respect and obedience toward prison officials over the years has helped build an outstanding reputation and has continued to keep the doors open for the Weekend of Champions program.

When all of the coordinators finish their check-outs, they return to the hotel for a meeting to make any last-minute adjustments or changes. Quite often, like dominoes, if a change is made at one prison, it will directly affect the others. Once the schedule is finalized, the team spends a great deal of time praying for a successful weekend. They also put together a packet of literature that they'll provide for each counselor on their team.

### Transporting Counselors and Platform Guests

Throughout the day on Thursday, counselors and platform guests arrive at and check into the hotel. Another key volunteer position comes into play here. Our housing director works closely with the hotel staff to make sure all guests are in the right rooms, know their assigned prisons, are aware of the meeting times, and have any other questions answered. This same person is also in charge of setting up the meeting rooms for large group gatherings as well as break-out rooms for each specific prison team.

The housing director's job is very demanding as counselors sometimes arrive late into the night and early the following morning. This person also works directly with the churches that are feeding us, making sure everything is ready for the two banquets. There are a number of other odd jobs assigned to the housing directors, and they stay busy all weekend, concluding with finalizing the hotel bills.

Transporting people to and from airports and prisons takes a tremendous amount of volunteer help and precise planning. There are times when the institutions provide transportation for us, but we can't always count on it. Then we must organize vehicles and drivers to move people around all weekend. Not only must the counselors be transported back and forth each day, but the platform guests must also be on time for all of their scheduled programs throughout the weekend. The larger the number of facilities we are working in, the greater the number of transportation needs. All of this is coordinated by the transportation director from a central control room at the headquarters. Although many of the transportation needs are arranged prior to the weekend, frequently last-minute details must be taken care of as everyone arrives. The transportation director gets very little rest while monitoring this important aspect of a Weekend of Champions, finally relaxing when the last counselor is on the plane to return home. This area really requires a team effort, and everyone pitches in to ensure that vehicles and drivers are available all weekend for the Glass team.

### Freshman Orientation

Other than the preliminary meetings the coordinators have with the prison officials, the first scheduled meeting of the weekend is the Thursday night orientation session for all first-time, or "freshman" counselors. This two-hour meeting is designed to adequately prepare these counselors for effective ministry in this unique setting. Some come to the meeting having had some experience with prison ministry before, just not with the Bill Glass team, although most are going into a prison for their very first time.

There are basically three specific areas that are covered in freshman orientation: 1) the do's and don'ts in a prison, 2) the contents of the

*Four Spiritual Laws* booklets, and 3) how to use the booklets and share our faith with inmates.

The do's and don'ts list is about certain things we can do in a prison, and certain things we shouldn't do. It is a guideline for behavior and helps alleviate problems for security in the institution. Security officers have thanked Glass for incorporating this into our training, and it is a very important part of the weekend.

Campus Crusade for Christ has published a little gold booklet called the *Four Spiritual Laws*. Our counselors use it to help point out a person's need for a relationship with Christ and the necessary steps to begin that relationship. The second portion of the orientation session involves going through the booklet and learning how to use it.

The training is concluded by learning specifically how to work with inmates and reviewing the schedule for the weekend. Most freshman counselors feel the training is necessary and helpful. Often, veterans who haven't attended a weekend for quite some time will also sit in on this meeting as a refresher course and a chance to acclimate themselves again to the ministry.

### Spiritual Enrichment

Friday morning at eight o'clock is the first opportunity for the entire team to convene at the Spiritual Enrichment meeting. The purpose is to prepare each person involved in the weekend for the life-changing work that lies ahead. It is much like a coach giving the team a pep talk before they leave the locker room to compete. The first part of the meeting usually involves group singing. Then Bill Glass or a guest speaker brings a message designed to encourage the counselors and to help them focus on the importance of the upcoming task. After the message, time is spent in prayer, thanking the Lord for this wonderful opportunity to serve and asking Him to work through us to change lives.

Near the conclusion of the Spiritual Enrichment time, the platform guests are excused for their meeting to check the program schedule and establish departure times, etc. for each institution. A sense of family is created among the platform guests as many often work on the same weekends; a great deal of time is spent together as they travel from program to program and share their talents from the platform. Consequently, strong friendships are formed, and time is spent in this meeting praying for one another and other specific concerns that are brought to the table.

Since the counselors have already been pre-assigned to specific prisons by the Glass office, the coordinators are introduced. They assemble their teams and lead them to a private room where they can begin last minute preparations to work in the prison. Paperwork is completed, information on the facility is conveyed, the schedule and transportation are covered, and literature is distributed. This meeting can be short or long depending upon the number of counselors to check in and/or the complexity of the institution and the schedule.

Another important part of this meeting is to pair up freshmen and veteran counselors as prayer partners. This allows the freshman to be in the company of someone with prison ministry experience throughout the weekend, or at least until the freshman feels comfortable enough in the prison setting to strike out on his or her own. These prayer partners pray together at the conclusion of the meeting, and some have become friends for life through this initial meeting.

With what little time remains between the end of the coordinators' meeting and the departure time to the prison, counselors grab a quick bite to eat and change clothes, if necessary. Every prison we enter places clothing restrictions on us to ensure that we dress differently from the inmates; that makes it easier for security to keep an eye on us.

It's an awesome sight to see hundreds of lay people from all over the United States filling cars, vans, and buses, leaving the headquarters hotel, and heading out in every direction to the various prisons. Some have longer trips than others, but eventually all arrive at their facility to begin clearing security.

### Counselor Check-In

Checking a team of counselors into a prison is a vital part of the weekend. Everything possible is done in advance to make this a smooth process, but it still takes time as security personnel must thoroughly do their jobs on clearing us, treating everyone who enters exactly the same. I appreciate this, and know it's for my own and others' safety. Glass counselors have learned to be patient and let the officials do their job, cooperating in every possible way.

Once the counselors have been cleared, they usually attend a brief meeting with the warden and other key prison officials to be welcomed and reminded of any crucial security procedures that must be followed. Any last-minute questions are addressed, and then the counselors are dismissed to begin working in the prison–mingling with the inmate population, alerting them to the first program and who will be coming to share. The coordinator examines the program site to be sure everything is ready to go, and then goes back to the front gate to meet the platform guests to check them in for the first program of the weekend.

## Day One: Friday

The usual starting time for the opening program of the weekend is around 1:00 or 1:30 P.M. on Friday. Lunch is over and, except for the inmates who are in school or working a job, the rest of the population is free to attend. This opening program is the most challenging as the inmates don't know too much yet about a Weekend of Champions, but probably suspect it will be another church-type service. However, once it's completed, the word will spread very quickly that what lies ahead will be fun and something they'll really enjoy, and the crowds will tend to build.

The program provides a great opportunity for the counselors to begin building relationships with the inmates. By sharing in a common experience and laughing together, they have something to visit about, and it doesn't take long before an inmate asks the inevitable question, "What are you doing here?" This is a perfect lead question for counselors to begin a conversation directed toward spiritual concerns. These conversations occur in and around the programs throughout the three days we spend in the prison. Having several days to visit gives counselors ample time to build good relationships and patiently wait for the right time to share their faith.

While the counselors begin their work, the coordinator checks the platform guests out of the institution so they can return to the headquarters hotel for their next assignment.

A little later in the afternoon, the counselors eat with the inmates, giving them another fantastic opportunity to share. Inmates seem to appreciate the fact that we will eat with them and, of course, a lot of good natured kidding and joking occurs regarding prison food.

Unfortunately, there isn't too much time for conversation as inmates are usually required to eat quickly to make room in the cafeteria for others. Overcrowding has created this problem. I've been in institutions where a bell rings to signal that meal time is over and all must exit the chow hall whether or not they are finished eating.

Once all the inmates have been fed, everyone gears up for the evening program. Because dinner usually starts around 4:00 P.M. and it takes a couple of hours to feed everyone, the evening program doesn't begin until about 6:30 P.M. A new set of platform guests arrives for their program. Since school is out and working inmates are finished with their jobs, the crowd is now bigger. When the program is over, the counselors are given about a half an hour to visit with the inmates before checking out of the prison. The inmates look forward to Saturday's programs and the chance to see counselors they've gotten to know throughout the day.

Security begins the long, tedious process of checking each counselor out of the institution. Once everyone has been cleared and the numbers are correct, the team travels to the Friday night banquet.

The banquets are usually sponsored by area churches who feed us and allow us to use their facilities. The entire Weekend of Champions team from every prison meets at the banquet for an evening of good food and a time of reflection. Counselors share their day's experiences and how things are going in their particular units. This uplifting time builds a sense of team unity and togetherness. We feel a part of something so important and exciting and, although we are usually worn out and exhausted, this sharing time recharges our batteries and leaves us optimistic and eager to return to the prison on Saturday.

### Day Two: Saturday

The counselors spend Saturday morning in the prison. No programs are scheduled because many inmates sleep in on Saturday morning, and a large number of the population are involved with visits from the outside. Consequently, there would be a small turnout for a program, yet there's still plenty of quality time for the counselors to work one on one with the inmates and to continue witnessing. Lunch is usually served from 10:30 A.M. to 12:00 noon. Then another program is scheduled to begin around 1:00 or 1:30 P.M. By then, visiting hours are over, and work is suspended so we'll most likely entertain large crowds for the program.

Depending on the approval of the prison, Saturday afternoon also is when we bring in the motorcycles and members of the Christian Motorcycle Association (CMA). There is a lot of excitement generated when a pack of Harley-Davidsons comes roaring onto the prison yard and assembles near the program area. The CMA folks are fantastic, combining their love of motorcycles with their love for the Lord, and providing a tremendous witness in the prison. There are a number of inmates who won't get involved with our program until the bikers come, and that rings their bell. They'll spend all afternoon out by the bikes talking shop with the bikers, and it's inevitable that the CMA folks will be able to share the Gospel with them. Parking the bikes near the program staging area helps draw an even bigger crowd, and by 1:30 P.M. the place is rockin'.

In addition to the motorcycles, another real highlight on many of our weekends is the NASCAR race car that is made available to us through Joe Gibbs, former Washington Redskins coach, and Norm Miller, president of Interstate Batteries. When the car races onto the prison yard, the noisy engine rousts inmates off their bunks, and they rush to see what the racket is all about. It is a huge draw and an excellent way to attract inmates to our program.

As the enthusiasm continues to build, the Saturday afternoon entertainment really helps set the stage for the big program that evening, which always draws the largest crowd of the weekend.

At the conclusion of the afternoon program, the platform guests leave, but the bikes remain on the yard until it is cleared for the late afternoon count and evening meal. Of course, the counselors are busy again working the yard and the cell blocks—encouraging, witnessing to, and sharing their faith with the inmates.

Veteran counselors are also busy throughout the weekend working the lockdown blocks, death rows, hospital, and AIDS wards, sharing with the inmates who are restricted from attending the programs. In addition to the counseling, the best we can provide is walk-throughs with platform guests going cell to cell to at least say hello. Periodically officers allow small groups of these special needs inmates to gather together so we can share a brief program and message. My gifts are well suited to these areas as I can go cell to cell, do a little magic, and give them a little taste of what's going on out at the programs. These areas are actually prime for counseling since the inmates are confined to their cells and there are no distractions—just a counselor and the inmate and a lot of time to visit.

Inmates confined to a lockdown area are usually there for one of two reasons, disciplinary or protective custody. Consequently, they are extremely appreciative of a visit with someone who cares about them and the pain they are experiencing.

As the population leaves the yard Saturday afternoon, the motorcycles exit the institution and the counselors eat again with the inmates. After dinner, the Saturday evening program is presented and is concluded with an invitation, encouraging inmates to make a commitment and trust Christ as their Lord and Savior. The combination of great programs and one on one witnessing the past two days has helped bring many inmates to the point where they accept the invitation, and many decisions are made. Inmates who respond are directed immediately to counselors; they help the inmate affirm this decision and provide some follow-up literature, encouragement, and prayer. Any decision made during the weekend is logged on a counselor card and given to the chaplain to assist in follow-up classes, which are set up for them after we leave. Those classes usually last about eight weeks.

After the counselors are cleared from the prison, everyone on the Bill Glass team attends and shares at the Saturday night banquet. The cross presentations are a major highlight of this banquet. Once a counselor has volunteered on five weekends, he or she is awarded a cross set in a wooden base in appreciation for dedicated service to the ministry. The cross, which is cut out of a piece of prison cell bar, is a great conversation piece and opens doors to share about the weekend when others inquire about it. This is a special plateau and serves as an incentive to counselors to continue their involvement. I remember receiving my cross and how special it was to me. It still sets on my desk in my office at home.

### Day Three: Sunday

One more trip is made to the prison on Sunday morning for our final program and to meet with the inmates one last time. Most of the time our program is separate from the regular Sunday morning worship service, but once in a while we combine efforts and work directly with the chaplain in their regular worship experience. Occasionally the prison choir or inmates provide music, and this is always appreciated. At the conclusion of the service, goodbyes are exchanged with inmates and security officers. It's amazing how friendships have been built in such a short time, and it's common to see inmates and counselors weeping as they hug and say goodbye. The Weekend of Champions has given these inmates hope and a newfound purpose and direction in life, and they are grateful. Addresses are exchanged; some inmates and counselors correspond with each other for years, maintaining their friendship. I keep in touch with many inmates I've met over the years, and I know mail call is a high point in their day.

The coordinator assembles the counselors and collects the decision cards for the chaplain, takes care of any last details, and moves the team out of the prison. After checking out of the hotel, counselors return home–tired, but thankful for the opportunity to serve and eager for the next time they'll be able to come.

## Why the Weekend of Champions Works

Almost every Weekend of Champions follows this format. I believe there are three main reasons why the Weekend of Champions program is so successful. First, all of the participants go at their own expense. This speaks volumes to the inmates, many of whom just can't believe someone would contribute that kind of time and expense to spend three days in prison. Second, the programs we take in are so good and the inmates have such a great time that it creates an environment conducive to sharing. And last, but not least, we get to be on their turf. If we were confined to the chapel or a visiting area, we could never contact the entire population, especially the inmates who are the most difficult to reach. By being able to go to the cell blocks, eat with the inmates, and hang around in the yard, we have access to everyone and can encourage inmate involvement.

# CHAPTER 2

# RON'S FIRST
# PRISON WEEKEND

*V*isiting a prison was never on Ron Kuntz's list of things he always wanted to do. As he was growing up, Ron dreamed of traveling around the world. He read all kinds of books about different places in the world and longed to visit them someday. He also loved sports, but he was small and wasn't usually able to participate. One of his other main interests, however, was photography, and Ron tackled it with a vengeance, becoming good enough to land a job with United Press International (UPI) in Cleveland in 1953. This vocation then paved the way for him to pursue his sports interests, shooting pictures at many major sporting events all over the globe, thus satisfying his dreams of seeing the world. That is what Ron Kuntz always wanted to do.

Some of Ron's photography career highlights include coverage of eight Olympic games, the Ali-Foreman fight in Africa in 1974, the World Cup soccer championship in Argentina in 1978, the Pan Am games in Caracas, Venezuela in 1983, the Pope's trip to Canada in the fall of 1984, and in 1986 he was one of four media people selected to go to the South Pole. In 1958 and 1959, Ron made two trips above the Arctic Circle traveling on a ship for two months shooting pictures of the resupplying of the DEW Line, and he also spent four months on Greenland's ice cap six hundred miles from the North Pole. Ron was becoming one of the world's premiere photographers and loved combining his interest in travel with his camera skills. At this point in his life, the last place he thought he would ever take pictures would be in prisons.

Ron covered almost every major sporting event in and around Cleveland, including the Cleveland Browns' football games. It was through this assignment that he met Bill Glass, the all-pro defensive end on the team. Bill, a sincere Christian, spoke in many Cleveland area churches, including Ron's church. Ron admired his strong Christian convictions, and through their love of sports and the Lord, they became good friends. However, when Bill retired from the NFL in 1969, Ron lost track of him.

Four years later, Bill called Ron and asked if he would like to go to prison. Ron's immediate response was, "Not particularly. What do you have in mind?" Bill then explained his idea of combining programs and counseling to share the Christian faith with inmates, and invited Ron to the upcoming event in Mansfield, Ohio. Ron learned that another media friend, Watson ("Waddy") Spoelstra, would be going. Waddy was a writer for the Detroit News. Eager to work with Waddy and to see Bill again, Ron agreed to go.

As Ron stood staring at the large stone walls surrounding Mansfield Prison, he thought, "What in the world am I doing here?" Later, as he cleared security and entered the inner sanctum of Mansfield, he again questioned if he had made the right call. All he knew about prison was the movies he had watched and the horrifying scenes of guys getting beat up. To make matters worse, it was usually the little guys who got beat up—little guys like Ron. He figured he'd be a prime candidate to be some inmate's Friday afternoon sparring partner.

When Waddy and Ron arrived in the big yard for the first program, three inmates approached them, and one of them asked, "Is this the first time you two have ever been in a prison?" Ron and Waddy looked at each other and then admitted, "Yeah." Another inmate continued, "We thought so. You guys don't look too cool in here." What a welcome, huh?

The inmate population at Mansfield was seventeen hundred. Once the initial shock of being surrounded by so many inmates wore off, Ron began to experience some amazing things, especially the response of the inmates to the programs—they were interested and attentive.

Between the afternoon and evening programs, Ron went into one of the large, tiered cell block areas to visit. The place was filthy, and he was not surprised that the prison had actually been condemned about fifty years prior to their visit. The smell was bad, and the cramped living conditions were hard to believe. Eventually, Ron found himself at one of the cells conversing with an inmate who was interested in Ron's cameras and work as a photographer. Although Ron's job was to take pictures of the platform guests and counselors, he couldn't resist this opportunity to chat for a little bit with an inmate. As they were talking, the inmate confided, "You know, if you had tried to talk to me on the street, I wouldn't have given you the time of day. But since I've been locked up, I've had a lot of time to think about the things that put me behind bars." Ron had the opportunity to help this inmate come to a saving knowledge of Jesus Christ, and it proved to be the highlight of his weekend. Ron now had a taste of how the Lord could use him to share his faith with those in real need of the love of Christ, and he was hooked. He also began to see God's hand on each weekend.

At the Friday night banquet, a counselor mentioned that he was asked to look up an inmate in Mansfield. The inmate was a member of a family the counselor knew in the northwestern part of Ohio. As he sat down in the bleachers for the first program, the counselor thought, "How in the world am I ever going to find this one inmate in a prison housing almost two thousand men?" While waiting for the program to start, the counselor asked the guy sitting next to him if he knew this particular person. The inmate looked surprised and said, "Yeah. That's me." And Ron knew that a "coincidence" like this one was definitely a God-ordained appointment. (We'll share more "divine appointments" later.)

Ron also recalls a couple of interesting experiences with platform guests on his first weekend. McCoy McLemore ("Mac"), a former basketball player on the Milwaukee Bucks world championship team, was speaking. During his message a group of inmates began acting up, yelling, and disturbing Mac's program. Suddenly Mac stopped, looked over at them, and calmly said, "It's better to remain silent and be thought a fool than to speak out and remove all doubt." Oddly enough, it quieted down the inmates, and Mac continued.

Also on the platform that particular weekend was Paul Anderson, the World's Strongest Man. After his program, Paul was sharing with a group of inmates when an officer told Sam Bender, one of the counselors, that the count was going to take place and the inmates should return to their cells. Sam raised his hand to signal Paul that he had two minutes left and shaped his fingers in a victory sign.

Anderson asked Bender, "What is that? The peace sign?"

Sam replied, "No, you've got two minutes."

Paul responded, "I'll take as long as I want."

Sam turned to Ron and simply shrugged his shoulders and said, "What am I gonna do?"

This was Ron's first experience with the Bill Glass Prison Ministry and was only the beginning of many weekends. Since that initial visit, Ron has participated in over 150 weekends and visited over six hundred prisons across the country. In addition to taking pictures, he always makes time in his schedule to share his faith with many inmates.

# CHAPTER 3

# RICK'S FIRST
# WEEKEND OF CHAMPIONS

*B*unny Martin, the Yo-Yo Champion of the World and the man who introduced me to magic and taught me how to entertain, had encouraged me for years to attend a prison ministry weekend. I was always curious and somewhat interested in taking him up on his offer, but the weekends were "come at your own expense," which presented a problem for me. While I was teaching and coaching, I had no time and no money, and later while working as the Iowa State Director of the Fellowship of Christian Athletes, I had less time and less money. Consequently, I was never able to participate. Bunny had been involved from the beginning serving as a platform guest, and had entertained in many prisons before I met him in 1976. Unfortunately, it wasn't until 1984 that I was finally able to take him up on his invitation.

When I first began to speak and entertain full time, I finally had the time to commit to a weekend, but still no finances. Consequently, I needed to find a weekend I could afford within driving distance, and Indianapolis, Indiana offered me that. An added incentive was an opportunity to visit my friend, Steve Alford, a basketball All-American from Indiana University, who had just returned from the Olympics where he had helped lead the USA to the gold medal. Steve lived in New Castle, which wasn't far from Indianapolis, and he was going to be home after the weekend. Bunny told me if I could put the gas in my car, I could room with him and he would take care of my on-site expenses, making it financially feasible for me to attend. It was finally going to happen. I was going to prison for three days. Bunny probably wasn't aware of it at the time, but I was more excited about the opportunity to be with him and to learn more about magic than I was about counseling in a prison. However, I figured I could survive the prison experience and that it would be somewhat interesting.

On the ten-hour drive from Des Moines to Indianapolis, my initial thoughts were on how great it was going to be to see Bunny and spend some time with him, and hopefully continue to develop my skills as a magician. But as I got closer to Indianapolis, I began to wonder about visiting a prison. I wasn't really nervous or scared at the thought of going into a facility, but wondered how well I would relate to the inmates. More importantly, how would they relate to me? Although I had been a Christian since 1968, I hadn't really done a lot of one on one witnessing and sharing my faith, and to think about communicating this part of my life with inmates made me nervous. Bunny told me there would be a two-hour training session for first-time counselors, but I wasn't sure they could prepare me that quickly.

Bunny wasn't scheduled to arrive until after the training session, so I grabbed a quick bite to eat, signed in, and reported to the rookie meeting, joining close to one hundred other folks who were also attending their first prison weekend. The two hours went by quickly as we reviewed the many details involved in going into a prison. We discussed the schedule and the approach of using the platform guests to present an entertaining program, which opens the doors for the counselors to share. A considerable amount of time was also spent teaching us how to use the *Four Spiritual Laws* booklets. I learned quickly that they were referred to as the "little gold books." Although the session was helpful, it still didn't totally eliminate my anxiety of entering a prison and mixing with inmates. I'm not sure there is any way to describe what that first time in a prison is like. It seems a person just has to experience it first hand. And chances are good it won't be anything at all like what was expected.

I stopped at the registration desk to see if Bunny had checked in, and they told me he was in the restaurant. Excited to see him again, I hustled over to the coffee shop. I noticed a large group of people gathered around a table in the corner, most of them laughing and having a good time. I knew Bunny was there, doing what he does best–entertaining and doing magic. Once things began to settle down, I broke through the crowd, gave Bunny a big hug, and sat down to visit. He thanked me for coming and said how glad he was to finally see me attend my first prison weekend. We didn't have much time to talk, however, because Marvin Johnson, three-time light heavyweight boxing champion of the world, suddenly walked into the restaurant.

Marvin lived in Indianapolis and was one of the scheduled platform guests. He and Bunny were good friends, and it was a thrill for me to meet him. He had one of his world championship belts with him, and I'll never forget the excitement of holding it and seeing it up close. Needless to say, it was impressive.

I could have sat at that table for weeks visiting with Bunny and Marvin, but it was getting late and Bunny knew we needed a good night's rest. (Three days later, that certainly proved to be true as the weekend wore me out.)

Even though it was late and I was tired from the long drive, Bunny and I stayed up and visited, and as has always been the case, Bunny showed me some new tricks he had learned and magic he had been working on. I made a perfect guinea pig and was bound and determined to learn all I could about magic and become good at it. I knew we wouldn't have a lot of time for magic instruction, so I was willing to stay up all night if Bunny consented to work with me. We stayed up later than we should have, considering the grueling weekend schedule ahead of us, but I savored every minute. Then, as tired as I was, I still couldn't sleep trying to remember everything he had shown me. But pure exhaustion won out, and I finally managed to get three or four hours of shut eye.

Talking magic with Bunny had totally taken my mind off visiting the prisons, but the early morning wake-up call was a sobering reminder that I was in Indianapolis to serve as a prison counselor and had an important meeting at 8:00 A.M. By Friday morning, the entire prison team had arrived and assembled for the Spiritual Enrichment time. The purpose of this meeting was to prepare ourselves for the upcoming work. Bill Glass or a special guest speaker delivered a message to empower and encourage us to minister in the various prisons we were working. The platform guests and leadership team were introduced, and time was also spent in prayer. I could sense the enthusiasm of the "veterans" and discovered I wasn't alone in the anxiety I was feeling about actually going into a prison and sharing with inmates. Several other freshmen felt the same way, but many long-time counselors quickly assured us we'd be fine and would feel very comfortable in the prison soon after we checked in. These people were very eager to help us, and their interest and concern were deeply appreciated.

At the conclusion of the meeting, the coordinators were introduced. These men and women were in charge of each particular institution that we were visiting that weekend. They worked directly with the counselors and prison officials–coordinating travel, schedules, programs, and follow-up. The Glass office had already predetermined the counselor lists for each institution, so the next step was to read off the names of each counselor assignment institution by institution. I was assigned to a facility named Pendleton, and my coordinator was Bill Pruitt from Visalia, California. Bunny told me Bill was a veteran coordinator and very good at his job. Little did I know at the time Bill and I would later work together as coordinators on many prison weekends and he would become one of my closest friends.

After they called out the names of the members of our team, we assembled in one of the meeting rooms at the hotel to fill out the necessary paperwork for clearing security at the prison, and Bill filled us in on the specifics of the Pendleton facility. It was a maximum security institution with a history of problems, including a recent riot that left several dead and many injured. Hearing that news didn't do much to help ease the increased anxiety I felt about going in, and as we got closer to departure I was becoming more nervous.

At the conclusion of our meeting, we were assigned a prayer partner; rookies were always paired with veterans. This is an excellent concept and gives a freshman counselor someone to work with in the institution until the freshman begins to feel comfortable in the prison setting. After spending a considerable amount of time in prayer with my prayer partner, we broke for lunch. I had a bite to eat, went back to my room to make sure I had everything I needed to take to the prison, and changed clothes to meet the security requirements at Pendleton. All prisons have clothing restrictions for visiting groups like ours, and they want us to be dressed totally different from the inmates. Having completed my checklist, I headed for the lobby of the hotel to board the bus for Pendleton.

On this particular weekend the institutions were providing transportation, and I had my first taste of prison life riding the Pendleton prison bus to the institution. Despite not wearing handcuffs or foot shackles, it was still eerie being locked in. There was metal fencing around all the windows and a bench down the middle of the bus with small metal loops so the inmates could be locked directly to the bench. I can't say it was the most comfortable bus ride I'd ever taken, but it did get us to Pendleton, and the hour-long trip gave me plenty of time to visit with some of the other counselors on my team.

Upon arriving at the Pendleton parking lot, Bill instructed us to wait on the bus until he could let the officials know we were there. Then they'd give us specific instructions on entering the facility and clearing security. We waited for quite a while before Bill came back on the bus with the prison warden.

The warden greeted us, thanked us for coming, and then "dropped a bomb." Apparently there had been talk among the inmate population of taking one of the Glass team members hostage sometime during the weekend. Although the warden couldn't confirm it, he felt obligated to tell us and made it very clear that if anyone was uncomfortable going in because of this, prison officials would transport them back to the hotel. I thought there would be immediate panic and guys would be racing for the exits, but nobody moved. At this point it was easy to distinguish the veterans from the rookies. Those of us on our first weekend were white as ghosts and our eyes as big as saucers. The veterans just sat there patiently, almost deaf to the announcement and apparently unaffected by the situation. Bill scanned the bus, giving everyone ample time to respond, but nobody budged. He turned toward the warden and said, "We're ready to check in, Warden. Lead the way."

With that, we grabbed our information packets and climbed off the bus one by one, forming a single file line in alphabetical order in front of Pendleton's entrance.

We had already been well schooled by Bill on making sure we were squeaky clean at the gate. All we really needed was a picture I.D. and our materials to share with the inmates. Security officers tend to frown on pocket knives, nail clippers, and other items that could be used to make weapons. All of us going into the prison had been cleared ahead of time by the Indiana corrections system. Our applications had been sent in early for review, and if for some reason the institution spotted a red flag on a counselor, they notified the Glass office, who then informed the counselor that he or she could not enter that particular prison. Even with all of these preliminary checks, we still had to go through a metal detector and present our picture I.D.'s for clearance. Obviously, a count is very critical to prison officials as they want to take out the same number of counselors in the evening as they sent in that morning. This entire process took a great deal of time, but finally we were all stamped with invisible ink on the back of our hands, which was the final seal of approval to enter the facility. This ink can only be seen under a black light, and as I got more involved in prison work, I learned this is a very common security procedure at prisons across the country. After another brief meeting with the warden and a number of other officers and administrators, we were led to the gates that would take us into the unit.

I, like most people entering a prison for the first time, was somewhat startled when the steel bars slid shut and the lock caught, trapping me between two gates. And when the second gate shut behind me, it was a sobering reminder that I was now locked in prison, and the only way back out was through those two steel gates I had just passed through. I know I'll never forget this experience or those first few steps into the prison yard. Within moments I was transported into a whole new world–prison, and I was exposed to its community–inmates.

The large cell blocks at Pendleton immediately caught my eye, but when we rounded the corner of a building to head for the gym for our opening program, the rec yard, full of hundreds of inmates, came into full view. There's no way to adequately describe the feeling that swept over me when I first experienced this. So many thoughts ran through my head: tattoos, long hair, shaved heads, all men, all dressed alike, and I knew that they'd all been convicted of crimes ranging from drugs to murder. It took my breath away and left me with a lump in my throat. It was difficult to keep from staring. Fortunately, we continued moving toward the gym to wait for our first program Friday afternoon. They had already informed us that some programs would be in the gym and some on the softball field. I thought that once we got to the gym I'd be able to regroup a little bit, but the gym was also full of inmates, including a large number of men who were preparing for our programs by setting up a stage and sound system.

Since my work involves staging areas and sound systems, I decided to wander over there, hoping I would begin to feel more comfortable with the inmates. As I pondered how to approach them and what to say, suddenly I felt a tap on my shoulder. I turned around and a couple of inmates stuck out their hands to shake mine.

"Welcome," they said. "We're really glad you're here and are excited about the Weekend of Champions." They introduced themselves and treated me as if I were a long lost friend. I was astonished at how polite they were, and also how interested they were in knowing all about me.

It wasn't long before I felt very comfortable in Pendleton and noticed that every one of the counselors on our team was engaged in conversation with an inmate. The time went by quickly, and all of a sudden I noticed the gym was packed full of inmates who had assembled for our first program. I could feel the excitement in the air, and I was surprised to see the smiles and joy on so many of the inmates' faces. I had imagined they would all look like tough guys, frowning and gritting their teeth. So far, everything I had imagined about a prison environment was incorrect. To be honest, I had even envisioned many of them licking their chops to get a chance to beat up somebody like me, but how wrong I was. They were really thrilled to see us and were very grateful for the type of program we had brought into their institution.

Many inmates came up to me, introduced themselves, thanked me for coming to their home, and expressed their enthusiasm about the upcoming weekend. Several inmates handed me a small slip of paper with their cell number on it and encouraged me to come visit them while they were locked down in their cells. It was obvious how lonely many of these men were, and how so many of them were receiving very few visits while doing their time. It was hard for me to imagine going through one of the worst scenarios in life–being incarcerated, and not ever having anyone from the outside to see every now and then. I later learned that this was not uncommon at all with many men and women who are doing time.

It was a little past 1:30 P.M., and the Pendleton gym was full of inmates. I found myself seated right in the middle of them, and although I was still a little uncomfortable, I was a lot less nervous and frightened than when we first entered the prison. The veterans were right; with each passing minute, I felt very safe and at home in a prison setting.

As I was visiting with the inmates on either side of me, suddenly everyone's attention focused on the entrance door to the gym, as Marvin Johnson arrived to do our first program. Everyone went crazy and stood up and applauded. Since Marvin was a local hero, these men all knew who he was and were certainly aware that he had won the light heavyweight boxing championship of the world three times.

Because so many inmates wanted to shake Marvin's hand and meet him, Bill Pruitt immediately got on the microphone and asked everyone to please stay in their seats until after the program, and then they could meet Marvin and take a look at the world championship belt he had brought with him.

Once again, I was astonished because I figured these guys would just ignore Bill's directions. Instead, they immediately filed back to their seats and eagerly awaited Marvin's message. I could sense the excitement in the crowd. This was a real thrill for these men to have a world class boxer in their institution.

Bill thanked the men for coming to the first program and welcomed them to the Bill Glass Weekend of Champions. He introduced all of the counselors and reminded the inmates we would be available all weekend to visit with them. He covered the program schedule, told a little bit about each platform guest, and when they would be coming to Pendleton for their particular program. As he named each guest, the crowd got even more excited, anticipating the opportunity to meet these special people. It became very obvious to me that what was about to occur the next three days at this prison was an extremely rare occasion, and the inmates were already pumped up and ready for something outstanding.

Bill finally introduced Marvin, and the guys gave him a standing ovation. Marvin's program was well received as he told of the journey to his first world boxing championship. Since Marvin mixed plenty of humor in his message, the inmates began cracking up, many of them giving each other high fives after some of his more hilarious stories. I realized right away how the programs broke the ice and created an atmosphere conducive for sharing later one on one with the counselors. The inmates were having fun, and as officers later told me, many of them were laughing for the first time since their incarceration.

Marvin closed by briefly sharing how his faith in Christ had helped him through some of the rough times in his career, and encouraged the inmates to visit with one of the counselors sometime during the weekend and discover first hand how the Lord could help them through this valley of their life.

After another standing ovation, Bill closed by announcing our six o'clock program later that day. Inmates poured out of the bleachers for autographs and to take a close look at the world championship belt Marvin brought with him. Needless to say, they were impressed, and his autographs on their Bibles or on small slips of paper were like gold to them.

Eventually the security officers began to clear the gym and lock the inmates back into their cells for the afternoon count. Since Marvin was to appear at another prison later that day, he had to leave, and correctional officers escorted him to the front gate to keep him on schedule. I noticed that they, too, got his autograph and were thrilled to have a chance to meet him and briefly visit with him.

At Pendleton the officials made a decision to keep us out of the cell blocks during count time. I learned that counts are taken several times during the day and can be time consuming, depending on the size of the institution. Obviously, this is a very important procedure and of great concern to the correctional staff. To be honest with you, I was amazed at how quickly they were able to do this, considering the large number of men they had to account for.

Once the count had cleared, we headed for the dining hall. One by one, cell blocks were dismissed for the evening meal. It was early, but I learned that the meal schedule in most prisons is totally different from the hours we normally eat. Dinner at Pendleton began around 4:00 P.M. and lasted several hours due to the limited amount of seating and the large number of men to be served. Also, the inmates were allotted a certain amount of time to eat and were then required to vacate the area to make room for the next wave of hungry men. Because of this, food was consumed quickly, and there wasn't much time for dinner conversation.

Bill had already reminded us to eat with the inmates rather than with each other, so I waited for the dinner line to form outside the dining hall and then fell into place. Bill also told all of the rookie counselors that we owed it to ourselves to eat at least one meal in prison, despite all the stories we had heard about the food.

The afternoon program had completely eliminated all of my nervousness and fear about being in a prison, so I quickly introduced myself to the inmates standing in line with me, and they began to tell me how foolish I was to even attempt to eat the food at Pendleton. Over the years working in prisons, I've learned that inmates in every institution in America complain about the food and how bad it is. These guys had me laughing as they went on and on describing in vivid detail some of the disasters the cooks had created, and begged me to "just say no" to dinner at Pendleton. Nonetheless, I was game to give it a try and decided that surely it couldn't be nearly as bad as they described it.

When we finally arrived in the chow hall, the smell almost knocked me out. Were these guys right after all? Words cannot begin to describe the main dining hall at Pendleton. It looked like a tornado had whirled through there. The floor was covered with food, it was so noisy we could hardly carry on a conversation, and my first sight of the food slopped on a plate that looked like a hospital bed pan certainly curbed my appetite. I felt like I was in a war zone. It was utter chaos. However, not wanting to offend my inmate buddies in line next to me and making good on a promise I made to Bill Pruitt that I would eat at least one meal, I forged ahead. Another lesson I learned quickly in prison was that I couldn't really pick and choose what or how much I wanted to eat. Instead, I just grabbed my tray full of food at the end of the line and looked for a place to sit down and eat.

Once again my buddies I'd met in the chow line were looking out for me and invited me to eat with them. We set down our trays, and I asked the guy next to me what choices I had for drinks. Their raucous laughter brought down the house. If they didn't know I was a rookie yet, that comment certainly gave me away.

In the middle of this big dining hall was a large Igloo cooler with a tray of metal cups next to it. Believe it or not, they actually looked like the cups you see inmates rubbing across the cell bars in the movies, and from the shape they were in, apparently some had been through that kind of abuse. A sticky liquid substance covered the floor around the cooler, and I could hardly keep my footing as I stepped forward to fill my cup. I pushed the pour knob in, and out came a sort of pale red liquid that reeked of sugar. It looked sort of like what I had seen in hummingbird feeders. Chances were good it probably tasted the same. Of course, I needed to fulfill my commitment to eat a meal in prison, so I filled it to the top and carefully sloshed my way back to the table.

About the only thing I actually recognized on my plate was the dinner roll, and I had to examine it closely to be absolutely sure. So far everything I'd heard about prison food was true. As if my first question about the drink choices wasn't enough proof I was a rookie in prison, my next question really proved my ignorance and had the inmates shaking their heads in disbelief. I asked for the salt and pepper and if it was possible to get some ketchup or steak sauce to liven up (or cover up) the mystery meat on my plate. My comrades explained to me that I was lucky to get plastic silverware, and if I didn't stop asking questions and start to eat, I'd go hungry, reminding me there was a time limit for meals.

As I watched these guys choke down their food, it suddenly dawned on me that this was it for them until breakfast. They couldn't head to the fridge later that night for a midnight snack or a bowl of ice cream. I knew that once we left the prison that evening, I could go out and get anything I wanted to eat. They couldn't. And I was convinced now that this statement is true: "If it's all you've got to eat and you're hungry, you'll eat just about anything."

I did my best to clean my plate, but there was no way I could. The food was awful and so full of starch that I felt bloated after eating very little. I washed it all down with a couple of quick swigs of the bug juice, but it nauseated me. I'd have given just about anything at that point for some Rolaids and breath mints, but things like that weren't allowed in Pendleton so the best I could do was to get some fresh air—pronto.

Just getting out of the noise and confusion, plus the pats on the back from the inmates that I had given it the old college try made me feel better. One good thing about this horrible experience was that I had bonded with a few of the men. I had made them laugh and provided dinner entertainment for them. One inmate in particular befriended me and invited me to go back to his house to visit awhile. We had some good fun at the dinner table together, and he seemed like a friendly enough guy, so I told him I'd be delighted to come.

Pendleton allows us to visit the prisoners in their cell blocks, which really helps us as counselors, because it gives us total access to them, as well as more time to share one on one. We can also be on their turf where they live, which makes it a bit more comfortable for the inmate, and it allows them to share a little more personally with us, as most of them have pictures of family in their cells, or items of personal interest that they like to show us.

Even though I had seen movies or television shows that were filmed inside prison cell blocks, when we walked into the huge building and I saw the high tiers of prison cells that house the inmates, I was in awe. This wasn't the movies. This was real. And I really felt like I was in prison in this environment.

It was hard to believe that in every one of those 5' x 7' cells lived two and sometimes three men. The sounds fascinated me. I had never experienced anything like it. By now the fear had completely worn off, and I was excited about actually going to a cell and getting to visit with the inmate I had met at dinner. At least I was excited until I learned where his house was. Unfortunately, he lived on level six, which was the top tier. For me, this presented a real problem because I'm afraid of heights. There were no elevators so we had to climb the set of stairs at the end of the block. This would be comparable to being on the sixth floor of a building, except that once we got to our floor, we weren't in a room looking out a window with a view. No, once we reached our level, we had to walk along a very narrow concrete catwalk running the entire length of the block, providing access to the inmates' cells. In this case, a crude railing ran along the edge of the catwalk, but there was still plenty of room between the two steel rails for someone to end up six stories below, right onto the concrete floor. Needless to say, I was petrified, and all of this right after I filled my belly with prison food. My stomach was churning.

Not wanting the inmate to know how scared I was of heights, I suggested we maybe sit down to visit at one of the card tables on level one. He quickly informed me that within a few minutes, they would lock down the inmates until our evening program and possibly do another count sometime between now and then.

It was decision time. Although I wasn't thrilled about it, I knew I only had one option–to head to the stairs and begin the long climb. I did my best to cover up my fear, but I'm sure it showed. I engaged my friend in conversation all the way up, hoping it would help me to relax. Once we reached the top, we began walking to the inmate's cell. I wish I could tell you that he lived near the end by the stairs, but unfortunately–you guessed it–he lived right in the middle. Experiences like this definitely enhance a person's prayer life, and as I crept along the narrow walkway, I prayed for strength, courage, and especially that I wouldn't throw up.

We finally arrived at the inmate's cell and chatted outside for a second. I was intrigued by the inside of his house and gawked at the conditions. It was so small and the two beds nearly filled the entire cell. The small sink and commode were old, dirty, and disgusting, and some of the inmates' personal effects were crammed into what was left of the available space. This was another prison experience that I won't ever forget.

Remembering we were told not to go into any cells but that we could visit directly outside them, I told the inmate I couldn't come in, but once they were all locked down I'd be glad to stay and visit. Shortly after that the buzzer sounded, and within minutes inmates scrambled into their respective cells, waiting for the doors to lock. The clang of hundreds of doors being locked echoed through the big cell block house and signaled that the inmates were confined to their cells.

I stood in front of the cell and stared straight inside. The last place I wanted to look was behind me, knowing it was like looking over the edge of a cliff with a steep drop-off. Shifting my weight from side to side and beginning to visit with the inmate, I found myself tiring quickly. There was no air conditioning in the cell block, and being at the top of this huge area on a hot August day, I began to sweat profusely. The prison food, a hot cell block, being up that high, and now facing an extended stretch of one on one communication made me feel weak.

Sensing this, the inmate stuffed his pillow through the bars and invited me to sit down. I thanked him and settled down on the pillow directly in front of his cell, where we could look each other squarely in the eye. We began talking and the inmate made it easy for me by asking a number of questions. As he did, it was natural for me to ask him the same questions, and before long we were visiting as if we'd known each other for years. I became so engrossed in our discussion that all the fear of being up so high temporarily left me. I was captivated listening to this man's life story and all the problems that eventually landed him behind bars. We talked about everything–prison life, families, crime and punishment, sports, magic, and eventually spiritual concerns. Oddly enough, as we were visiting, periodically inmates walked behind me on the catwalk. I didn't say anything, but it seemed odd since I knew that the inmates were supposed to be locked in their cells. And the foremost thought in my mind was that any one of those guys could grab me by the back of my shirt collar and with one swift tug send me over the edge of the railing six stories down for an appointment with a concrete floor.

After about the third inmate had filed past me, obviously without any incident, the inmate in the cell abruptly stopped in the middle of a story and said, "You're nervous about those guys walking behind you, aren't you?"

"You got that right!" I responded.

He continued, "You think one of 'em might toss you over the railing, don't you?"

"You're a mind reader!" I said.

"Listen, Rick," he assured me, "I know every guy in this block, and if I see one coming that I know would throw you over the edge, I'll warn you in plenty of time." We both laughed and it did help relieve my tension and concern. He explained that even though the inmates were all supposed to be locked up, there were a few who had gained some unwritten privileges and were allowed to move freely in the cell block to visit with other inmates, and some were running various errands for the officers.

As much as I enjoyed visiting with this man, I have to say I was relieved when the buzzer sounded for the inmates to be released for our six o'clock program. Prior to leaving, I invited the inmate to the evening program, and he told me he had enjoyed the afternoon session with Marvin Johnson and wanted to attend again. I moved quickly down the catwalk to the stairs at the end of the block and to the bottom. It felt good to be off the top and back on solid ground.

The evening program was moved outdoors to the softball field, so I joined the group of inmates headed that way and found a good seat. The crowd had grown a little bit from the afternoon session, and I learned this was common. Word gets out quickly within the prison community that the programs are very entertaining and not a "church service" as they suspected. Also, by Friday evening most inmates are finished with work or school and are free to attend.

After a great evening program, the inmates were dismissed first, and then once the yard was cleared, they counted counselors and moved us to the front gate. The officers were particularly concerned about getting the inmates locked down before it got dark, so they moved us out last. Leaving the institution was just as tedious as checking in as we marched through the metal detector, collected our picture I.D.'s, and placed our hands under the all important black light for the final approval to vacate the facility. Once everyone had been cleared, Bill Pruitt met briefly with the security officers to review Saturday's schedule, and then escorted us to the bus.

It felt good to sit down and be back on the outside. The atmosphere on the bus had certainly changed. Going to Pendleton that afternoon there was a somewhat somber, anxious mood, but now the counselors buzzed with excitement as they exchanged interesting stories about their experiences that day and rejoiced in the many opportunities they'd had to share their faith with the inmates. Once everyone boarded the bus, Bill quieted us down and led in prayer, thanking the Lord for our day, especially that there weren't any hostage incidents. We then left Pendleton to attend the Friday night snack and share time at an Indianapolis church.

At the conclusion of each day in the prisons, all the counselors from each facility gather together to eat and to share highlights of their day. It's incredible to hear the fantastic reports of changed lives and God-appointed visits. The banquets really charge our spiritual batteries and boost our faith, not to mention how they build a wonderful sense of community and team spirit. We close the session with a sense of joy and gratitude, and anticipation for the next day.

I couldn't wait to get back to the hotel to see Bunny and he, of course, was eager to hear about my first trip to prison. In spite of our weariness, we talked way past midnight, and exhaustion finally caused us to fall asleep. I slept well that night, but not for long as the alarm sounded early. By 7:30 A.M. I was back on the bus and ready to spend an entire Saturday in Pendleton. Veteran counselors had told me to eat my Wheaties that morning because Saturdays were long and tiring. As worn out as I was just from Friday afternoon's visit, it wasn't hard to convince me they were right.

By now our team was well-versed in the security procedures to check into the institution, and we actually were processed a lot quicker than on Friday. The security officers seemed more comfortable with us, and they became confident that we were not going to cause problems for them, but instead help create an atmosphere in Pendleton that made their jobs easier.

As we were waiting to clear security, I got my first taste of visiting day. We were being processed through a separate entrance, but next to us was a huge room full of people. Saturday morning was set aside for inmate visits, and most of these people were families of the men incarcerated in Pendleton. My heart ached as I stared into their faces. I could feel the loneliness and pain as they patiently "jumped through all the hoops" to have a little bit of precious time with their loved ones. It's no small task to process all of these visitors, and they, too, had to pass through metal detectors, store their personal effects, and be cleared on the inmate's list of visitors. When I looked into the faces of wives and little children, all I could envision was how difficult their lives must be without a daddy, and how hard it must be for them to have to see a husband and father serving time in prison. I watched the little ones enter a small room to be searched by officers. I couldn't imagine how humiliating that would be for a child, yet also understood the importance of this procedure, as contraband could easily be smuggled into the institution through a youngster. It was obvious how difficult this experience was for all of them.

Once we cleared security and entered the prison, the large visiting area on the other side of security processing was full of inmates and their visitors. Again I felt a flurry of emotions as I viewed this unique setting. For every smiling face there was a hurting face. While love and concern seemed present in some visits, anger and hatred spewed out in others. What touched me the most, however, was seeing the children sitting on their daddy's lap and sharing all the love and affection possible in the short amount of time they would be together. Odds were it would be at least one week, or maybe longer, before they could enjoy this privilege again.

It was probably good that they quickly moved us on into the institution to get ready for our morning program because the whole visiting area scenario really left me with an empty feeling. After all the years and Saturday mornings I've entered prisons, seeing the visiting family members and the visitation area always affects my emotions and is very difficult.

By now I was familiar with the layout of Pendleton, and the officers were more relaxed so they basically left us on our own to spend our day in the institution. Other than the flurry of activity in the visiting area, Pendleton was quiet. It was Saturday and most inmates slept in because they didn't have to go to work.

Bill Pruitt encouraged us to head to the cell blocks and remind the inmates of our 9:30 A.M. program at the softball diamond. Making a quick run through the blocks probably helped drum up a few more guys to attend the program, but it was obvious that our crowd would be a little smaller that morning. Most of the inmates were either asleep or had a visitor.

Although the crowd was a little thin, those who did attend weren't disappointed as Bob Cole from Tallahassee, Florida shared his program. In the famous movie, *The Sting*, Robert Redford played out the life story of Bob Cole. Bob was a con man in Chicago and was constantly running from the law. He is deadly with a deck of cards or a pair of dice; the inmates were fascinated as he told them of his days cheating suckers out of their money until, as an older man, he was converted to Christ. Bunny had told me about Bob's ability to handle cards, and I was intrigued watching him interact with the inmates, showing them moves he learned with cards that won him a lot of money in high stakes games. I was sorry he had to leave right after his program because I would have really enjoyed spending time with him. Once again, little did I know that Bob would soon become a very close friend and we would spend years working as teammates on prison weekends all over the country.

My inmate buddy from Friday afternoon wasn't at Bob's program, so afterwards I headed to his cell block to see him. Mustering up my courage again, I climbed the stairs to level six and hurried down to his cell, only to discover he had a visit that morning and wouldn't be back until after lunch. I quickly returned to the bottom floor and began to go cell to cell to look for an inmate to share with.

I hadn't gotten very far down the row until I came to a cell where an inmate was working on an unusual project. I saw hundreds of neatly stacked Popsicle sticks, a bucket full of little pebbles and stones, and a pile of old cans. The inmate was busy working over a little makeshift bench. I introduced myself and told him I was one of the counselors from the Bill Glass Weekend of Champions. Sensing my curiosity with his project, he handed me one of his finished products and proudly showed me a wishing well fashioned out of the sticks, stones, and cans. He had glued tiny pebbles around the outside of the can and then formed a little roof with Popsicle sticks. As crude as these were, they served a very important purpose. The inmate told me he sold them at the craft store in front of Pendleton and used the money to help his wife while she tried to make ends meet for their two children and herself. Although it wasn't a great deal of income, he said that just the fact he was doing something to help was enough to hold his marriage together, hopefully until he was released. He mentioned that when he first began to build the wishing wells, it took him almost a week to finish two or three, but presently, if he had enough supplies, he could make several dozen in that same time.

I was inspired as he beamed with pride in his accomplishments, and I was impressed at his willingness to work and to be attentive to the needs of his family. I promised him I'd buy one of his wells when we left later that day. This experience made me think of the old saying that one man's trash is another man's treasure, and also reminded me again of how difficult it must be for the families of people who are incarcerated.

We visited briefly while he continued to patiently glue pebbles onto the old cans, until the lunch bell rang and the block began to clear as the inmates left to eat. I invited him to attend our afternoon program at one-thirty and thanked him again for showing me his work. I also asked if he would mind if I prayed for him and his family, and he quickly accepted my offer. I grabbed his hands through the cell and asked the Lord to help hold his marriage together until his release. This was the first time I prayed with an inmate, and I discovered that this means a lot to them. Over the years I've worked in prisons I've had very few men refuse to let me pray for them. Most are grateful and appreciate this type of support. Reaching out to this stranger also helped build my confidence in sharing my faith within the confines of a prison. These men were truly hungry for a friend and some love and affection.

I know this may be hard to believe, but I skipped lunch and opted for cookies and some punch in the break room the prison officials had set up for our counselors. After a short break, I hustled over to the gymnasium for our one-thirty program. I didn't want to miss it since Tanya Crevier, the world's greatest basketball handler, was scheduled to perform. Tanya is a very close friend, and we'd done many programs together over the years. Her show is unbelievable! Spinning and dribbling basketballs with enthusiasm and a smile that will melt hearts, she immediately lights up a crowd. People admire her skill, but they are more impressed by the person. She is a dynamic Christian, and people all over the world have been blessed through her performances.

With visiting hours over and most of the population finally out of bed, we had a huge crowd for Tanya's show. Just like the veteran counselors said, the enthusiasm and interest did build, and it was reflected in the size of the crowds.

As Tanya performed, I marveled at the smiles and laughter on the faces of these men. As they watched her entertain, for a few fleeting moments they forgot about their situation and their problems and relished the joy they were experiencing. Once Tanya finished she had earned the respect and attention of every inmate, and they listened intently to her as she spoke of her love for Christ and desire to share her faith with the world through her basketball skills. She challenged the inmates to invite Christ into their hearts and allow Him to produce the change that they so desperately needed in their lives. Her sincerity and conviction touched a large number of inmates because counselors were very busy afterwards dealing with men who were eager to explore the claims of Jesus Christ. I'll never forget looking out over the gym and seeing inmates and counselors sharing and praying together. It was almost hard to believe we were in a prison.

After Tanya signed autographs and the security officers began to move us out of the gym, I hurried over to her, gave her a big hug, and thanked her for a terrific program. Tanya had also encouraged me for years to attend a prison weekend, and I know she was glad I'd finally been able to come. We chatted briefly, as she had an evening program later that day and needed to report back to the headquarters hotel for her transportation for the six o'clock program in another institution.

Leaving the gym I headed toward the rec yard, which was open until the late afternoon count. Having played college basketball and still playing regularly to keep in shape, I was attracted to the game going on at the basketball court. They were going at it tooth and nail, and I marveled at the intensity of their play. Standing on the side lines, I'd only watched a few minutes when an inmate approached me and asked if I wanted to play. He said they needed one more guy to get five up to take on the winners. I told him I'd be glad to, but jokingly warned him I liked to shoot. He just laughed and said, "Good luck. So do we!"

Once our game started, I discovered that the rules of pickup basketball are a tad bit different in prison than the rules I learned playing competitively throughout high school and college. Being a guest and thinking any one of these guys could be doing time for assault and battery, or possibly even murder, I played unselfishly and courteously. I had a great time because now I was really in my element–playing basketball! My ability to shoot well and my college basketball scholarship paid great dividends that day as I helped keep our team on the court for five straight games with the "winner stays on" rule. By then it was time for the inmates to go back to the cells for count before being dismissed block by block for meals.

My four teammates gave me hearty high fives and encouraged me to rob a bank before I left Indiana, then beg the judge to sentence me to Pendleton so they could sign me up on their team for league play. I begged off and asked them to do me a favor instead. I told them that Bunny Martin was coming for the evening program at Pendleton and requested that they attend. I promised them they wouldn't see better entertainment anywhere, especially while doing time at Pendleton. Noting that Bunny was an excellent magician, they promised to come, expressing their interest in magic. This was just the beginning of how I learned that magic would be a wonderful tool, giving me the opportunity to share the Gospel in prisons for years to come, and acquiring the respect and attention of inmates. They love being entertained and they love magic.

Playing basketball had worn me out. So instead of going up to the cell blocks, I went back to our break room to cool off and get something to drink. The Pendleton officials had provided some snacks, so I ate in the break room rather than in the cafeteria. I enjoyed visiting with other counselors, especially the ones who had been counseling for years. They told me incredible stories, and I was inspired by their enthusiasm and commitment to Christ. Their greatest joy in life was to share their faith with others, especially those in prison.

Time passed quickly and I was really looking forward to our evening program since Bunny Martin was the scheduled guest. I knew the inmates would love his show and have a great time. I'd been to many of his programs and always enjoyed watching him work. His yo-yo show is one of a kind, and the man truly knows how to entertain.

I arrived at the program area early to wait for Bunny. When he came, we had time to do some card tricks for the inmates prior to Bunny's program, and I was so proud that he asked me to help him. I was a bit nervous, but also excited about the opportunity to perform. I love to entertain, especially to an extremely appreciative audience. We had a blast, and once again I watched my mentor as he gave me a lesson on how to interact with inmates and use the magic as a tool to open doors for sharing the Good News. Doing just a trick or two got me hooked on how much fun it is to do magic for inmates in a prison. We were having such a good time that I was almost sorry the program had to start.

As Bunny was preparing for his show, Ron Kuntz, a photographer from Cleveland, Ohio arrived, and Bunny introduced us. Bunny asked Ron to take a picture of the two of us with some inmates. He told me Ron was a real pro and had covered a lot of major sporting events. At the time, I had no idea our brief meeting would develop into a strong friendship and this book.

Bunny put on a super show, and our Saturday night crowd was the largest of the weekend. The inmates had a great time, and Bunny's brief but penetrating message at the conclusion of his program touched the hearts of a lot of the men, and many were eager to visit with counselors after he finished. Bunny and I worked with several men afterward, and one man made a commitment to Christ while the others rededicated their lives to Christ. I paid very close attention to how Bunny led the inmate who trusted Christ in the sinner's prayer, and I learned a lot. My confidence was building as I took part in this encounter, and I was amazed at how eager the inmates were to receive the claims of Christ. For many this was brand new, and I couldn't believe someone could grow up in America and have little or no knowledge of Christianity.

As we concluded our visit, we encouraged these men to get involved with the follow-up program. Then we had a wonderful time of prayer, thanking the Lord for the commitments that were made and asking Him to give these men strength and courage to put shoe leather on their faith during their incarceration. They gave us big hugs and high fives, and I fought back the tears. I was beginning to understand now why so many counselors kept coming back on these prison weekends. This was exciting and important life-changing work. I began to think about how I could get back on another weekend as soon as possible, and asked the Lord to begin opening the doors.

Bunny invited me to ride with him to the Saturday night banquet, so we checked with Bill Pruitt to make sure it was okay and not foul up his counselor count since I'd be leaving earlier than the other counselors. Bill had no problems with our plan, and it was nice to have an opportunity to spend a little extra time with Bunny, not to mention the fact I wouldn't have to ride in the prison bus or wait in the long line to clear security out of Pendleton.

Bunny and I have always had great times together, but this night was extra special. We were both excited about my first prison weekend and the joy we had just experienced serving together after his program. It was an evening I will long remember and was the first of many mountaintop prison experiences we would share in the years ahead.

I was anticipating the good food at the Saturday night banquet since I had lived off the break room snacks all day at the prison. The testimonies of other counselors from the other units were uplifting and exciting. There were many decisions, and it was obvious the Lord had been at work through His faithful servants throughout the weekend. It felt good to be a part of this team effort and the victories we shared.

Back at the hotel Bunny and I discussed his program and some of the tricks he had used. I soaked it all up like a sponge and knew that I would bring my magic skills into the next prison I visited. We worked on magic a little bit, but mostly just talked about the weekend and my initial months of working full time as a professional speaker and entertainer. We looked at the prison schedule and tried to select another weekend that I could attend. I knew that I'd be participating again as soon as possible. It's a good thing I was so physically worn out because I had so much on my mind that night that it would have otherwise been difficult to get to sleep.

Sunday morning we returned to Pendleton for one final program and a brief period of counseling time. This was also a chance to say goodbye to the inmates we had gotten to know the past two days. We joined forces with the normal Sunday morning worship service, and I received my first dose of church in prison. Let me tell you, it was fantastic! The music was incredible; this time of praise and worship meant a lot to the inmates. This was truly a time to reflect on what the Lord had done and was doing in their lives. I was touched by the sincerity and conviction of these men and wanted to bottle up the atmosphere and send it to every church in America. The service really ministered to me. I was becoming more convinced that if inmates sincerely trusted Christ and made a commitment to follow Him, lasting change could occur in their lives.

Several of the men I had gotten to know over the course of the weekend had attended our final program, and we had a brief visit and time of prayer before I had to leave Pendleton for good. It was hard to believe that in three short days I could develop a relationship with these inmates and find it very hard to say goodbye. They asked me to pray for them and for their families. As we held hands and prayed, I could hardly hold back the tears. This was a special moment and a great way to close my first Bill Glass weekend in prison. Giving these men one last hug and handshake of encouragement, I took my place in line by the exit to clear security and leave Pendleton. By now this procedure went very quickly and smoothly as the officials had become accustomed to checking us in and out.

As we cleared security and boarded the bus, I thanked the correctional officers for their help. Bill Pruitt took care of the final details to make sure we were ready to go back to the hotel. Then the Pendleton officials cleared all their records with the proper numbers to be sure no one was left in the institution or had forgotten their picture I.D.'s.

The bus ride back to the hotel went quickly as we shared success stories of our weekend and exchanged goodbyes. We had truly become a team and grown close to one another. Getting off the bus at the hotel, Bill Pruitt shook our hands and thanked us for coming and for our efforts. As I shook his hand, I reminded him that we got through the weekend without a hostage problem. He quickly replied, "I knew we would. The Lord always watches out for us."

I caught Bunny just before he left for the airport and thanked him again for making it possible for me to come. He knew I'd be back again soon. When people come the first time, it's very unusual for them not to come back. I told him I'd look at my calendar and let him know the next weekend I'd attend.

I packed very quickly, eager to drive over to New Castle to spend some time with Steve Alford. In less than an hour I pulled into his driveway. It was great to see him again, especially after he had helped lead the USA to a gold medal in the Olympics. We had a fantastic time together, including some great games over at the high school gym. What a thrill to play with an All-American and admire his unbelievable work ethic. Very few basketball players worked harder at the game than Steve did. His commitment to excellence certainly paid off as he later led Indiana to a national championship and played four years in the NBA. Throughout his career he made it a priority to use his athletic platform to communicate his faith in Jesus Christ and walk his talk when it came to Christianity. It didn't surprise me because this was a commitment he had made his junior year in high school when we first met and shared these dreams at a Fellowship of Christian Athletes conference in Northfield, Minnesota at St. Olaf College.

As I write this, Steve's success has continued. As a former coach at Manchester College in Indiana, he totally turned around a struggling program, leading several teams to conference championships and into the national playoffs in Division III. In 1995, Manchester College finished second in the NCAA Division III tournament, closing the season with a 31-1 record. Steve is preparing for his second season as a Division I head coach at Southwest Missouri State in Springfield, Missouri. He and his wife, Tanya, have two boys, Kory and Bryce, and they continue to make Christ the center of their lives. They support my work, and I have helped Steve at many of his summer basketball camps by speaking to the conferees. I'm sure it's just a matter of time before Steve will also join me on a prison weekend, sharing about his athletic career and strong Christian commitment with the inmates we serve.

The drive back to Des Moines from New Castle took all day, but seemed to go quickly as I reminisced on all the events of my time in Indiana. And I prayed about which weekend I would be able to attend next, at this time not knowing I would end up attending almost every Weekend of Champions for nearly a decade.

# CHAPTER 4

# PLATFORM GUESTS—
# PAST AND PRESENT

*T*he first time **Bill Glass** spoke in a prison, he immediately noticed the large crowds a professional athlete could draw within the confines of the prison walls. He also was impressed with their thirst for spiritual insight and direction, and recognized that the combination of a celebrity guest athlete to draw a crowd and counseling after the program could be an extremely effective way to communicate the Gospel. Bill realized that if the platform program entertained and interested the inmates, it would more effectively open the door for counselors to best convey their Christian witness. So Bill talked football and tried to take the inmates right into the locker rooms and onto the playing fields of the NFL, wrapped up his program with his testimony of how he came to faith in Christ, and encouraged the inmates to visit with the counselors regarding these important spiritual issues.

Since 1972 this concept hasn't changed, and the platform guests continue to present entertaining programs that help build enthusiasm and excitement into the weekend, plus provide tremendous incentive for the inmates to begin developing relationships with the counselors. The only major difference from the early concept of an athletic clinic with a professional athlete has been to incorporate other types of entertaining programs, as long as they are appealing to inmates and give them an opportunity to laugh and have a great time. Of course, athletes and coaches have continued their involvement and are always a favorite with the inmates.

Bill Glass has always been on the platform and has probably given more programs in prison than anyone living today. Not far behind, however, are two other individuals who, like Bill, continue their involvement on most weekends–**Bunny Martin**, the Yo-Yo Champion of the World and a great magician and entertainer; and **Bob Cole**, a former con man who became well known through the movie *The Sting*, when Robert Redford played Bob's life story in the film.

Bunny's skills with a yo-yo and as a master magician, coupled with his uncanny ability to entertain, have kept inmates laughing for years. In addition to doing programs since the early 1970's, he also served as the prison ministry director from 1987 to 1994. His wife, Mary Etta, also participated as a counselor and coordinator.

Bob's background in the world of high stakes card games and gambling kept him close to the possibility of prison time, not to mention nearly losing his life on several scams gone awry. He is deadly with a deck of cards or a pair of dice, and uses these skills to attract large crowds of inmates so that he can relate the incredible story of his life in the fast lane, but more importantly his conversion to Christianity as an older man. He and his wife, Betty, are actively involved with the prison ministry.

Several others who participated with Bill in the early years include **Chuck Colson, John Westbrook, and Bob Anderson**. After being released from prison for his activity in the Watergate scandal, Chuck Colson participated in a number of weekends. As a result, Chuck felt led to get involved in prison ministry on a full-time basis and started Prison Fellowship. This unique ministry now reaches into prisons all over the world providing significant ministry to inmates and their families. Most people associate Prison Fellowship with Chuck Colson, but the organization has also become well known through the Angel Tree program. This unique aspect of ministry provides Christmas gifts for children whose moms or dads are in prison. Thousands of gifts are delivered annually by Prison Fellowship volunteers, thus opening the door to also share the Gospel with families of those who are incarcerated.

John Westbrook was an outstanding football player at Baylor University. Known as the man who broke the color barrier in the Southwest Conference, John was an All-Southwest Conference running back his sophomore year. Unfortunately, injuries cut short a promising career and after graduation from Baylor, John entered seminary. He eventually became the senior pastor at Antioch Baptist Church in Houston, where he served for many years before his untimely death. In addition to his athletic accomplishments, John was a great singer and often broke into song while on the platform. Westbrook was usually accompanied by Bob Anderson, an organist who played for all of Bill's crusades. John and Bob made a great team, and inmates really loved their music.

## Power Lifters

Over the years, probably the most well-received celebrity athletes have been power lifters. At one time, **Paul Anderson** held the title of the World's Strongest Man. He won the gold medal in weight lifting at the 1956 Olympic games, and for years demonstrated incredible feats of strength while also delivering a powerful message of his faith in Christ. Paul always drew large crowds of inmates and officers for his program which began with bending nails and climaxed by back lifting a table full of men weighing thousands of pounds. As a matter of fact, Paul holds the Guinness World Record for lifting the greatest weight ever raised by a human being—6,270 pounds in a back lift. Paul served with Bill for years before finally retiring and managing his youth homes with his wife, Glenda. Paul has since gone on to be with the Lord and has been greatly missed.

With inmates' continued high interest in weight lifting, others have followed in Paul Anderson's footsteps to provide this type of program. **Paul Wrenn** won the World Power Lifting Championship in Calcutta, India in 1981, and presently, at age forty-nine, reigns as the Masters Division Power Lifting World Champion. In addition to performing outstanding demonstrations of strength, Paul is an excellent evangelist, so he's just as strong as a platform speaker.

Some of Paul's earlier programs included lifting large inmates with his teeth or pulling a pickup truck full of inmates, also with his teeth. However, several years ago, while lifting a 385-pound coal miner, Paul's five bottom teeth came out, thus putting an end to this part of his show. To this day, though, Paul still demonstrates the squat lift and challenges any inmate to a contest. At one time he held the squat lift world record of 975 pounds. He also drives a nail through two boards with his bare hand, bends nails, lets the toughest inmate in the prison give his best punch at his stomach, and does a push-up with a heavy inmate on his back.

The highlight of Paul's show is letting the largest inmate in the prison jump off a bench onto his stomach. This stunt alone draws huge crowds of inmates, as almost every prison we work in has at least one inmate weighing over three hundred pounds. Although Paul's stomach is large, it is solid muscle and hard as granite.

**Anthony Clark** of Pasadena, Texas got involved with the Weekend of Champions, joining the team as a more recent World's Strongest Man. Tony always attracts gigantic crowds as he demonstrates world record setting lifts. One of his strongest lifts is the reverse-grip bench press, and his world record lift is 775 pounds. He also holds the world record of 1,100 pounds in the squat lift. One of Tony's most impressive stunts is to lift the back of an automobile and push it across the prison yard like a wheelbarrow.

Tony relates very well to inmates as he speaks about the struggles in his own life, and how he overcame them through his faith, eventually reaching his goal of being the strongest man in the world. Like Paul Anderson and Paul Wrenn, Tony silences the critics who believe Christianity is for wimps and sissies.

### Basketball Stars

The list of platform guest celebrities has continued to grow in the last decade, and new superstars have begun to serve as regulars on the Weekends of Champions. One of the most popular performers is **Tanya Crevier**, the World's Greatest Female Basketball Handler. After a stellar high school career and being voted the top athlete at South Dakota State University, Tanya played three years in the Women's Professional Basketball League before taking her basketball show on the road full time. Her ability to spin, dribble, shoot, and pass basketballs, coupled with her infectious enthusiasm and zeal for Christ, make her programs unforgettable. Tanya's talents have taken her all over the world, but she still manages to include a large number of prison weekends. Inmates fall in love with her and respond favorably to her invitation to follow Christ.

Tanya's younger brother, **Bruce Crevier**, became interested in Tanya's career, and she began teaching him all of the tricks she had spent years mastering. A quick learner, it wasn't long before Bruce was on the circuit doing his own basketball show, and he developed new tricks and skills that Tanya couldn't do. In 1994 Bruce set a Guinness

World Record at the NCAA Final Four by simultaneously spinning eighteen basketballs on his body.

Although Bruce and Tanya are both extremely busy, once in a while they participate on a weekend together and have developed a program that allows them to combine their incredible skills as a team and incorporate new displays of their basketball wizardry into the program. Like Tanya, Bruce is also a dedicated and committed Christian, and he uses his talents to present the Gospel.

**McCoy McLemore** was an All-American basketball player from Drake University in Des Moines, Iowa, who later played on the NBA World Champion Milwaukee Bucks with Lew Alcindor (Kareem Abdul-Jabbar). At 6' 9", "Mac" always draws huge crowds when he challenges the best player in the prison to a game of one on one. Inmates form a huge circle around half court, cheering for the inmate and laughing at all the cheating Mac does to assure victory. Long lines of inmates assemble after the game to look at the world championship ring Mac proudly wears. McCoy is very active with the Weekend of Champions, attending at least a dozen weekends annually. His short but powerful message opens many doors for counselors to share their faith. This gentle giant has been a valuable asset from the platform throughout the ministry's history.

Another basketball legend who participated, prior to his untimely death, was **"Pistol" Pete Maravich**. Pete also played one on one with the inmates, or took them on in shooting contests. He "ate their lunch" and earned their utmost respect with his incredible abilities as a player. Pete's message was powerful, as he had experienced a dramatic conversion to Christ, and left this earth as one of the most dynamic and committed Christians I've ever met.

**Michael Jordan, Al Wood, and John Lotz** are three University of North Carolina basketball celebrities who have joined us on Weekends of Champions. Michael and Al played college basketball together at UNC, and Lotz was an Assistant Coach under the legendary Dean Smith before taking the head basketball job at the University of Florida, where he received Southeast Conference Coach of the Year honors. Lotz is back at North Carolina as an Assistant Athletic Director and, in addition to being a platform guest himself, he has been able to involve a number of well known Tar Heel athletes over the years. An outstanding shooting clinician, Lotz loves to shoot against the inmates, and rarely loses a contest.

Jordan joined the Glass team on a weekend in North Carolina in 1982 shortly after leading North Carolina to the national basketball championship. Needless to say, huge crowds came out to meet him and were dazzled by his uncanny shooting skills. But the most memorable moment of Michael Jordan's first involvement occurred while he was assisting karate expert Mike Crain during one of Mike's performances. Crain performed a trick that began by placing a watermelon on Jordan's stomach, while Michael was lying on his back on a bench. Crain then blindfolded himself with his black belt, pulled out a large samurai sword, and proceeded to cut the watermelon in half. Jordan, staring in amazement, held up half of the watermelon as the inmates cheered and applauded his courageous effort. However, as Glass, Jordan, Ron, and a Department of Corrections official were driving to another unit for their next program, Jordan told the driver that he felt something unusual on his stomach. As Michael lifted up his shirt, the driver looked at him and exclaimed, "You're cut!" And sure enough, Crain's sword had gone through the rind of the melon and Michael's shirt, leaving a small cut on the left side of his stomach.

When Glass saw it, he almost hit the roof and insisted they return to the unit to have Michael's wound checked by a counselor who was a doctor. Dr. Rex Whiteman examined Michael and suggested he be taken to a nearby emergency room, where he received three stitches. As he left the hospital, Michael turned to Ron and said, "I'll never eat watermelon again." Later on in Jordan's career in the NBA, he saw Ron while playing in Cleveland. When Ron encouraged him to come back with us on a weekend, Jordan asked, "Do you still have that crazy guy with the sword?"

Al Wood attended a weekend following his NBA career, and after surviving a history of drug problems throughout his playing days. It was as a result of the drug struggles that Al eventually made a commitment to Christ and developed a zeal to communicate his life-changing experience with others. Through overcoming his drug addictions, coupled with his stellar athletic success, Al was very well received in the prisons and brought a message of hope to inmates who were also on the long road of recovery from drug abuse. I was inspired and impressed with his deep Christian commitment.

Other celebrities from the world of basketball have included **Meadowlark Lemon**, former clown prince of basketball and star of the

Harlem Globetrotters, and **Bill Chaffin**, a shooting superstar and motivational speaker who holds the Guinness World Record for sinking 190 out of 208 free throws in ten minutes.

## Dallas Cowboy Legends

Bill's background as a player in the National Football League gave him many connections with football players and coaches. With the prison ministry's national office in Dallas, it was convenient to have members of the Dallas Cowboys on the platform. Two of the more well-known guests were coach **Tom Landry** and quarterback **Roger Staubach**. Not only did Landry and Staubach bring great athletic achievement to the platform, both were also very committed Christians. Other Cowboys who periodically participated were **Bob Bruenig** and **Charlie Waters**.

## Other Football Heroes

Former All-Pro Chicago Bear **Mike Singletary** drew huge crowds in the Chicago area prisons while still competing and has stayed involved even though he has retired from the game. Another All-Pro **Reggie White**, while playing with the Eagles, had the same effect as Mike Singletary when we visited New Jersey area prisons. There weren't many inmates left in the cell blocks when Reggie arrived, and the man known as the "Minister of Defense" can preach as well as he plays football.

Quarterback **Trent Dilfer**, the 1994 number one draft pick of the Tampa Bay Buccaneers, joined us while still playing at Fresno State. Trent went the "second mile" throwing pass after pass to inmates running patterns in the prison yard—all of this shortly after coming off shoulder surgery. Although his arm was sore, Trent enjoyed the inmates' smiles as they caught passes from an All-American and soon to be NFL star. In addition to impressing the inmates with his athletic achievements, Trent stood tall in his Christian commitment and had no trouble getting their attention as he talked about his love for Christ and the importance of "taking a stand."

A number of other outstanding NFL players have also lent a hand to this ministry. They include: **Cody Reisen** and **Oscar Roan** of the

Browns; **Jeff Kemp** of the Seahawks; **Bruce Collie** of the Eagles; **J. D. Hill**, all-pro from the Buffalo Bills; **Cody Carlson** of the Oilers; **George Rogers**, 1980 Heisman trophy winner from South Carolina, **Bubba Paris** of the 49ers, who played in three Super Bowls, and **Dave Washington**, who was All-Pro three times.

During the early years, other NFL players who were involved in numerous weekends were: **Mean Joe Greene, Bobby Bryant, Mike McCoy, Earl Campbell, Billy Whiteshoes Johnson, Rex Kern, Mike Stensrud, Mike Barber, Jerry Stovall, Bill Krisher, Rosie Grier, and Randy Gradishar**.

In addition to these outstanding athletes, coaching greats **Sam Rutigliano, Don Shinnick, Mike Ditka, Raymond Berry, Grant Teaff, and Gene Stallings** have also volunteered their time in the midst of already overloaded schedules. Inmates always have plenty of great questions for them, and love to pick their brains regarding the world of football.

### Baseball Greats

The Glass team has also been fortunate to have several major league baseball players volunteer, including pitchers **Frank Tanana** and **Buddy Groom** of the Detroit Tigers, **Rick Krueger** of the Boston Red Sox, **Al Worthington** of the Minnesota Twins, and **Jose Alvarez** of the Atlanta Braves. These outstanding pitchers gave inmates a chance to experience the thrill of trying to get a hit off a big league pitcher. I might add, not too many got a hit.

Others outstanding baseball players that have been platform guests on prison weekends include: former New York Yankee star **Bobby Richardson**, catcher **Jim Sundberg**, and former Cleveland Indian great **Andre Thornton**.

### Boxers

**Earnie Shavers** and **Marvin Johnson** have been extensively active in the prison ministry. Marvin was a three-time light-heavyweight world champion, and inmates love to listen to his story of getting to the top, plus admire the world championship belts he always brings with him. Earnie fought twice for the heavyweight championship, losing both times, but many in the sport feel he threw the hardest punch of any boxer in the history of boxing. Muhammad Ali once said, "When Earnie hit me, my kinfolks in Africa could feel it." Earnie has a powerful testimony of how the Lord changed his life, rescuing him from situations that could have ruined his life or left him dead.

### Other Special Athletes

Another outstanding athlete who continues to help is **Kyle Rote, Jr.** Kyle was a professional soccer player and one of the stars of the game, but probably became best known for winning the Superstars competition three years in a row. Top athletes from a variety of sports competed in different athletic events, totaling points for meeting certain goals in each contest. Kyle beat many incredible athletes to win again and again. He now has his own business working as a sports agent for professional athletes but still volunteers his time on several weekends a year. He is a dynamic communicator and solid Christian gentleman.

Karate, kick boxing, and other forms of the martial arts always attract the attention of a lot of inmates. **Denny Holzbauer**, a five-time world karate champion and 7th degree black belt, has demonstrated his world class skills on numerous weekends over the years. His professional fight record is 32 wins and no losses. Although retired from the sport and over fifty years old, Denny continues to teach karate to maintain his skills and physical condition so that he can demonstrate this unique sport during his program. He often brings his students on prison weekends to assist him and to help witness to inmates. One of the highlights of Denny's program is flying through the air over four or five bodies and breaking boards with his feet while two inmates hold the boards firmly at chest level. Inmates are impressed with Denny's karate skills but are often more inspired by his message. This is a man who has traveled life's rocky road. In spite of a painful divorce, being shot and left for dead, losing a child, and battling cancer on and off through his career, Denny's faith in Christ has sustained him and has been an integral part of his rising above so much adversity.

**Johnny Spinks**, a professional kick boxing champion who has knocked out every opponent he has fought except one, also shares his skills and message.

From the sport of track and field, gold medal marathon runner

**Alberto Salazar** talked track and field, and then ran with any inmate who wanted a good workout.

Early on, **Madeline Manning Mims**, Olympic gold medal track star and outstanding gospel singer, was a regular on many weekends. Madeline had a lot to offer as she not only had the athletic credentials, but her music and communication skills always attracted large crowds for her program. One of the more unique platform celebrities is **Tully Blanchard**. Oddly enough, Tully spent much of his athletic career on the pro wrestling circuit, and was one of the original "four horsemen." Wearing his famous cape, Tully takes the inmates into the ring and shares what the world of pro wrestling is like, and then relates how Christ came into his life.

### Special Celebrities

**Gary Bender**, a sports broadcaster and the voice of the Green Bay Packers, participated in the early years, and was a big hit in a number of Wisconsin prisons. Gary has had an illustrious career, covering many major sporting events as a broadcaster.

**Pat Williams** joined us on a number of weekends when he was the general manager of the Philadelphia 76'ers. This noted author and outstanding speaker is now the general manager of the NBA's Orlando Magic.

Former Miss Americas, **Terry Meeuwsen** and **Kelly Cash**, have offered their help over the years and always entertained large crowds in both men's and women's facilities. Also, **Varetta Heidelberg**, a former Miss Black America and multi-talented singer, musician, and composer, was a favorite with her incredible musical abilities.

**David and Lynda Pendleton** work full time with Campus Crusade for Christ and are always well received as platform guests on our weekends. David is one of today's premier ventriloquists and has delighted audiences across the nation with Otis, Aunt Tilly, and Buford the Dog. He has been performing since he was eleven years old and has been a guest on several television shows.

**Herbie Shreve**, president of the Christian Motorcyclists Association, has a dramatic testimony of how his interest in motorcycles served as an attempt to bridge the ever-increasing gap between him and his rebellious teenage son who was making bad choices at each of life's crossroads. This unusual move eventually brought Herbie into relationships with members of the CMA and, through their witness for Jesus Christ, Herbie's life was transformed. In addition to being a powerful speaker, Herbie brings with him hundreds of other CMA members who bring their bikes, their faith, and a strong witness onto prison yards all over America with the Bill Glass Weekends of Champions.

Two of the ministry's favorite guests are **Kathy Golla** and **Sandi Fatow**. These two women are both outstanding speakers, and their pasts have given them platforms to which inmates can really relate. Kathy was abused by her father when she was a little girl; she shares a powerful story of how her conversion to Christ helped bring her out of the pain of her childhood. She now works in a clinic with people who are struggling with chemical dependency, abused pasts, etc., and is a true professional in this area. She touches on issues that many inmates can identify with and offers hope through faith in Christ.

Sandi Fatow may be the most dynamic speaker in the history of the Bill Glass ministry. Growing up, her life was hardly a rose garden. Sandi certainly lived in the fast lane, hanging around many of the rock bands of the 70's, gaining and losing boyfriends who ended up either in prison or dead. Sandi's conversion to Christ is an incredible story, and I have watched her hold many audiences of inmates in awe as she relives her scarred past, and the change faith brought into her life. She loves people and is concerned for their spiritual condition like no one I've ever seen. She relishes every opportunity to share the Gospel in and out of prison.

Two other regulars, who for years have been a part of almost every weekend, are **Jack Murphy** and **Harold Thompson**. Both of these men spent a number of years in prison and are now in full-time ministry–Jack working with Bill Glass, and Harold with Campus Crusade for Christ. Further details on their unique backgrounds can be found in the chapter on ex-offenders who are or have been involved in this ministry.

### Great Musicians

Numerous musicians and bands have provided music from the platform on many of the weekends. Some that have been actively involved include **Johnny Ray Watson**, a 6' 9" former basketball star who suffered a career-ending injury only to become one of the world's top gospel artists. **Ray Hildebrand** and **Paul Land** from Kansas City, Missouri, travel coast to coast sharing their unique brand of music and humor. Ray wrote and sang the number one pop song, "Hey Paula," in 1963, and he and Paul continue to compose much of their own music. **Bill Michael** led the singing at many of Bill Glass's city-wide crusades, and also spent hours singing for inmates in prisons across America. **Tom and Edna Jones** have also contributed musically. Inmates enjoy Tom's soulful saxophone artistry and Edna's beautiful voice. Country music star, **Wanda Jackson,** was a big hit on a Missouri prison weekend, and **Clifton Jansky,** who wrote a number of country music hits including "Amarillo By Morning," has also been a featured entertainer. Music has been and will always be something inmates and counselors really enjoy.

Although I've mentioned many individuals who have served as celebrity platform guests with Bill Glass, I'm sure I've missed some. I've tried to list many that Ron and I know, and apologize to those who have been involved but haven't been included in this chapter. Even as you read this, there will continue to be many new guests who will discover the joy of serving in this capacity. These are very special people who serve only because they love the Lord and want to play a part in sharing the Gospel with those who are lost, incarcerated, and need a new direction and purpose in life. It is a labor of love and hard work, with little or no payback, yet so critical to the overall success of a Bill Glass Weekend of Champions. What a thrill it has been for Ron and me to work together in prison ministry with these champions in Christ.

# CHAPTER 5

# COUNSELORS, COORDINATORS, AND PRISON MINISTRY DIRECTORS

*T*hree of the key positions on a Bill Glass Weekend of Champions are the counselors, coordinators, and prison ministry director.

The director is the only paid staff member involved in the Weekend of Champions. The counselors and coordinators are volunteers who pay their own way to come and serve. This is an especially large commitment for the coordinators, who sacrifice five days of their time, plus have a great deal of work to do in "directing traffic" at their assigned institution. To maintain a sharpness at their job, coordinators are required to attend at least four weekends a year, which can really place some financial burdens on them. I served as a coordinator for a decade, attending almost every weekend, and can certainly attest to the high level of commitment involved with this particular assignment. Fortunately, my position as president of Blueprint For Life allowed me to invest the time and finances necessary to serve in this capacity.

### Counselors–the Heart and Soul of a Weekend of Champions

In my opinion, the real heroes of the Weekend of Champions are the lay counselors who give of themselves so unselfishly to serve on the team and carry out the nitty-gritty work of one on one evangelism with the inmates. They, too, pay their own expenses, and this speaks volumes to inmates as to their love and concern. The counselors really do care about the inmates and are willing to make this kind of sacrifice to come. Counselors give in every way–physically, financially, mentally, and emotionally, and the Lord blesses this type of commitment. These are individuals who love to share their faith, and have a special passion for those who are hurting. They come from all walks of life and range in age from eighteen to ninety. Many retired individuals are able to give a lot of time to the prison ministry, and their involvement tends to rejuvenate them and give them a real sense of satisfaction and contribution. It always amazes me how these elderly counselors seem to relate so well to younger inmates. Perhaps they represent a father figure to them, or a grandfather they never had. Regardless, senior citizens are invaluable to the Weekend of Champions and truly are an inspiration to Ron and me.

Early in the ministry, **George Joslin** led the charge of the elderly and was still serving at the age of ninety. This feisty soul winner wasn't intimidated by any inmate and would never miss an opportunity to share his faith with them. George is now deceased, but many veterans of the Weekend of Champions still tell stories about his relentless efforts to reach inmates with the Gospel. In addition to his counseling skills, George was an avid prayer warrior. Ron recalls visiting George's apartment and seeing long lists of names on sheets of paper covering the walls. The lists included many inmates and prison counselors, and above each list was a day of the week, indicating which people he would pray for on that particular day. One of the funniest stories about George was the time he filled out his name and address at a banquet, and after "zip" he wrote "yes." George certainly proved that age was not a factor serving in prison ministry.

An elderly couple who served well into their ninety's were **Carl and Mabel Hamlin** from Florida. These tireless volunteers traveled all over the country to serve, including one four-day trip all the way from Florida to California. Carl needed a cane to get around, but once he was settled in at a facility, he was constantly surrounded by inmates who helped him. Carl often commented that he hoped the Lord would be kind enough to allow him to die while witnessing on a prison yard. Unfortunately, his failing health placed him in a hospital the last days of his life before he passed away. Mabel's poor health prevents her from attending any more weekends. Carl and Mabel touched lives in prisons all over America and certainly earned the respect and admiration of the Bill Glass team.

**Harmon Oates**, affectionately known as "Harmon the Great," has been serving with Bill Glass for many years. Being a senior citizen hasn't deterred Harmon from the rigorous challenges of the prison weekends. Harmon is a magician and a delight to watch as he mesmerizes inmates with his skills and amusing patter. You can always find inmates begging Harmon to show them another trick. They love him! His wife, **Ruby**, is also a faithful counselor attending many weekends with Harmon when we are working in female institutions.

Two elderly gentlemen from South Carolina enjoy giving their time for prison weekends. For years **Joe Danielly** has stuck to his commitment to talk about the plan of salvation with at least one person every day of his life. His gentle, loving approach has allowed him to reach many. **Albert McMakin** has the distinction of being instrumental in Billy Graham's conversion to Christ when he allowed Billy and his pals to drive Albert's pickup truck to a local crusade. Billy Graham gave his life to the Lord that evening and has since become one of the world's most dynamic evangelists. Albert was a tremendous asset to the prison ministry as well, and hoped he would find another Billy Graham among all of those with whom he shared.

**Hazel Wilson** is a remarkable woman from Forest, Ohio. She is also a great example of faith in action and has given her life to tell inmates all over America about the love of Christ. Ron and I recall a unique experience we had with Hazel as she was ministering to the women on death row in Texas. Watching Hazel work with these ladies was inspirational. Many times Hazel's health prevented her from attending a weekend, and she often remarked how difficult it was to be absent from her "prison family." She also took "freshman" counselors under her wing and taught them how to minister effectively with inmates and initiated them to prison ministry.

**Fred Carter** of Fort Valley, Georgia, has volunteered his time on hundreds of weekends. As a retired pastor, he has all the tools necessary to reach inmates with the Gospel. Despite his age, Fred's enthusiasm for sharing his faith is at an all-time high, and he seems to be effective with inmates of all ages.

**Warren New** and **Fred Spencer** are also two elderly gentlemen and veteran counselors from Fresno, California who have given "second mile" efforts throughout central California to help us prepare for the Weekends of Champions. I always loved having Fred and Warren on my team because so many of our freshman counselors benefitted from their example. They were always thinking about others and eager to serve. I enjoyed watching them encourage the freshmen, and I told their prayer partners how lucky they were to be with two of the very best warriors on the Weekend of Champions team.

Several other outstanding counselors who give a great deal of their retirement time to the Weekend of Champions are **Charles Ashton** from Indiana, **John Chinni** from Texas, and **John Simons** from

Tennessee. These experienced prison ministry veterans have served faithfully for years and have touched the lives of thousands of inmates through their involvement. All of these men would quickly agree that their lives would seem somewhat empty if they couldn't attend prison ministry weekends on a regular basis. John Simons' daughter, Sandi Fatow, began coming as a platform guest and quickly realized the prison ministry weekends were a perfect environment for her father to do what he loves best–share his faith. This father and daughter travel together all over the United States witnessing to many people both in and out of prison.

These are certainly just a few of the many counselors who haven't let their age restrict them from sharing their faith on our Weekends of Champions, and our hats go off to all of them. We hope these folks will be granted many more weekends of service.

It would be impossible to mention every counselor Ron and I have worked with throughout the years, and each one who comes is very special to us. We would, however, like to tell you about some of the individuals with whom we have worked closely, because we believe their stories will inspire you.

One of my priorities upon returning from my early weekend experiences as a counselor was to recruit as many new counselors as possible from my church. I needed to find a weekend on the schedule that was within driving distance that offered opportunities for both men and women. Although many from my church would come to me from time to time and tell me how they'd like to go "sometime," I was usually able to sort out who was serious and who wasn't. When it got right down to filling out the application form and making travel plans, most suddenly had other obligations. It's real easy not to go; it takes a serious commitment to join the team.

A few years after my first weekend, however, I was finally able to recruit eleven church members, including my wife, Jan, to join me on a weekend in the Chicago area in June 1988. It was exciting to watch them, and the most amazing part was that each person was involved in an inmate's decision to trust Christ as Savior. For most, this was their first time to witness and to have an individual respond to the invitation to accept the Lord. This weekend broke open the flood gates because these volunteers spoke of their experience in church the following Sunday, and since that day there have been many prison volunteers from Meredith Drive Reformed Church in Des Moines, including several regulars who attend three or four weekends annually.

**Denny Lillard,** one of my dear friends from Meredith Drive, always used to tell me how great it was that I volunteered so much time in prison ministry, but he was sure it wasn't for him. Knowing Denny, though, I was certain that he would be an excellent counselor and would love serving in prisons. However, I've never pushed anyone, and have always felt that an individual must have the desire to go, rather than do it as a favor to me. And I never pressured Denny, but told him to let me know if he ever changed his mind. As you've probably guessed, he did a few years later. He approached me one day after church and said, "I have to go on a prison weekend." Apparently in his Bible reading he came across a verse that spoke to him of the importance of getting involved, and he and I quickly looked for the next opportunity.

I'll never forget Denny's first weekend. He absolutely loved the experience and discovered what I had suspected—he had a gift to share his faith with others. We couldn't shut him up, and I'm sure he didn't get much sleep that weekend because of the excitement of being in a prison delivering the Gospel message. Denny's enthusiasm was the best thing that ever happened at church as he was the type of individual who decided *everyone* ought to go on one of these Weekends of Champions and boldly began to recruit, and still does today. His initial apprehension about going is a strong selling point to many individuals who also get goose bumps when they think about entering a prison. I love Denny, and it's always great to watch him work in a prison. He's become a real pro.

Another first-time attender on that particular weekend was **George McVicker,** a teacher and coach at Valley High School in West Des Moines. George and I laugh today about his indoctrination into prison ministry. He was assigned to Stateville Prison, the unit in which I was a coordinator. Stateville is one of the largest, roughest prisons in the state of Illinois, and also houses death row. I was told by several officers that one cell house on the complex was the largest in the United States, housing over sixteen hundred inmates. Not only was this particular cell house over crowded, but it was summer time and the temperature was over 100 degrees. Also, there was no air conditioning and very little ventilation, so the smell was almost unbearable. Tiers of cells packed full of inmates reached six stories high, and with the combination of blaring noise from televisions and radios, stifling heat, and stale, smoky air, this was truly a hell hole.

On Saturday afternoon, I invited George to work this particular block with me. As we entered the cell house, he was astounded at the deplorable living conditions in this huge warehouse crammed to the rafters with inmates. I said to George, "There are plenty of men in here to visit with. Let's meet back here at the bottom in one hour. Good luck, and I'll be somewhere in the block. If you need me, find an officer and he'll show you where I am." With that, George took off, eager to explore this fascinating new world that he was in, and look for an opportunity to share.

Later I learned that George beat me to the exit because of an interesting encounter at a cell on one of the higher tiers. As George was visiting with an inmate, the man asked him, "Aren't you scared to be clear up here?"

"Not really, I'm sure the officers are keeping a close eye on us," George responded.

The inmate explained, "Buddy, you must be nuts. There are never any officers up here. They're smarter than that. Most of them know they're asking for trouble hanging' around on these upper levels. They could get killed up here. This is dangerous turf."

After dissecting this encouraging news, George immediately reached into the cell bars and asked the inmate if he could pray for him. It may have been the shortest prayer George ever prayed, and after a hearty "Amen," he informed the inmate that he was late for a very important meeting, quickly raced down the stairs, and hustled over to the exit to wait for me. After the hour had passed and I met George, I asked him how things went. He said, "I got here a little bit early." When I asked him why, he told me about his short-term visit with an inmate on a dangerous, unguarded tier, and that he was born on a weekend–but not last weekend, prompting his early return.

Thankfully, this unnerving initiation into prison ministry didn't deter George from continuing his involvement on future weekends. As a matter of fact, it enhanced his enthusiasm and interest, and he eventually received his prison cross for serving on five weekends.

Another member of Meredith Drive Reformed Church, **Buck Groenendyk**, has led the charge in continuing to invite other friends from his church, and has attended well over twenty weekends. Buck and his wife, **Grace**, travel all over the United States to participate. He has found a niche with the prison ministry since sharing his faith with others has always been a vital part of his life. Through his recruiting efforts, Buck's influence has not only been felt by the members of his own church, but by Christians in other churches as well.

**Darrell Hines** was approached about becoming a counselor by Denny Lillard, Buck Groenendyk, and me, and eventually attended his first weekend in Jefferson City, Missouri. Like George McVicker, Darrell had an unforgettable experience during his first prison visit. Darrell was assigned to the facility I was coordinating. One specific dormitory in this unit housed inmates with AIDS, and fifty percent of these men were drag queens. It's tough enough for a first-time counselor to be in a maximum security prison, let alone to be thrust into an environment of this nature. Had Ron Kuntz been with us when we first entered this segregated area, he could have had a Pulitzer prize-winning picture of the look on Darrell's face! Fortunately, Darrell adjusted very well to this unique situation, and his strong faith in the Lord and desire to share the Gospel allowed him to look beyond the physical abnormalities and see deep within these men's hearts to their tremendous spiritual needs.

I'm always looking for others, especially my friends, to join me on prison weekends. Another very special person I was able to bring was Kris Fabeck, now **Kris Parlee**. Kris is a customer service agent with Northwest Airlines in Des Moines. Constantly flying out of a smaller city like Des Moines, I tend to become fairly familiar with the airport employees, and I had seen Kris while checking in for many of my flights. One day while returning from an engagement, she happened to be sitting next to me on the plane, and I introduced myself and mentioned that I recognized her as a Northwest employee in Des Moines. She made the mistake of asking me what I did that caused me to fly so much, and I began doing card tricks, and showing her Ron's pictures of my work in the prisons and telling her about my many experiences. Kris told me a little about the struggles at that time in her life, so later, whenever I checked in for a flight, I dropped off books and articles for Kris to read. I had a real desire to try to help her overcome her problems and prayed for her regularly. All of this eventually paid off when one morning as I arrived for a 6:00 A.M. flight, she beamed at me from across the counter. I kiddingly said, "Kris, it's too early in the morning for anyone to be that happy. What's up?"

And she leaned over the counter and said, "I got saved, Rick. I invited Christ into my life this weekend." I almost missed my flight that morning as we talked about this wonderful decision and change in her life. To meet Kris today, it's hard to believe she has been through so much as she is one of the most committed Christians I know. I discipled her along the way and told her that sometime I'd really like to take her to prison with me.

Eventually, in 1993, she was able to join me in Chowchilla, California to work in the largest women's prison in the world. The scars of her past life became invaluable tools in helping her reach out to the women who were incarcerated, and she was a super counselor. Seeing Kris sharing her faith in the prison yard brought tears to my eyes because I knew how far she had come. There is nothing greater than sharing one's faith with another and seeing those labors come to fruition when that person becomes a Christian and joins the team.

Interestingly enough, Kris's experience in prison ministry paid off on a missions trip to Thailand in November 1995. Out of the goodness of her heart, Kris provided companion passes to help fly two missionary friends from her church to Thailand to prepare them for future ministry to these people. The airline's rules for companion passes necessitated that Kris accompany her friends on the flights, and since she has a real heart for missions anyway, she was glad to help make this possible. To her surprise, a great portion of her time in Thailand was spent ministering in prisons with another missionary who was involved in full-time prison ministry there. Kris said that the Weekend of Champions experience gave her the confidence she needed to be an effective witness and proved to be invaluable when she suddenly found herself thrust into service in Thailand's prisons.

I'm sure Kris will soon join me on another prison weekend, and in the meantime she continues to help me with my travel needs. Kris and her husband, Jim, are special friends and have brought much joy to my family and me.

Having been involved since high school with the Fellowship of Christian Athletes (FCA), I developed a close friendship with **Ed McNeil**, a teacher and coach from Fort Dodge, Iowa High School. As a baseball coach there for thirty years, Ed was the best! His teams were always great, and it will be a long time before many of the records he set will be broken. Ed and his wife, Sharon, helped build the FCA ministry in Iowa, giving countless hours of their time to this fine organization. It was a thrill for me to eventually become the first full-time paid staff person for FCA in Iowa, and it was made possible because of the extensive groundwork done by Ed and Sharon. As I became involved on the prison weekends and explained to Ed how exciting they were, he began to dream of going. He already knew Bill Glass because Ed was the chairman of the city-wide crusade that Bill led in Fort Dodge in the early 1970's. With teaching and coaching obligations, it didn't look like there would ever be time for Ed to be part of a Weekend of Champions. However, when he opted for early retirement, suddenly Ed was free to go. When I offered him a "frequent flyer" plane ticket to attend a weekend in Texas, he was as good as there.

Ed really loved the prison weekend, and inmates flocked around this lovable old coach, especially when they discovered he had won more baseball games than any other coach in Iowa high school baseball history. They also responded favorably when he shared his faith and were drawn to Ed because of the obvious love he had for Jesus Christ and them. Ed couldn't thank me enough for inviting him to go and looked forward to attending as many of these weekends as possible in his retirement. Unfortunately, that never happened as Ed died several months later. His was one of the toughest funerals I ever participated in as I loved Ed McNeil very much. He had a fantastic influence on my life. The day we buried Ed, I recalled the many mountaintop experiences we had been through together, but thought especially of the prison weekend in Texas, which Ed had told me was one of the major highlights of his life.

I also enjoy bringing younger people to the weekends. A counselor must be at least eighteen years of age to participate. There is a group of related families in Pella, Iowa whose children became involved in prison ministry with me once they turned eighteen. **Bob and Lois Vermeer, Dale and Mary Andringa, and Stan and Alma Vermeer** have been friends of mine for many years and faithful supporters of my work. Bob, Stan and Mary are siblings, and Bob and Mary work together at Vermeer Manufacturing Company in Pella. The company was founded by their father, Gary Vermeer, who invented the hay baler, and then began building all kinds of large machines for use in the agricultural and industrial industry. This large and very successful company employs well over 2,000 people and services customers all over the world.

Bob and Lois's son, **Dan**, while still a senior at Pella Christian High School, was the first to join me on a prison weekend. His enthusiasm spread, and the next year he brought three of his classmate buddies with him. Dan has received his prison cross, a special award given to those who volunteer on five Weekends of Champions. Now married, Dan's wife, **Tricia**, has also participated, and they have plans to continue to serve as time permits. When Dan came home and shared the exciting stories of serving as a prison counselor, his younger sister, **Heidi**, began counting the days until she turned eighteen and could come with me. The summer after her senior year, Heidi attended the Seattle, Washington Weekend of Champions and, like Dan, she was an excellent counselor. She is a recent graduate of Calvin College in Grand Rapids, Michigan, and has mentioned that she would like to serve again. Dan and Heidi's younger sister, **Allison**, is just entering high school, but odds are pretty good that when she becomes eighteen she'll follow in her brother's and sister's footsteps and join me in prison.

Dale and Mary have two children, **Jason and Mindi**. I remember the day Mary called and told me Jason had turned eighteen, and asked when he could go on a weekend. Jason also served during his senior year at Pella Christian High School, and his cousins, Dan and Tricia, joined him in Florida. It was really fun to have all three of them serving together, and Jason also had a fantastic experience, echoing what Dan had said all along–that this was an experience he would never forget. Jason is also attending Calvin College. His sister, Mindi, an outstanding basketball player at Pella Christian, has promised me she'll be ready to help once she's eighteen. I'm looking forward to that day and expect to still be actively involved then.

Stan and Alma's son, **Jonathan**, recently got his feet wet in prison ministry while attending Wheaton College in Wheaton, Illinois. Jonathan was a freshman counselor in September 1995 at our huge Weekend of Champions in the Cook County Jail in Chicago. On that particular weekend, over five hundred counselors and platform guests ministered to over ten thousand inmates in this enormous jail complex.

I'm thankful these families have been able to make this type of an investment in the lives of their children, and they all testify that this experience has played a very important role in strengthening the spiritual foundation of their lives. I'm also extremely appreciative of their support of Blueprint For Life, as it has enabled me to give a large amount of my time to prison ministry over the last decade.

**Mike Baldassin** played football at the University of Washington and then linebacker for the San Francisco 49'ers for four years. After leaving pro ball, Mike became a police officer in Oakland, California, working the streets on assignments that were very dangerous and required a tremendous amount of physical and mental exertion. I met Mike at an FCA camp in Ashland, Oregon while he was still playing with the 49'ers. We built a solid friendship at the camp and stayed in touch through the years.

Looking ahead one year at the prison schedule, I noticed we were going to be in San Quentin in San Francisco. I called Mike to see if maybe we could get together. As I explained the prison ministry to Mike, he expressed a genuine interest in serving as a counselor, so I sent him an application, his schedule cleared, and Mike joined me in San Quentin. Although he had been a police officer a number of years, he hadn't spent much time in prisons, so visiting San Quentin was something he looked forward to—at least until he got inside.

Believe it or not, the first four inmates Mike ran into were all guys he had busted on the streets. Although it was uncomfortable for all of them at first, eventually Mike was able to witness to them and share his love for the Lord. Later that evening we were reminiscing about how amazing it was that on his first visit to a prison he would immediately meet guys he'd arrested, and Mike was pleased that those men could get to know him when he wasn't wearing his badge and know that his faith was an important part of his vocation. This initial Weekend of Champions paved the way for Mike to attend future weekends across California.

There are a number of other terrific counselors who have become good friends to Ron and me. **Jack and Rosie Jacob** from McComb, Ohio are two of the best on the team. Jack is at his best in lockdowns and spends his whole weekend counseling in them, when possible. He just can't get enough. A painter by trade, he often works extra long days to make room in his schedule for prison ministry. His wife, Rosie, is also top notch and has attended almost every weekend when women counselors are permitted to come. Jack and Rosie credit the prison ministry for helping keep their marriage intact through a rough stretch of their lives together. Their involvement isn't limited to weekends with

Bill Glass as they correspond, visit, and help inmates across the country whom they've met. Sharing their faith with inmates has become a way of life for this special couple.

It's always great when pastors join us, and one of the best is **Kent Reynolds**, a Methodist minister from Georgia. Kent and his wife, **Sandy**, have brought a number of counselors from their congregation, providing them hands-on experience in witnessing. With their busy schedules, pastors who come make quite a sacrifice, and most return home late Saturday night facing a full slate of duties ahead of them beginning early Sunday morning.

**Pastor Ray Castro**, from the People's Church in Fresno, California, is another Weekend of Champions warrior and, as one of the premier instructors of Evangelism Explosion, loves the prison ministry and encourages many of his students to begin using the principles of sharing their faith on a prison weekend. When we're in California, we can count on Ray and many of his Evangelism Explosion faithful to make an effort to be a part of the team.

Every pastor who attends remarks how beneficial prison ministry has been for their church and how the excitement of the weekend is usually brought back and shared with the rest of their congregation. Many who gain confidence and skill in witnessing on prison weekends return to their communities and realize the importance of sharing with neighbors and friends, and are bolder and better equipped for the challenge.

**Jimmy Haney**, although not a pastor, has served as a volunteer chaplain in many prisons and jails across Alabama, particularly near his hometown of Athens. He has also hosted a radio show and many of his programs have included stories of his Weekends of Champions adventures. Jimmy's humble, easy-going presence and servant's heart help him to make friends quickly with inmates, and he presents the Gospel in such a comfortable way that many of them respond favorably to trust Christ. Another Weekend of Champions warrior who is heavily involved in jail ministry in his hometown is **Tom Stone** from Reno, Nevada. Tom spends hours at the county jail ministering to the men and women incarcerated there and goes the "second mile" to meet their special needs as they await their trials and possible sentencing.

One of the ministry's best counselors is **Dr. Ted Monnier**, a chiropractor from Clearwater, Florida. "Doc" really got turned on at his first prison weekend and now attends on a regular basis. Like Jack Jacob, Ted is also a pro in the lockdown areas. He loves the environment that allows him to go one on one with inmates with very few distractions. The Lord has gifted Doc Monnier with an incredible ability to share his faith with others. He knows the scriptures, and he is truly concerned about people. He is willing to spend hours at a time with any inmate to make absolutely sure he has done everything possible to communicate the Gospel and answer any questions the inmate might have. Because of these gifts, inmates usually understand their need to let Christ direct their lives and pray to receive Him into their hearts.

Then, as if the day in the prisons wasn't enough hard work, Doc's hotel room is usually full of counselors with aches and pains from the day's activities, and he has used his chiropractic skills in the evenings to help those who are hurting. I once kidded him that he had treated more patients on a prison weekend than he did during the week at his office in Clearwater. He didn't disagree with me.

The sacrifices that many of these counselors make to come is incredible. Ron recalls one woman who spent all of her money on bus tickets and arrived at the weekend flat broke. She was so convinced the Lord wanted her to serve, by faith she trusted Him to meet the remainder of her financial obligations. Ron discovered the woman's dilemma while sitting next to her at a meal. He noticed she wasn't eating. When Ron asked why, she explained that she had exhausted all of her resources on bus tickets and that it had taken her three days of riding buses to get to the weekend. As usual, the Lord did provide, and she said it was probably the greatest weekend in which she had ever participated.

Another one of our good friends is **Lois Spees** from Fort Myers, Florida. After hearing about Lois's wild past, we wondered how she managed to stay alive. Living in the fast lane would be putting it mildly. As a young woman, she was a blackjack dealer in Las Vegas, and when she wasn't working, she was partying. Hitting bottom on a number of occasions, Lois pulled herself up by her bootstraps, relocated, and found new friends and a new environment to start over. Unfortunately, her lifestyle stayed the same and it was just a matter of time before she was fighting for her life again on a daily basis. She was on the brink of suicide when she finally found hope and a new direction for her life and made a commitment to Christ. Slowly becoming the new creature He promised He would make her, she began to use her scarred and ugly past as a platform to share her faith with others. The prison ministry became an ideal setting for Lois, as many of the inmates can totally relate to her, and she to them. Lois has lived where most of them have lived and she doesn't mince any words when she confronts them with their only option for hope—faith in God through Jesus Christ. She also has come on many weekends wondering where the finances would come from, yet knowing she was to be obedient and faithful to serve when called for duty.

**Dick Hickman** from Okeechobee, Florida is a walking miracle. He has been involved for years with the Weekend of Champions and is a faithful and gifted counselor. Over the past decade, however, Dick has fought a multitude of serious health problems that have set him at death's door many times. The fact that death's door never opened to Dick has astounded doctors as he has recovered time and time again from their terminal diagnoses. I have watched in amazement as this incredible man of God has stood in front of his peers at banquets on many of our weekends, sharing how the Lord miraculously had given him a second (and third and fourth) wind with his health to be able to participate on yet another prison weekend. Dick's positive attitude, optimistic outlook, and gratefulness to God are an inspiration to everyone involved in this ministry. What amazes me the most is that on the weekends Dick was given the least likelihood of attending, he had some of his greatest moments as a counselor, and many inmates' lives have been changed for eternity because of his courage, dedication, and perseverance.

Another counselor who fought the good fight was **Dr. Frank Wong**, a dentist from Fresno, California. Frank was one of the most enjoyable men I've ever been around, and he attended almost all of our California weekends over the years until his untimely death. He had an uncanny ability to bring a smile to the face of some of the most hardened inmates and won many to the Lord. In addition to recruiting a number of counselors from his church, Frank was most proud of introducing his entire family to the ministry, and on many weekends the Wong family comprised a great percentage of our overall counselor list. I'm sure Dr. Wong's patients heard incredible stories of his involvement in prison ministry while he filled cavities, since he was so proud to be a part of the team and loved to counsel.

One of the more incredible counselor stories that I was involved with occurred in San Diego while preparing to work the Richard Donovan facility near there. I was serving as a coordinator at the time, and at the beginning of my meeting with the counselors, I instructed each member of my team to take thirty seconds and briefly introduce themselves to the group. One of my counselors was **Nieves Ramirez** from Visalia, California. I had worked with Nieves before and he was a terrific counselor, and especially helpful to our team in California because he was bilingual in English and Spanish. He introduced himself, and then about ten counselors later, another Hispanic counselor named **Carlos Chavez** stood up to introduce himself. Before he told us his name, however, he looked across the room at Nieves and asked, "Were you in a bar fight in the mid-1970's?"

"Yes," Nieves responded, and then his eyes lit up as he put two and two together. Nieves recognized Carlos as the man who had taken a knife in that fight and almost disemboweled Nieves, leaving him for dead at the bar. Carlos knew for sure they had fought, and I think he was just thankful that Nieves had survived. After the fight, they ended up living in the same town for years, but their paths never crossed, and both had since become Christians. Now, years later they met again, only this time to share their faith and serve as prison counselors on the same team on a Weekend of Champions. The two walked to the center of the room, embraced, and proudly proclaimed that they would now fight together as brothers in Christ to help others. There weren't too many dry eyes in the room when that happened, and both of these men continue to work with us on almost all of the California weekends, especially enhancing our success with their ability to speak Spanish. Ron and I have become great friends with both of these men.

As I mentioned on the Acknowledgments page, a very dear friend, **Irma Beekman**, edited the manuscript for *Doin' Time*. It seemed only fitting that she attend a prison weekend to help make the book come alive for her. Also, Irma loves the Lord and is not only a natural-born counselor, but has chosen teaching and counseling as her vocation, so I knew she would feel "right at home." Upon her return from a Texas Weekend of Champions, Irma documented a few of her experiences so they could be shared with others. I asked Irma if we could include her story in our book in order to bring the perspective of prison through the eyes of a first-time counselor. *Thanks, Irma, for letting us share your personal thoughts.*

## Memories and Reflections of a Weekend in Prison
## Weekend of Champions – Huntsville, Texas
## March 29-31, 1996

Who would have ever thought that proofreading Rick Nielsen's and Ron Kuntz's book, *Doin' Time*, would land me in prison! Not me! But it did. . . and I'll be forever grateful for the experience. That special Weekend of Champions in prison has added a new dimension to my life and my counseling and teaching career. It has positively affected who I am and what I do.

As I proofread *Doin' Time*, I was introduced to and learned about the Bill Glass Prison Ministry in which Rick and Ron have been involved for many years. Then, thanks to Rick's invitation to join the prison ministry team as one of almost a thousand volunteer counselors, I was privileged to experience first-hand a weekend in nine prisons in Huntsville, Texas. Rick's primary goal was to "make the book come alive" for me via this huge Weekend of Champions. That initial goal definitely was met. Many of the names that I read about now have faces and personalities. Because special arrangements were made for me to be on the "all prison list," I visited many units and now have visible images of prison environments. *Doin' Time* is truly alive!

Throughout the weekend I saw how Rick's special ministries, Blueprint For Life, Inc. and the Bill Glass Prison Ministry, complement each other. That fact also confirms and strengthens my prayer and financial commitment to Blueprint For Life. I consider it a privilege to be part of the team of financial supporters who enable Rick to use his "magical" interpersonal talents in Blueprint For Life's vital ministry, and also encourage his continued involvement on Weekends of Champions.

Personally, I can never thank Rick enough for making arrangements for my Weekend of Champions experience. In addition to my own personal and spiritual enrichment via counseling that weekend, I appreciated the opportunity to watch Rick and Ron in action. These two men personify caring and sharing; they're compassionate individuals with genuine servant attitudes. That's what makes them so effective in their specific roles–Rick, as a popular platform guest, and Ron, as the official photographer for the prison ministry.

One of the first things I noticed, even before going into the prisons, is that Rick doesn't pass up an opportunity to witness and share his faith. It's a natural part of his personality.

For example, our plane landed at the Houston airport shortly before 10:00 P.M. on Thursday. This was after a long day for Rick, which had included speaking and entertaining in several Nebraska schools, driving to the Omaha airport, flying to Minneapolis and then on to Houston. Therefore, I was surprised when he began entertaining two clerks at the Hertz Rent-A-Car counter at that time of the night. Most exhausted people would have either just sprawled in a chair or leaned on the counter while they waited for their car. However, that's not Rick's style. This was an opportunity, and he made the most of it–first doing some magic, and then giving each woman a Christian tract. Talk about making them feel special! I looked back as we left to get the car. Both were totally engrossed in reading their tracts. That's making a difference when and where it really counts.

During the weekend I repeatedly watched the subtitle of Rick's book come to life–*An In-Depth Look at Life Behind Bars Through a Window of Hope*. That "window of eternal hope" is what Rick, Ron, the other platform guests, and the volunteer counselors bring to and open on the Weekend of Champions.

My first Weekend of Champions was fantastic and often overwhelming. It's difficult to describe the variety of emotions and impressions I had that weekend. Words like *exhilarating, exceptional, emotional, and exhausting* come to mind; however, it's something a person has to experience to fully appreciate.

Each time I entered a program area, I saw a sea of white prison uniforms as hundreds of inmates gathered for the entertainment. At first all the inmates' facial expressions were basically the same–very somber, non-smiling, almost melancholy, and they were hardly conversing with each other or the counselors who were sitting among them.

Then a dramatic change occurred as Rick captured their attention with his entertaining magic and juggling. What a thrill to see the anticipation of the next sleight of hand or another type of magic replace the vacant expressions in the inmates' eyes. I can still hear their hearty laughter above the cacophony of heavy clanging locks on gates and doors mixed with the shouts of inmates and security personnel echoing through the prison. It was touching to hear officers make remarks like, "This is the first time "Sam" has laughed, or even smiled, in months."

The inmates' passive actions soon turned into "high fives" after a particularly challenging trick–and especially when fellow inmates (Rick's "assistants") were the objects of good-natured jokes. For a short time, it seemed like they forgot where they were, why they were there, and the circumstances that separated them from families and friends.

By the time Rick completed the entertainment segment, he had won the inmates' confidence and many were primed to hear his Christian testimony and to meet one on one with the counselors. Then that sea of white reminded me of a field that had been tilled and prepared for planting–it was ready for the seeds of the gospel.

There are always positive responses to Rick's Christian testimony because he doesn't use high-pressured, emotional, preachy techniques. In his personal, sincere invitation, Rick simply tells the inmates how they "can receive the love of the Lord." That's what this mission is all about; and that's how countless lives are touched and changed in the name of the Lord.

There were many outstanding experiences that weekend. It's impossible to include all of them in these reflections. However, a couple of inmates made permanent impressions on me and reminded me how God's timing is always right and precise. These were not coincidences. I'm convinced that these were "divine appointments."

I had the privilege of sharing some special time with Rick, Ron, and Kevin Hamilton, a young inmate who is in the final stages of terminal cancer. (The story of Ron and his son, Joshua's, unique friendship with Kevin is included in this book.) When we arrived at the Estelle Unit, Ron unexpectedly discovered that Kevin Hamilton had recently been moved from the hospital to the prison infirmary. So Ron eagerly took Rick and me to meet Kevin.

As we approached Kevin's cell, we could see him sitting on his bunk, reading his Bible. We were all blessed by Kevin's marvelous testimony! Although it was extremely difficult for Kevin to speak because he had just completed a round of chemotherapy, he wanted us to know that God was helping him through this rough time and that he was completely at peace with his situation. There wasn't a dry eye among us as we joined hands through the prison bars and prayed together. Since no one had tissues, Kevin unselfishly shared a valuable commodity with us– his roll of toilet paper.

When it was time to leave Kevin's cell area, I witnessed a memorable, sad, yet hopeful "goodbye" between Ron and Kevin. Kevin assured Ron, "I know I'll see you again. If not on this earth, I'll see you and Josh in heaven." Most likely Kevin will no longer be living the next time Ron visits that prison. He'll be gone, but certainly not forgotten. None of us will ever forget Kevin Hamilton and our emotional visit with him.

As Rick concluded his magic-juggling program in the Estelle Unit, he shared his testimony with the crowd of inmates, officers, and counselors gathered in the prison yard. Rick explained how he and his wife, Jan, were able to survive losing their infant son, Jeffrey, because God's love sustained and carried them through that difficult time. God's "peace that passes all understanding" enabled them to become better instead of bitter as a result of that major obstacle in their lives. Rick testified that God helped them make sense out of something that made no sense at all.

Immediately after the program, a young inmate rushed up to Rick. "I know just what you're talking about, Mr. Nielsen," he said, and he pointed to a beautiful little girl's photo that he was wearing on his uniform. "This was my daughter. She was killed in our house fire in January. And today would have been her fourth birthday. Tears filled his brown eyes and his voice broke as he continued, "Thank you so much for reminding me that God will help my wife and me deal with this tough time."

As Rick and this heartbroken inmate prayed together, I thought about God's perfect timing. This grieving young father needed to hear Rick's assurance of a loving God on that specific day–his daughter's birthday. Coincidence? No way. It didn't just happen that Rick was assigned as a platform guest to Estelle that afternoon, and that this prisoner was in the audience.

When I returned home, many people asked if I was afraid in prison. I can honestly say that fear was not one of the many emotions that I experienced during the weekend. I felt completely safe even in the lockdown area in the Wynne Unit where the toughest criminals are in maximum security. As we stood out in the prison yard among the inmates, watching and waiting for a sky diver to drop into prison, I wondered, "How many of these convicts out here are murderers, rapists, and thieves." Yet I wasn't apprehensive. God was in control.

One of the things that consistently impressed me was the courtesy and gratefulness of the inmates in every unit. Many men and women sincerely thanked us and other members of the Weekend of Champions team for spending time and sharing the good news of the gospel with them. Things that we take so for granted meant very much to them. Needless to say, I learned a valuable lesson on gratitude while I was in prison.

I'm not the same person that left Minnesota on Thursday, March 28th, and I'm thankful for that. That memorable weekend in prison has positively changed me. I pray that there will be more prison ministry opportunities in my future. Meanwhile, I'll continue to pray for and support faithful servants like Rick Nielsen, Ron Kuntz, and others on the prison ministry team who are committed to opening that "window of hope" for those who are *doin' time* behind bars. They are putting love into action every time they fulfill Christ's mandate: "I was in prison and you visited me."

### Full-Time Volunteer Staff

Another very important group of individuals who deserve special recognition for investing their time on a majority of the Weekends of Champions are the full-time volunteer staff. These men and women are involved in almost every weekend on the schedule. They oversee some extremely important facets of the ministry, and their expertise and dedication are critical to the overall success of the ministry.

**Don Lykins** from Paris, Kentucky has probably served on more prison weekends than any other volunteer. Don was one of the original coordinators, leading many of the first groups of volunteers into prisons and traveling all over the country to promote the ministry and encourage prison officials to invite Bill and the team for a weekend in their institution. Don's business and sales background gives him the necessary skills to open many doors for opportunities to serve. His warm smile and pleasant personality win him friends all over America, and he is an individual who knows how to ask for help, seldom receiving a "no."

As the ministry began to grow in the early 80's, Don sensed a need for someone to oversee a central control room and coordinate all of the transportation required on the weekends. Don graciously accepted this behind-the-scenes position and has done a magnificent job of handling it. As you can imagine, moving counselors and platform guests to and from all of the different institutions is no small task. Although it has kept him from actually getting into the prisons and sharing with inmates, Don's servant heart reminds him of his important role. In recent years, Don's wife, **Jane**, has accompanied him on the weekends, and she has become like a mom to many of us, fixing snacks in the control room and helping Don with much of his work.

As if monitoring all of the transportation wasn't enough, Don also has gone to the weekend sites ahead of the team. He has visited churches and encouraged them to allow us to use their facilities for evening banquets, plus provide food and servers to feed the entire Weekend of Champions team. On some of our larger weekends, this isn't easy, yet Don has come through time and time again in amazing ways.

An excellent communicator, Don also does a superb job at the freshman orientation meetings of getting the rookies prepared for service and excited about how *they* can make a difference. His warm, sincere smile and genuine love and enthusiasm for the Lord help relax many anxious first-time counselors. Don and Jane Lykins have contributed greatly to the many victories over the years through the Bill Glass Ministry. As I write this, they have every intention of serving until it becomes impossible to handle the rigorous travel schedule and time commitment. The prison ministry team has truly become their family.

Another very important behind-the-scenes job is the position of housing director. This person works directly with the hotel staff to ensure that all of the team's lodging needs are met and that the meeting rooms are ready for our large and small group meetings. The housing director also assists with some of the transportation needs and many other "odds and ends" details to keep the schedule running smoothly.

Two special volunteers who have become housing director pros are **Art Gamsby** from Newark, Delaware and **Sally Brock** from Fort Smith, Arkansas. Art and Sally put in long hours, especially the day when everyone arrives, often staying up late at night to check in late-arriving team members.

While I was working as a coordinator, I recall many late night trips to the airport with Art to pick up counselors or platform guests whose flights were delayed. Art and I knew that traveling together and visiting kept us from falling asleep at the wheel. I cherish many of these late night runs with Art and have grown to love him as a dear friend and brother in Christ. Art has a big heart and loves the prison ministry. Like Don Lykins, Art also started as a coordinator, then unselfishly volunteered to serve as the housing director when the ministry grew and the need arose. He misses dealing directly with the inmates but realizes the important contribution he is making to the overall success of the weekends. Periodically things run smoothly enough that he can slip out to a prison for a while and counsel.

Sally Brock first became involved with the ministry as a counselor, then worked as a coordinator, and was eventually asked to serve as a housing director when the ministry expanded to eighteen to twenty weekends annually. Her background in the hotel industry and "people person" personality made her a natural for this job. She'd be the first to tell you that one of the requirements of this position is the ability to function on very little sleep. Sally loves the counselors and makes an extra effort to welcome them, tells them how special they are, and reminds them of their importance on the weekend.

On some of the larger weekends, especially when we are using two or three hotels, Art and Sally both come to serve. I would be remiss in failing to mention Art's wife, **Dot**, and Sally's husband, **Ron**, who are also involved in the ministry. Dot is a faithful counselor, and Ron has worked as a coordinator. It's a family affair for these couples.

**Roger Hoss**, a businessman from Freeport, Texas, has also gone the "second mile" to assist on prison weekends. It's hard for me to imagine how much Roger has contributed by purchasing all of the food for the control room on numerous weekends through the years, and also purchasing and preparing all of the food for evening banquets on prison weekends across Texas.

Roger loves to cook; his philosophy is that the best fellowship always occurs when there's a table full of good food. In March 1995, Roger and a couple of his associates cooked dinner for both evening banquets for a thousand team members on the largest weekend in the history of the ministry. Not only did everyone get plenty to eat, but there was food left over. Roger is a super idea man, and is always brainstorming for ways to make the ministry more effective and to generate enough finances to meet the needs of expansion. You just won't meet a finer individual than Roger Hoss. I'm thankful for what he has contributed to the Weekend of Champions and am also proud to call him my friend. I might add that Roger's fervor to talk about his faith doesn't just occur on prison weekends. Many locals in Freeport, Texas have told me amazing stories of how his generosity, witness, and love for others have helped touch lives throughout his community.

In the chapter on ex-offenders involved in the ministry, you'll meet **Harold Thompson** and his wife, **Mary**. As prison ministry directors for Campus Crusade for Christ, they are in charge of all the follow-up after the Weekends of Champions. Another individual who contributes greatly in this important area of service is **Howard Hardegree** from Atlanta, Georgia. A former police officer, Howard became a Christian a number of years ago, and eventually joined the staff of Campus Crusade for Christ. He works directly with Harold and Mary on the follow-up, and spent considerable time writing the follow-up booklet that the inmates use after the weekend. Once again, behind the scenes, Howard spends hours on the phone prior to our weekends, contacting prison chaplains across the country, assisting them in preparing for the follow-up, and also monitoring the follow-up once the weekend is over. His goal is to make sure everyone involved in this aspect of the ministry has all the tools needed for its ultimate success. This never-ending job requires someone with a strong commitment and a vision for success. Howard Hardegree has been a real pro and a great part of the team.

## Coordinators

The role of the coordinator is to direct the activities in a prison over the course of the entire weekend. This person works directly with the prison officials, counselors, and platform guests to ensure everything is done by the book regarding schedules, programs, and especially security. Starting with the check-out meeting on Thursday afternoon with the prison officials, the coordinator helps instill confidence in the prison staff that we are there to work *with* them, and that the coordinator will make sure every aspect of the weekend is followed exactly as planned. The coordinator acts as a liaison between the prison staff and the Glass team. The lines of communication and instruction from the prison are given to the coordinator, who in turn relays this vital information to the counselors and platform guests. If there is a problem during the weekend, the prison officials will work through it with the coordinator, who then handles it. The goal is to keep everyone happy, but ultimately to make absolutely sure the prison officials are comfortable with the activities of the weekend.

In addition to keeping an eye on the counselors, the coordinator is in charge of getting the platform guests in and out of the prison, and emceeing the program in the facility. Being a "people person" is critical for this job, and being knowledgeable on how prisons work is vital. Having served as a coordinator for a decade, I found that the more I learned about the prison system, the better coordinator I became. My goal was to set up everything in such a way that it would allow us to be the most effective, yet make sure the officials were totally comfortable with my plan, and didn't feel as if I were attempting to take over their jobs. We are always guests, and they always have the final say, and this must never change. Making sure this philosophy is a top priority has helped build solid relationships with prison staffs around the country, ensuring our continued invitations to their facilities.

A coordinator occasionally discovers that the prison staff is the easiest to work with while the counselors present a bigger challenge. This requires "kid gloves" treatment, as counselors are volunteers and are not paid to serve. Once in a while, a counselor wanders into a restricted area or does something that is strictly forbidden, and the coordinator must deal with the infraction. One serious slip-up could literally shut down this ministry in prisons all over America, so counselors must be lovingly reprimanded and reminded of the far-reaching effects of their mistakes.

A coordinator works hard. When I filled that position, I returned from the weekends exhausted from all the responsibilities. I completely gave of myself for five long, hard days and sometimes prayed at night before going to bed, "Lord, somehow give me eight hours of rest on four hours of sleep."

Throughout the years, Ron and I have become very close friends with many of the coordinators. They are fantastic individuals and real servants.

One of these servants, a true man of God, is **Bill Pruitt** from Visalia, California. He owns an orange grove and a gas station in Visalia. Bill was my first coordinator when I was a counselor, and has probably filled this role longer than anyone involved in the ministry. In addition to coordinating all over the country, Bill has organized many of the weekends in California, traveling all over the state, meeting with prison officials to discuss the Weekend of Champions, and opening doors for our program.

Bill Pruitt recruited **Warren Sargent**, also from Visalia, and Warren has helped on a consistent basis for a number of years. Warren's concern for those who are struggling goes beyond prison walls as he gives unselfishly to work with the homeless and "down and out" in the Visalia area. Two other California coordinators are **John Searcy** and **Bob Ellis**. John and Bob started in prison ministry as counselors and eventually gained the skills necessary to become coordinators and lead teams of counselors into the prisons.

**Cliff Schmidt**, a Fort Worth, Texas businessman, is another veteran coordinator. One of his contributions has been to pay the way of seminary students in the Dallas-Fort Worth area who want to attend a weekend. On many occasions Cliff has covered the bill for as many as a dozen students just so they could serve. This is a valuable asset in their seminary training. Interestingly, some of the students have become so turned on that they have pursued prison chaplaincy rather than serving as a pastor in a church.

**Ed and Helen Kilby** from Indianapolis, Indiana have also served for years with Bill Glass and after retiring have given even more time to the ministry.

Dallas, Texas is home for **Perry and Charlotte Bodin**, another husband and wife team who have given countless hours as coordinators. Perry owns a successful concrete business, and he and Charlotte often take the time to attend prison weekends.

**Carl and Agatha Williams** from Starkville, Mississippi are two of the sweetest folks you'd ever meet, as are **Sid and Kay McHaney** from

Huntsville, Texas. These couples are regulars on many weekends. When no women coordinators are needed, Carl and Sid are often encouraged by their wives to go without them. For the Williams, serving as coordinators has become a family affair as their son, **Marc**, and his wife, **Jean**, volunteer on many occasions, and they are as good as Dad and Mom in this role.

It's also a family affair for **Frank and Ila Green**, who live in Fortesque, New Jersey. This wonderful couple met through ministering in the prisons, and eventually married. As a matter of fact, the preacher who helped them tie the knot was strongman Paul Wrenn, whom they had grown to love while working together in the prison ministry.

**Steve and Ginny Jackson** travel from Houston, Texas to attend more weekends every year. Steve works as a coordinator, while Ginny loves to help in the control room and assist with many of the little emergency problems that arise, lending a hand with transportation, banquets, lodging, or any other number of areas where somebody needs extra help.

Another terrific husband-wife team is **Charles and Velma Lawson,** whose home is in Tallahassee, Florida. Charles was a member of the Florida Parole Board and still serves as a coordinator on many weekends, as does Velma. His knowledge of the prison system and his connections have been invaluable to Bill Glass.

**Eunice Sundberg**, a pastor's wife from California, was one of the best female coordinators the ministry ever had. Eunice had a lot to offer not only to the inmates but also to the counselors. She was actively involved in prison ministry outside the Glass weekends. She also has a gift in teaching and training and often presented material at the annual coordinators training meetings. She is now busy helping her husband, Wes, pastor a church in Minnesota.

Other special women who have given a considerable amount of time serving as coordinators are: **Mary Etta Martin** from Dallas, Texas; **Henree Martin** (not related) and **Peggy Williams** from Tallahassee, Florida; and **Pauline Boyd** from Lithonia, Georgia. These women are pros who do a super job of leading and serving on the Weekend of Champions. Mary Etta is the wife of former prison ministry director, Bunny Martin. When Bunny performed in the unit in which Mary Etta was working, it was always very special for her to introduce her husband to the inmates.

Early in my involvement there were some terrific men who volunteered regularly, and still serve occasionally. **Charles Darnell**, from Knoxville, Tennessee, owned a moving business and was a die-hard Tennessee Volunteer fan. **Randy Poe**, a Roseburg, Oregon dentist, often shut down his office to attend a Weekend of Champions. He always brought a number of friends from his church and community, and provided a large bus from their church that met a number of our transportation needs. **Charles Wilson** represented the state of New Mexico, and **Gary Hinkle** traveled all the way from Alaska to help serve on weekends. **Chet MacMillan** from Louisiana and **Jim Gibson** from Missouri were also active coordinators in the early days of the ministry.

Two other faithful and talented coordinators are now deceased– **Dick Stump** from Indianapolis, Indiana and **Rick McDonald** from Visalia, California. These two dear friends gave a tremendous amount of their time and resources to coordinate.

There were a handful of men who worked with me regularly during my ten years as a coordinator. Many of these men are still serving on a regular basis and do a fantastic job working with the ministry. One man in particular literally worked himself into a full-time staff position with Bill Glass. **Emory Wilson** from Fort Valley, Georgia, spent time behind bars, but when meeting him today, a person would never believe it. He is one of the finest men I've ever met. A tireless crusader for the ministry, Emory is *always* recruiting volunteers and sharing about prison ministry. Although I have prided myself in bringing new guests to the weekends, I can't hold a candle to Emory. He has probably gotten more people involved than anyone in the ministry. When Emory left the furniture business, Bill Glass saw a great opportunity and hired Emory to help raise finances and promote the Weekends of Champions. He is often kidded about his Georgian accent and our inability to understand him, but he is loved by everyone on the team and is one of my closest friends.

Other outstanding individuals from Georgia who have served as coordinators include **Frank Daniely, Kim Cassell, Dr. James Kirkwood, Frank Mellette, and Jerry Word. Dave Walker**, also from Georgia, gave his time to assist with transportation for many years.

**Paul Flory** from Orlando, Florida and **Jack Gould** from Dallas, Texas are two businessmen whose large companies require a tremendous amount of time and commitment. But despite the constant demands of their work, Paul and Jack always seem to make time for these weekends. What an advantage to have men with their business and leadership skills working as coordinators. Both of these gentlemen have told me a number of times how great it is to take off their ties, throw on their jeans and tennis shoes, and share the Gospel with inmates. They say it is a pleasant change of pace from the hectic world of business, and actually more exciting than many of their million-dollar deals.

Earlier in this chapter I mentioned **Hazel Wilson**, one of our elderly veterans. Her son, **John**, also from Ohio, serves as a coordinator and does a first-class job of working with counselors and prison officials.

With the Glass office in Dallas, a large number of coordinators come from the state of Texas. **Dick Dunham**, a Dallas businessman, volunteers regularly, and is also a member of the board of directors. **Rusty Harden**, an insurance salesman from Houston, has used his position as a coordinator to meet a number of prison officials and inmates, and work with them to help inmates find work and a church in the Houston area after they are released. **Larry Cowart** played football with Bill Glass and found Christ after his life and marriage were nearly destroyed by alcohol. Larry is a gentle giant who is a dynamic, solid believer and is one of the best coordinators on the team. **Ted Farrar** of Richardson, Texas, is a retired IRS agent who always managed to commit to a half a dozen weekends annually even while working with the IRS. And **Clarence McDaniel** from Borger, Texas, has become so enthused he comes to almost every weekend. His simple prayer is, "Lord, I want to serve every time, if you will provide the resources." And his prayer has certainly been answered as Clarence has been able to come consistently. **Franklin Scott** from Grand Prairie, Texas, is another outstanding Texan who serves, as does board member **John Saville**. John may be the most positive individual I've ever met–always looking on the bright side, and he's a real encourager. Other coordinators from Texas include **Bill Wilson, Clyde Caylor, Ken Jerome, Wendell Hoffman, and Mike Goodman.** (Oddly enough, Mike got started in prison ministry through his son's incarceration.)

Although unable to give as much time now as he used to, **Paul Holcomb**, a Columbia, South Carolina banker, opened the doors for this ministry to come into the South Carolina system, and also joined me on many weekends when I served as a coordinator. **Bill Kronemeyer** from Hilton Head, South Carolina, also was an active coordinator in the 1980's.

**Jerry Morris** from Springfield, Missouri and **Earl Wright** from Kingsport, Tennessee were two of Bill Glass's very best counselors through the years, and although counseling was their "first love," as the ministry expanded they graciously agreed to lend their skills and veteran experience by serving as coordinators.

There are others who served before I became involved and many new faces who continue to volunteer, and all of these people bring joy and delight to the ministry team. They play a critical role in the overall success of a Weekend of Champions, and their efforts have helped this ministry grow and continue to maintain positive credibility throughout prisons nationwide.

## Prison Ministry Directors

Since I became involved with Bill Glass in 1985, there have been a number of prison ministry directors. This is the only paid staff position, and the director is responsible for setting up and organizing the weekends. There is no way to adequately describe how difficult this job is. I know firsthand what is involved in making this work as I served as a director on six weekends in 1993 to assist in the ever-expanding schedule.

At a minimum, prior to the actual weekend, a director needs to make two trips, and sometimes three, to the facilities in which we'll be working. While the director is there on the initial visit, he meets with the officers at every institution to plan the schedule and gather all the important information about that particular facility. The director's goal is to have as many prison officials as possible at the meeting, and to make sure they all understand what will be necessary for the program to work. The number of inmates and staff will directly affect the number of counselors we will be allowed to bring in. The layout of the prison itself dictates other details such as program sites, lockdown or death row units, boot camps, or even breaking larger prisons into sections, having programs in as many as five or six sites at one time for specific inmates in those areas.

Just the details and information at the prisons alone occupies a large portion of the director's time on the check-out trip, but the director must also reserve a headquarters hotel and visit churches to plan food and facilities for the evening banquets. The prisons and churches are also encouraged to help with transportation, if possible. The goals are to find a hotel that is located in the proximity of all the prisons we are serving and to obtain an inexpensive group rate. Once the maximum number of counselors we can bring is established, it is easier to try to estimate the number of motel rooms and meeting areas we will need, plus give the churches a rough idea of how many they will need to feed.

Once again, volunteers who live in the area will often do some of this leg work prior to the director's arrival, saving him quite a bit of time and effort.

Coordinating all of these meetings with busy prison officials requires time on the phone and a commitment from the officials to be flexible so that each unit can be visited on one trip over a few days.

After the check-out has been completed, the information is then brought back to the Dallas office and all of the arrangements are confirmed in writing with each prison. An information letter and application forms are then put together to be sent to the entire counselor mailing list.

As the platform guests are confirmed, posters are designed especially for the weekend in that specific area. The posters are mailed to the institutions well in advance so they can be placed throughout the prisons to begin alerting the inmates and staff of our upcoming visit and to start building interest and enthusiasm.

From the check-out all the way up to the weekend proper, lines of communication are kept open between the prisons and the Bill Glass office, and many times adjustments need to be made to coincide with the ever-changing prison environment.

Of course, two or three months later, the director will return to actually direct the weekend and stay on top of all of the activities and schedules that are taking place. The actual weekend is even more taxing than the check-out trip as the director is going non-stop from early in the morning until late at night, monitoring every aspect of the occasion.

All of this is for just *one* weekend; but remember, there are twenty-plus weekends like this annually. Consequently, as soon as the director finishes either a weekend or a check-out, he is off again to do another weekend or another check-out, constantly meeting important calendar deadlines that must be kept to give the office and the prisons ample preparation time for the event. Without the volunteer help along the way, it is almost impossible to meet the never-ending demands of the job. When I did this, it almost wore me out, so I admire and respect the individuals who have served and continue to serve in this capacity.

The first year or so of my involvement, **Dan Leary** from Indiana was the director, and then **Bunny Martin** took over the position. The majority of the time I've been a volunteer, Bunny has been the leader of the team. After he took the position of director, he immediately invited me to serve as a coordinator, and through our close friendship I became heavily involved in working directly with Bunny on a number of projects to try to make the ministry more effective and bring new ideas that would upgrade the professionalism. It was during Bunny's seven-year term as director that the ministry really expanded, jumping from seven or eight weekends annually to twenty-four a year. He did an unbelievable job of staying on top of this huge undertaking and, believe it or not, also continued to serve as a platform guest on the weekends, in addition to directing them. What a thrill it was for me to work so closely with my good friend, Bunny, during these super years! His infectious enthusiasm, sense of humor, and love for others helped build a sweet spirit among the ranks, and Bunny gets a well deserved pat on the back for a job well done.

When Bunny stepped down in 1994, **Jim Lang** took over, and he has also done an incredible job of leading the charge. His wife, **Bonnie**, also came on board, serving as a secretary in the office. And eventually, when the Bill Glass office realized that the demands of the job were just too much for one staff person, **Jake Minton**, a retired funeral home director from Borger, Texas, was hired to assist Jim as prison ministry director. **Donna Morris** also helps with secretarial duties, and **Kim Zabinski** also works full time with the ministry out of the Dallas office. About the time Jim Lang was hired, **Gene Ellerbee**, a top level businessman from Proctor & Gamble, decided to leave his position and become the chief operating officer of the Bill Glass Ministries, bringing his business expertise with him to help bring focus and direction to the ever-expanding association. **Dick Plowman** also works full time for the ministry in the area of development, and loves to join us on as many weekends as possible to serve as a counselor.

I'd also like to mention two very special friends who for many years gave their lives to the prison ministry through their positions on Bill's staff. **Dick Rohrer** and his wife, **Colleen**, recently retired, but only after twenty years and twelve years, respectively, of working on the staff. Dick and Colleen helped organize many of Bill Glass's city-wide crusades and contributed greatly to the prison ministry. During a number of the transition periods between directors and also in the expansion, Dick directed many weekends and did a fantastic job, as did Colleen, of keeping the boat afloat. This is a couple who are loved and admired, and are well-known friends of the Bill Glass family.

Another wonderful lady named **Ruth Hale** served as Bunny's secretary during most of his years as director. With the rapid growth, you can imagine the tremendous amount of extra time and effort that Ruth put in to keep the wheels on the bus. Many counselors often talked about how great it was to call the office and visit with Ruth. In addition to handling their questions about the prison weekends, she had a deep personal concern for them and became a friend to many on the team, praying for them and helping many through difficult times in their lives with her love and encouragement. Ruth has been sorely missed since she and her husband moved to Oklahoma.

Everyone who has served in a staff position deserves a big "high five" for his or her invaluable contributions over the years. They have helped the Weekend of Champions program to grow and to be effective in bringing the Gospel to prisons all over America.

As I mentioned earlier in this chapter, a whole book could be devoted just to counselor stories and experiences. We've attempted, however, to inform you of the specific roles the counselors, full-time volunteer staff, coordinators, and prison ministry directors play on a Weekend of Champions, and introduce many of the key leadership personnel with whom we've served over the years. These are all very special teammates, and our hats go off to them. We share our love and gratitude for all they have given and continue to give to this unique ministry.

In closing, a number of years ago, Nathaniel Clark, an inmate at the Goree Unit in Huntsville, Texas, wrote a poem. He presented it to prison counselors **Bob Kocmoud** and **Kevin Hatton** at the conclusion of our weekend to thank them for visiting the Goree Unit, and especially for the love and concern they had shown him. Through Bob and Kevin's efforts, Nathaniel trusted Christ, and his poem seems to best convey the positive impact that counselors do have on inmates and serves as an important reminder that counselors truly are the heart and soul of a Bill Glass Weekend of Champions.

### Is Nothing Ever For Free?

I met a group of men one day
And went to hear what they had to say.
They spoke of Jesus, the Son of God,
And of the love they had in their hearts.
They were lawyers, teachers, businessmen,
But they treated inmates like people, even friends.
They laughed and talked with them, even ate,
They talked about their past lives,
their misfortunes, their old hates.
They spoke about religion and of the sacrifice
And how God gave his only Son
the Lord Jesus Christ.
They talked about heaven and the way to get in,
Said Jesus had died for all of us to free us from sin.
Although I only got to talk with but two,
Somehow deep inside, I think I knew
They had found something good
and would take nothing less,
For in their eyes I saw love, peace and happiness.
I won't say that I truly understand
But it has given me another perspective on
the creature called man.
Never before have I seen anything like it,
nor did I ever think I would–
People caring about other people,
trying to do some good.
Everybody does something for something–
nothing is ever for free.
**It's the first time in my life**
**somebody has given me something**
**and didn't ask nothing from me.**
We bowed our heads and together we prayed,
So good luck, Mr. Glass, in your crusade.

# CHAPTER 6

# PRISON STAFF—
# OFFICERS AND CHAPLAINS

*I*n July 1992, I was the coordinator at Somers Correctional Institution on one of our weekends in the Hartford, Connecticut area and had just finished loading my team of counselors on the prison bus that would transport us to the Friday night banquet. We were right on schedule, and everything had gone smoothly all day. Everyone was present and accounted for, so I went back into the security entrance of the facility to let the captain of security know our numbers were accurate and we were ready to leave. But as we were checking our lists, suddenly there was a flurry of commotion at the security booth, and within seconds officers were pouring into the area. The captain told me to sit tight and await his instructions once he assessed the situation. As the moments passed, I was concerned about my counselors but realized there was nothing I could do to explain the delay to them but only stay put and wait for further direction from the Somers correctional staff.

I knew there was a major disturbance when the officers opened a large room that was filled with weapons, handcuffs, and other items used to subdue inmates. Officers came running in, grabbing the equipment they needed, and preparing themselves for action. I'd been in enough prisons to know that one of two things had occurred—there was either an escape or a riot. It turned out to be the latter. Once the security captain had all the details, he informed me that a riot was in progress at the Enfield facility, which was five minutes down the road from Somers.

The first order of business was to quickly remove all of my counselors from the bus because the officers needed it to transport staff over to Enfield to beef up security there, and the bus would serve as somewhat of a battlefield headquarters for the officers.

We hustled to the bus, I told my counselors what was happening, and then quickly moved them into one of the nearby visiting areas. In spite of all that was going on, the officer I was working with made it top priority to take care of us first, and to make sure we were safe. Once we were taken care of, only then did his attention shift to the problem at Enfield. Thanking us for our patience, he told us some other vehicles were on their way to pick us up and transport us back to the hotel. Then he jumped into a waiting vehicle to join his fellow officers at Enfield.

What I remember most about this whole experience is watching the officers at the weapons room interact. I saw many of them hugging each other and expressing their love, realizing that in moments they would be thrust into a life and death situation that had no guarantees. It was like a football team in a locker room right before a big game; there each player prepares individually for his assignment, but also realizes the importance of teammates that he will rely on to achieve victory in the game. Although the atmosphere was similar, the situation was altogether different. This was not a game, but a situation where the stakes of winning and losing were much higher.

This whole ordeal reminded me that correctional officers put their lives on the line every day they show up for work. Because of the constant possibility of life-threatening situations, a strong comraderie is built among officers who rely so much on each other. If one fails to do his job correctly, the rest of the team will be affected and lives could be lost by a lack of attentiveness. This is a special breed of people, and I respect and admire them all.

On each Weekend of Champions we meet dozens of chaplains and officers. In this chapter Ron and I want to salute all of these special folks and mention a few who hold a special place in our hearts and who have become our good friends.

## Captain Bill Treadwell

One of the very special officers I will always remember is Captain Bill Treadwell, whom I met at the Jackson, Georgia Diagnostic and Classification Center while he was working on the death row cell block. This gifted man served on Georgia's death row cell block and had an uncanny ability to take care of the inmates in this challenging situation. Treadwell's motto was "Fairness, Firmness, and Respect." He knew how to do his job, yet capture the respect of the inmates. This is unusual in that most of the time there isn't a great deal of love and admiration between security officers and inmates. Captain Bill educated me on the mentality and personality of death row inmates and taught me a tremendous lesson on the power of the spoken word. This southern gentleman took pride in his work and bent over backwards to accommodate us while working the death row area on the Weekend of Champions. I am thankful to have had the chance to work with him.

On subsequent prison weekends that included this Jackson facility, Captain Treadwell always stopped by the control room at the hotel to say hello, and I spent many wonderful hours visiting with him over coffee. After his retirement, he was able to share in more detail about death row, and I sat fascinated as he reflected on the years he served in H-Block.

The influence Captain Treadwell had on my life is outlined in detail in the chapter about our death row experiences.

### Dick Hanley and Chaplain Skip Pike

Dick Hanley was one of the program directors at Central Prison in Raleigh, North Carolina. He was our contact at Central and coordinated the Weekend of Champions. On my first visit to Central in April 1990, I was the assigned coordinator and met Dick at my Thursday morning check-out meeting. After just a few minutes with him, I knew this was a very special man and that we were going to have a great weekend at Central. An added bonus was then meeting Chaplain Skip Pike, who also impressed me immediately and gained my respect as one of the top prison chaplains in the country. Dick and Skip had already spent hours preparing for our visit and had every base covered to accommodate us, including special programs for the death row inmates. This was especially exciting since the Weekend of Champions was not allowed on Central's death row a few years earlier. Dick Hanley comes about as close to being a saint as anyone I've ever met—kind of a Mother Teresa in a suit and tie.

Skip Pike does a fantastic job as prison chaplain in the largest prison in the state of North Carolina. Like Dick, Skip is a servant and has a heart for God and for inmates. The feedback from many of the inmates that weekend was all positive toward Chaplain Pike. He spent the entire weekend with our team, which is unusual. Sadly enough, on many of our weekends we don't see the chaplain all weekend. They often just disappear.

Dick and Skip became our close friends, and whenever Ron and I are doing a prison weekend in the state of North Carolina, we always call ahead and offer to do programs at Central, especially for the death row inmates who have very few opportunities for anything special. On several occasions, Ron has shown the inmates slides of many of the greatest photographs he has taken in his years with United Press International. John Lotz, a former Tar Heel coach and now the assistant athletic director at North Carolina, has joined us on several visits to death row at Central, and the inmates love John. He is a powerful speaker, and they love question and answer time with him about the athletic program at UNC.

Probably one of the most unique aspects of our many death row visits at Central is the fact that inmates are let out of their cells into the day room area for our program. This enhances our effectiveness to have a positive impact on their lives. I'm sure the respect that Dick and Skip have earned with the prison officials has helped make this possible. On most death rows we have to work cell to cell, and the security officers won't release the inmates in a group.

In the death row chapter, Ron relates interesting experiences he's had with several of the men on death row at Central. We were there together just a few weeks prior to a scheduled execution. Obviously the atmosphere was different and, although only one man was to be put to death, each man on death row had to deal with the situation, and *all* were affected. It felt good to know we had a positive impact on the population during this time.

In August of 1995, Dick Hanley retired due to health problems. He will be sorely missed, and I won't ever forget the influence he had on my life and on the lives of the many inmates he faithfully cared for and served. Chaplain Pike continues to minister at Central, and I look forward to working with him many more years.

### Memorable Commissioners

State commissioners who have gone the "second mile" to assist us with the Weekends of Champions are **Morris Thigpen** from Alabama and **Larry Meachum** from Oklahoma and Connecticut. Not only did these men hold positions of authority in the Department of Corrections, but they had strong Christian commitments and were strong believers in the Weekend of Champions program. Because of this, it was always a pleasure to work in their states as we could bet that everything we needed to most effectively run our program was taken care of, and first-class treatment was always the norm.

Commissioner Thigpen was incredible. In spite of all the pressures and responsibilities he had serving as commissioner in Alabama, he put on his blue jeans and tennis shoes and worked with us the entire weekend. In a very low-key, humble way, Morris did some of the more menial tasks like carrying equipment for the platform guests, making sandwiches in the break room, or helping drive program people to and from the institutions. He was a servant in every sense of the word and was almost embarrassed to take credit for his efforts. Not only did he ensure total cooperation at each institution we visited, but he also arranged for his church to provide the meals and facility for both of our weekend banquets.

I vividly recall Morris carrying Tanya Crevier's basketballs and equipment into the Holman Unit in Atmore, Alabama. He put his job on the line by allowing the entire death row population out into the yard to watch Tanya perform and to hear Bill Glass speak. Morris mingled with all of the inmates and was concerned for each of them. He really wasn't Commissioner Thigpen that day. He was Morris, a lay counselor and committed Christian who wanted to share his faith with inmates and bring some hope and good news into their lives.

**Ron Sutton** was Commissioner Thigpen's assistant, and he, just like Morris, participated all weekend with us and helped behind the scenes to make sure we had everything we needed. These two gentlemen developed many friendships with the members of the Bill Glass family and enabled us to reach thousands of inmates for Christ in the prisons in their state.

Larry Meachum served as the Commissioner of Prisons in the states of Oklahoma and Connecticut and was an avid supporter of the Weekend of Champions. Larry was totally committed to the program and believed rehabilitation occurred when an inmate accepted Jesus Christ and pursued the Christian faith. He understood our approach and knew what we needed in the way of cooperation from prison officials to bring our very best to the table. Consequently, he almost did our job for us by selling the facilities on our program before we arrived. Not only that, he briefed them on many of the things we needed from them to run the program. He was dedicated to his work and his faith. We always had great weekends in the states Larry served.

Being involved with the Glass Prison Ministry for over two decades, Ron has become acquainted with many prison officials and has sent them wonderful memories of our weekends through the pictures of them posing with platform guests and counselors. There are a couple of wardens who stand out in Ron's favorite recollections.

### Lieutenant Craig, Major Craig, and Warden Craig

In 1975, while visiting the Goree Women's Facility near Huntsville, Texas, Ron met Lieutenant Catherine Craig. She had been assigned to oversee the activities of the Weekend of Champions at Goree. When Ron arrived at the institution, he hit it off immediately with Catherine, and she was totally receptive to his visiting with inmates and shooting pictures. This seemed a bit strange to Ron as most officials are usually a little bit wary of cameras going into prison, even though clearance is established prior to Ron's arrival at the gate. Ron had a great experience at Goree and was especially appreciative of Lieutenant Craig's interest and cooperation.

Several years later, the women's unit was transferred to Gatesville, Texas, where it is located today. In the early 1980's, Ron was involved in a Weekend of Champions in the Gatesville area, and he learned that Lieutenant Craig had been promoted to the rank of major at a facility called Riverside. Between the Friday afternoon and evening programs, Ron–cameras and all–approached the unit and was met by the glares of three female officers. Staring at his equipment and then Ron, they asked him where he was going with the cameras. Ron told them he was the photographer for the Bill Glass Weekend of Champions and was there to shoot pictures of some of the counselors. At that point one of the officers said, "There's no way in hell you're gonna get those cameras in here!"

About that time, however, Major Craig strolled up the path, saw Ron, and gave him a big hug. She told the women officers to give Ron free run of the whole prison and to make sure he had everything he needed.

As the officers' jaws dropped in amazement, Ron waltzed into the prison, contemplating whether or not to rub it in, but wisely choosing not to. Just as Lieutenant Craig was now Major Craig, these female officers could very easily become wardens, and Ron might need them on his side someday.

By 1986 when the team returned for another weekend, Major Craig was now the warden at the Mountain View Women's Facility in Gatesville. This particular prison also housed the women on death row. Ron was planning to visit Mountain View on Saturday; however, the unit coordinator told him on Friday night that Warden Craig would be gone Saturday on a business trip. Saturday morning when Ron arrived at the prison, the assistant warden met him, and with a puzzled look on her face she said to Ron, "I don't know what kind of spell you have on Warden Craig, but she told me to tell you that you're free to go anywhere in the prison, including death row." And that opened the door for Ron to begin what would become an incredible relationship with the women housed there. (His experiences with them are described in further detail in the chapter on death row experiences.)

Ron has maintained his friendship with Warden Craig over the years, and on many of his overseas trips, he includes her on the long list of people to whom he sends post cards. In 1992, on a subsequent visit to Gatesville, she showed Ron all of the post cards and pictures he had sent her that she had saved and shown to others. As Ron became acquainted with the women on death row, he discovered the tremendous amount of respect and admiration they had for Warden Craig.

It's a pleasure to work with officials like Warden Craig, who share our Christian commitment. Their concern, cooperation, and encouragement help us to be especially effective in reaching inmates with the Gospel. Unfortunately, not all administrators are like this, and some reluctantly host our team. One of Ron's other memorable prison official stories occurred under this scenario.

### Warden Tom Jones

Tom Jones was the warden at Rivers Correctional Unit in Milledgeville, Georgia. When the team brought the Weekend of Champions program to this area in the early 1980's, Warden Jones was extremely uncomfortable with our visit and really didn't want us in his prison. He was afraid we were going to create havoc and all kinds of security problems. Despite his lack of interest and opposition, however, he was present and accounted for all weekend, keeping close watch on everything we were doing. Apparently he felt that he'd need to be there in case the wheels started coming off the bus.

An amazing thing occurred, however, through the course of that weekend. The Lord began to work on Warden Jones. As he observed the programs, counseling, and positive response of some of the most hardened criminals, his heart began to soften and his attitude began to change. Everyone was shocked when, with tears streaming down his cheeks, the warden walked to the front of the chapel after our final program on Sunday morning. Fighting to gain his composure, he eyed the room full of Bill Glass counselors and said, "I want to tell you people I really didn't want you here, but this weekend I have seen an unbelievable change in this institution. Normally I would have 150 DR's (disciplinary reports) on any given weekend. This weekend I only had three. You have turned this prison around and made a positive difference."

As he thanked the entire Glass team, it was obvious he was absolutely overwhelmed by what had happened. Ron learned several weeks later that Warden Jones accepted Christ through his involvement with a church in Milledgeville and since that time has become a staunch supporter of Bill's program.

On other weekends in Milledgeville over the years, Warden Jones has been with us from start to finish and helped open many other institutions for us to visit, including Reidsville, one of the toughest prisons in the system.

### Warden Lanson Newsome

Reidsville had very little programming, but Warden Jones told Lanson Newsome, the warden at Reidsville, that Bill's program really worked and he ought to invite the team in at the first opportunity. Ron happened to be at the first weekend in Reidsville and knew of its reputation for numerous incidents, riots, and murders. Warden Newsome, who is also a believer, stood tall in his position and was well respected for his leadership in this tough environment. Ron was impressed at his availability to the inmate population, and his positive attitude toward the Weekend of Champions. That first weekend at Reidsville went very well and, like the experience at Rivers, had a calming effect on the entire prison population.

## Chaplains to Remember

Prison chaplains have a difficult job. They work in an extremely negative environment, catching those they serve at low tide in their lives and often with very little spiritual dimension in their past. Chaplains are normally in charge of all religious programming in the institution, so they must deal with a variety of faiths and issues. To the strong evangelistic chaplain, this presents a great challenge, and it takes a very special person to accommodate each group of inmates. Chaplains have to deal with deaths, either of inmates or relatives of inmates on the outside. Losing a loved one during a time of incarceration is twice as tough, and the chaplain is usually the bearer of bad news. I recall one incident that vividly reminded me of how tough a chaplain's job can be.

I had concluded my Thursday morning check-out at Coffield Prison near Palestine, Texas. As I sat in the chaplain's office waiting for my ride back to the hotel, I learned that late the night before an inmate had committed suicide in his cell. I watched the chaplain begin calling a list of people he was to contact in a situation like this, establishing who would come and get the body. Believe it or not, he called every one of the seventeen names on the list, and not one of the contacts wanted anything to do with the body. Consequently, he told me the inmate would have to be buried in a graveyard near the prison that was used for unclaimed bodies of inmates. The chaplain would officiate at a service before the burial, and odds are only a few officers or friends of the chaplain would attend. I could tell that the chaplain was very distressed with this dilemma, and saddened by the fact that no one even cared that the inmate had committed suicide. I felt sick to my stomach just watching him make call after call in frustration.

Prison chaplains put in very long, hard hours and are really never off duty. They often have small budgets, and many institutions don't have a chapel to hold their services in on Sunday morning. They must improvise by moving chairs and sound systems to and from areas that will accommodate their prison congregations. Flexibility is certainly a common word in their vocabulary.

Prison chaplains learn very quickly not to be conned by inmates and how to exercise tough love. They must be consistent in the ways they handle the various problems and concerns that inmates bring into their offices. In addition, they are at the mercy of security and must be obedient to their authority and direction. There are numerous other problems prison chaplains have to deal with that don't exist in any local church. Obviously, chaplains who have a heart for the Lord and for inmates will be the most effective, and the best chaplains are those who feel called to this type of ministry, rather than being stuck there.

The support of the prison chaplain is an integral part of the success of a Weekend of Champions. Of course, we must have the backing of the administration, but having a good prison chaplain to work with can only make the weekend better. Ron and I have met so many outstanding chaplains in our years in prison ministry, and I'm sure we will continue to meet many new ones who will become friends and allies with us in the fight to win lost inmates to faith in Christ.

In other chapters the names of some of the chaplains we've worked with will surface through some of our stories, but here Ron and I want to mention a few prison chaplains with whom we have developed a special relationship through our years of service.

Some states have a head chaplain who oversees all of the other chaplains and the religious programming at every correctional facility in that state. Some of the best we've had the pleasure of working with are: **Emmit Solomon** in Texas; **Jim Dent** in Kentucky; **Bob Lynn** in Washington; **James Cook** in Connecticut; and **Ben Wright** in Georgia. Because of their strong commitment to our program, we've always been well received in these states and have had outstanding experiences. These gentlemen are all well respected by their fellow chaplains and correctional officials and have served faithfully as prison chaplains for many years.

**Austin Anderson** of North Carolina and **Paul Pedrick** of New Jersey are prison chaplains who also serve as coordinators on the Weekends of Champions. These outstanding individuals find time in their already busy schedules to serve with us, and their experience is invaluable on the weekends. Because they are prison chaplains, they have helped the rest of the Glass leadership better understand the mindset, personality, and challenges of this position. They have both assisted at annual training sessions and have provided great insight and help.

From a different perspective, there are several other individuals who became prison chaplains through their initial experience as counselors on a Weekend of Champions. **Steve Hankins** serves in Florida; **Bill Cleavinger** at a facility in North Carolina; **Jack Wilcox** in Texas, including extensive work with the death row unit at Ellis I; and **Nancy Dixon** in California. I truly believe the Bill Glass Ministry will be responsible for generating future prison chaplains who will serve in correctional systems someday.

Another unique individual, who is now deceased, but served faithfully with Bill was **Roscoe Plowman**. Roscoe was a prison chaplain for years, and then after he retired he served as a counselor on Glass weekends. The most fascinating part of Roscoe's life, however, was his experience as a circuit rider preacher. Roscoe rode a horse across the country and stopped at towns to preach at revival meetings. This godly, loving man attracted large groups of counselors and inmates on the weekends; they sat for hours listening to his fascinating stories of his days on the circuit, and also his work as one of the very first prison chaplains in the United States.

We occasionally meet prison chaplains who actually got their start in prison ministry as inmates, or through close brushes with the law. I remember a chaplain at Waupun, Wisconsin who took me to the cell in the prison where he did his time. One of the premier chaplains in America is **Earl Smith**, who serves at San Quentin in California. Earl's background was pretty shaky, but the Lord has used it to give him a great understanding of the lifestyles of the men he serves. Working San Quentin, one of the largest prisons in the country, is no picnic, and Earl has been there a long time and does a fantastic job. Whenever Earl is with our team, I love to sit down and visit with him as he is a person I respect and admire very much.

Another gentleman I have grown to love and respect is Chaplain **Roland Ruffin** who serves at the Tracy-Deuel Correctional Facility in Tracy, California. Always upbeat and with a real heart for service, Roland arranges some fantastic programs for the men he serves.

Also in California, Chaplain **Glen Davis** has a fantastic ministry at the Fresno City Jail, and because of his presence we have been able to do some outstanding programs there. This is a bit unusual since most of our work is done in state prisons. And across town at the Fresno Prison for Juvenile Offenders, **Ron Climer** is one of the best chaplains I've ever met who deals with young offenders. During his childhood, Ron experienced many of the same problems the youth he serves are facing, but his life's course was dramatically altered when he was introduced to the Lord.

**Charlie Davis**, a former University of North Carolina Tar Heel football player, has also provided outstanding help while serving as a chaplain and supervising the chaplaincy programs in prisons all over the western half of the state of North Carolina.

Two chaplains in the state of Missouri who contributed greatly to successful weekends over the years in their state are **Bob Bell** and **Larry Hines**. Whenever we participated in Missouri, Bob and Larry provided transportation for the prison ministry director and accompanied him to the check-out meetings at each facility. Assistance like this can only be provided by someone who knows the area and the key personnel, and we always appreciated their help. They also helped open doors for banquet arrangements and recruited counselors from nearby churches to participate.

Two other outstanding chaplains mentioned elsewhere in this book are **Skip Pike** who serves in North Carolina and **Tim Crosby** from Texas. These men always have the welcome mat out for our team and provide red carpet treatment. Ron and I have spent time with these chaplains on the death rows in their respective units.

And I can't forget **Chaplain Ray** of the International Prison Ministry in Dallas, Texas! Considered one of the pioneers in prison ministry, Chaplain Ray has provided an unlimited supply of literature to prisoners all over the world through his many books about former inmates and others whose lives have been changed through their relationship with Christ.

Another great friend of ours and of the Glass ministry is **Don Smarto**. Don worked in prisons before becoming the Director of the Institute for Prison Ministries, which headquarters at the Billy Graham Center in Chicago on the Wheaton College campus. Don is a brilliant man, and with his background working in the prison system, coupled with his strong Christian commitment and heart for prison ministry, he has become one of the most respected authorities on prison ministry in the world today. He has written a number of excellent books on crime, punishment, and ministry, and is in great demand around the world as a speaker. I'll always try to get a front row seat if Don is speaking at a Weekend of Champions event. He is super! He regularly brings large numbers of Wheaton students as counselors on the weekends. He also oversees the Colson Scholarship individuals on campus. Named after Chuck Colson, these scholarships are provided to ex-offenders who want to pursue a degree in a ministry-related field. Many former inmates apply and Don helps screen the applicants to determine the best candidates.

Having examined most of the five hundred prison ministries in America today, Don considers the Weekend of Champions program one of the best, if not the best, evangelistic prison outreach in America. Having an endorsement like that from Don has meant a lot to those of us who have spent years serving with the Glass ministry. Don also has great skills in the film and video arena and has produced several film projects featuring an on-camera look at the Glass Weekend of Champions. Needless to say, Don is a true friend of this ministry and deserves a big thank you for all he's done to help over the years.

It's impossible to list all the names of the officers and chaplains Ron and I have met through the prison ministry in numerous correctional facilities. We've tried to recognize a few extra special friends, but we appreciate all of the officials and chaplains in this country for their dedication and for the wonderful cooperation they have afforded us on prison ministry weekends through the years. There are many professionals out there who take a great deal of pride in their work and demonstrate a tremendous courage and conviction in their tasks. Ron and I look forward to continuing our visits to prisons and meeting new friends that serve as officers and chaplains.

ack Eckerd of Eckerd Drugs was a counselor at ome of the early weekends.

Often counselors don't leave the prison until nightfall.

3unny Martin is cuffed and arrested. He was harged with impersonating a magician.

Norm Miller, CEO of Interstate Batteries, helps provide a race car and also serves as a counselor.

Counselors enter a prison to begin a Weekend of Champions.

Officers pat down counselors during the security clearing process.

A ferry escorts these counselors across the inlet to the McNeil Island prison near Seattle, Washington.

A bus stops to drop off counselors at a Mississippi prison gate.

Counselors leave an institution after a busy day.

Inmates fill the yard for a Weekend of Champions program featuring powerlifter Paul Wrenn.

Bill Glass, founder of the Weekend of Champions, prays with a hurting inmate in the San Quentin chapel.

The NASCAR race car is made available through Joe Gibbs and is a huge draw when it roars onto prison yards.

Bikers from the Christian Motorcycle Association (CMA) enter a prison to witness and show off their bikes.

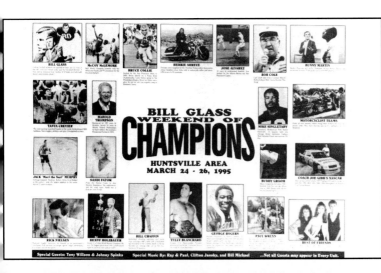

Posters listing the platform guests are placed throughout the institutions to promote our upcoming visit.

Bill Glass speaks to a large group of inmates on one of the first prison ministry weekends.

Motorcycles line the salleyport of this Connecticut prison for a security check.

Ron poses for a picture with Hugh Bob Majors who recognized Ron from a previous prison weekend.

Ron with former
death row inmate
Charles Stanley.
They first met on
death row in 1983.
Stanley's sentence
was later
commuted to life.

An inmate proudly
shows Ron a new
Bible he has just
received.

Ron shares
Scripture with an
inmate.

Watson "Waddy" Spoelstra, a writer for the Detroit News, accompanied Ron on his first prison weekend.

The entire Glass team that participated on Ron's first prison weekend. This photo was taken in Mansfield, Ohio in 1973 and was the third Weekend of Champions.

Paul Wrenn warms up with Rick before he hits the weight pile.

Rick with Pepsi Light!

A South Carolina
inmate gives Ron a
model airplane he
built in prison.

Bunny Martin with
Rick at Rick's first
weekend in
Indianapolis,
Indiana in 1984.

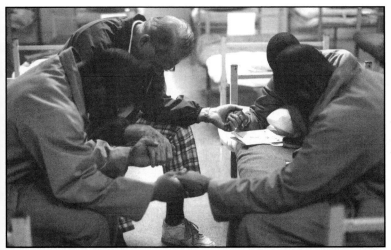

Praying is always
special to inmates
and counselors.

Rick receives his fifth weekend prison cross from Bill Glass and Bunny Martin.

Rick is juggling in Chowchilla, California–the largest women's prison in the world.

Rick points to the gold ace of spades on this inmate's tooth.

Bill Pruitt, Coordinator

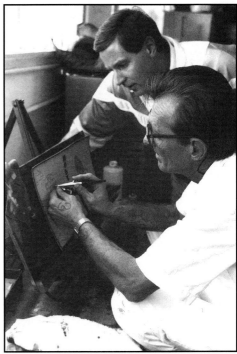

Observing an inmate working on a leather Bible cover.

Marvin Johnson, three-time Light Heavyweight Boxing Champion of the World, shows off his world championship belts in a youth prison.

Johnny Spinks, professional kick boxing champion.

Rick listens intently to an inmate in a Texas prison.

Inmates use mirrors to watch Rick's hands closely as he demonstrates a card trick on Connecticut's death row.

This Alabama inmate (nicknamed Popeye) lost all his teeth as a result of using drugs.

Bunny Martin, World's Yo-Yo Champion, strikes a match held in the clenched teeth of an inmate while Rick looks on.

Former Twins pitcher Al Worthington helps an inmate study the Bible.

Rick with Gene Stallings, Head Football Coach at the University of Alabama.

Country-Western singer Clifton Jansky stands in a prison cemetery near Huntsville, Texas where the bodies of unclaimed inmates are buried. The numbers on each grave marker signify the inmate's prison I.D. number. This prompted Jansky to write the theme song for the Bill Glass Prison Ministry - "They May Know My Number, But Jesus Knows My Name."

Bill Chaffin holds the Guinness world record for sinking 190 out of 208 free throws in ten minutes.

Terry Meeuwsen, former Miss America, presently works with the *700 Club* on the Christian Broadcasting Network.

Oscar Roan, Cleveland Browns.

Paul Wrenn, 1981 Powerlifting Champion of the World, lifts a correctional officer with his teeth.

Denny Holzbauer, six-time world karate champion, and 7th degree blackbelt.

Rick arm wrestles Earnie Shavers, former boxing great.

Rick and Reggie White, the "NFL's Minister of Defense," prepare to enter a New Jersey prison.

George Rogers,
1980 Heisman
trophy winner, and
Rick are held
captive by two
California officers.

ack Murphy, who
id time as a jewel
hief, studies Don
hinnick's Super
owl rings while
Rick warns Don to
eep a close eye on
hem.

Anthony Clark,
World's Strongest
Man, lifts the back
end of an
automobile and
pushes it across the
prison yard like a
wheelbarrow.

America's coach, Tom Landry of the Dallas Cowboys, without his hat.

Former NFL star Earl Campbell makes a point on a Weekend of Champions.

Baseball great Andre Thornton of the Cleveland Indians eats a prison meal.

Billy "Whiteshoes" Johnson does his famous touchdown dance while former Dallas Cowboy linebacker Bob Bruenig looks on.

Al Wood, former North Carolina standout and NBA star, discusses hoops and his faith.

Former All-Pro of the Dallas Cowboys Roger Staubach throws passes to inmates.

Pittsburgh Steeler standout Mean Joe Green takes the microphone.

Jim Sundberg had a great major league career as a catcher.

Former North Carolina assistant and SEC Coach of the Year at Florida John Lotz "shoots the eyes out" in this North Carolina prison yard.

Tully Blanchard, pro wrestler and one of the original "four horsemen."

Detroit Tiger pitching great Frank Tanana.

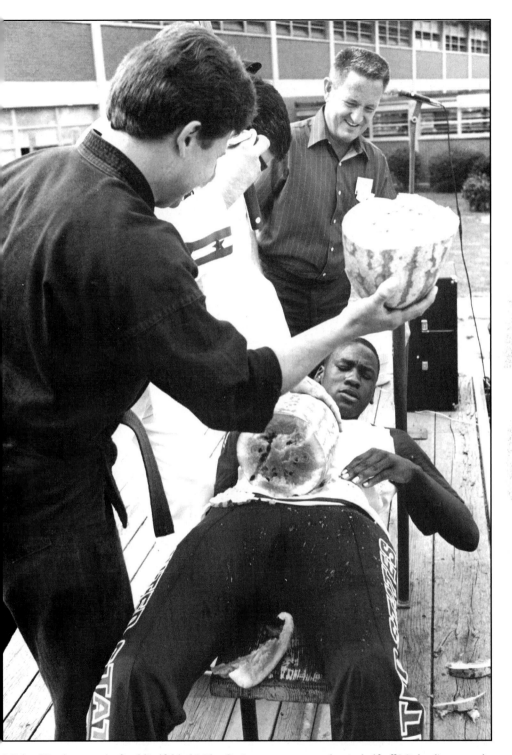

Michael Jordan reacts after blindfolded Mike Crain cuts a watermelon in half off Michael's stomach. Unfortunately, Crain also cut Jordan, sending Michael to the hospital for three stitches.

NFL coach Sam
Rutigliano discusses
faith and football.

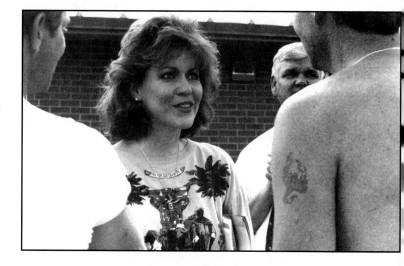

Kathy Golla visits
with inmates after
sharing her
incredible story.

Ray Hildebrand (r.)
and his singing
partner, Paul Land
(l.). In 1963
Hildebrand wrote
and recorded the
number one hit,
"Hey Paula."

Olympic Gold Medal winner Madeline Manning Mims.

Rosey Grier, former NFL star, can also preach.

Pat Williams, now General Manager of the NBA's Orlando Magic, shares while serving in the same capacity with the Philadelphia 76ers.

Mike Barber, former NFL great, now directs the very successful Mike Barber Prison Ministry.

Bubba Paris played in three Super Bowls with the San Francisco 49'ers.

Paul Anderson holds the Guinness world record for the greatest weight ever raised by a human being—6,270 pounds in a back lift.

Marathon runner Alberto Salazar (far left) takes a lap with these determined inmates.

NFL veteran and former Iowa State star Mike Stensrud talks to an attentive inmate.

Raymond Berry, former All-Pro receiver and NFL coach, leads Rick to a lockdown wing.

John Westbrook breaks into a song while Bob Anderson accompanies him.

Bob Cole tells of his days as a con man in Chicago before a dramatic conversion experience later in his life.

One of America's premier Gospel singers, Johnny Ray Watson.

Three-time Superstars champion and soccer standout Kyle Rote, Jr.

Boston Red Sox pitcher Rick Krueger throws one right down the middle to an inmate.

Sandi Fatow, one of the most dynamic speakers ever to take the platform on the Weekend of Champions.

Jose Alvarez, the fourth oldest rookie in major league history, was named Atlanta's Most Valuable Pitcher in 1988.

Tanya and Bruce Crevier conclude their incredible basketball show by each spinning ten basketballs.

Grant Teaff, former Baylor University football coach, leaves a prison with Bill Glass.

New York Yankee
second baseman
Bobby Richardson
(r) still holds World
Series records.

Buddy Groom,
Detroit Tiger
pitcher, assists Rick
with a card trick.

Jerry Stovall, NFL
star and successful
coach.

McCoy McLemore played on the NBA world champion Milwaukee Bucks.

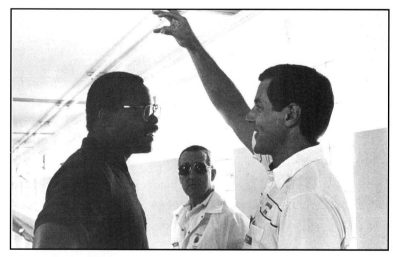

Discussing a magic trick with NFL All-Pro linebacker Mike Singletary, and Bunny Martin, World's Yo-Yo Champion.

Dan Vermeer (c.) started a family tradition of prison ministry counselors. He and Rick are intrigued as Bob Cole tells another one of his famous stories.

Trent Dilfer, star quarterback from Fresno State, and the number one draft choice of the Tampa Bay Bucs, on his first prison weekend.

Working with many senior citizen counselors has been rewarding for Rick on prison weekends.

Jason Andringa attended his first prison weekend as a senior at Pella, Iowa Christian High School.

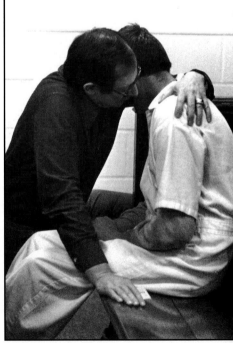

A hug seemed appropriate after this inmate gave his life to Christ.

This inmate must be trying to get a counselor to help him clean the floor.

Irma Beekman's memorable encounter with Kevin Hamilton.

One on one evangelism is the secret to successful prison ministry.

An inmate and a counselor visit while running during yard time.

Counselors wave goodbye after a busy day at the Mountain View Unit in Gatesville, Texas.

A relationship is slowly built during a game of checkers.

A counselor prays with an inmate through cell bars.

Charles Ashton, Counselor

Carl Williams, Coordinator

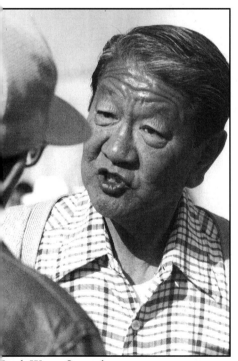

Frank Wong, Counselor

Dick Hickman, Counselor

Inside a large prison dormitory a counselor visits with two inmates.

Mark Jarvis from California settles in for a long visit.

A counselor with an inmate in Georgia.

Sharing the *Four Spiritual Laws.*

Art Gamsby,
Housing Director
and Coordinator

An inmate takes a break from his broom to visit with a counselor.

Sore feet tend to be the norm on a Weekend of Champions.

Often inmates enjoy sharing scripture with counselors.

The silhouette of an inmate and a counselor as they discuss their faith.

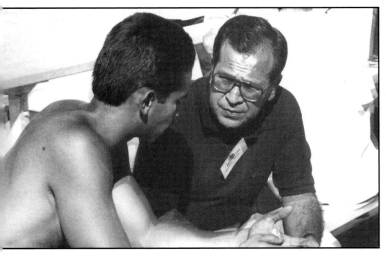

Pastor Ray Castro is one of the premier instructors of Evangelism Explosion.

Coordinator Charles Darnell announces an upcoming program from the control room.

Staff member Dick Plowman shares lunch with an inmate.

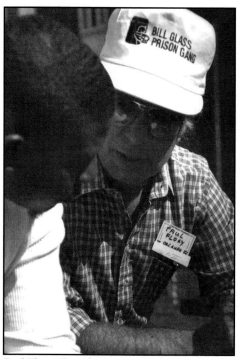

Paul Flory, Coordinator

Counselor Bryan Glanzer (l.) and Coordinator Jack Gould (r.) don flak jackets before entering a lockdown unit.

Jerry Morris, Coordinator

Eunice Sundberg, Coordinator

John Chinni,
Counselor

Emory Wilson, Bill
Glass staff

Henree Martin,
Coordinator

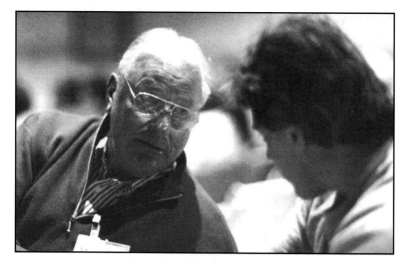

Warren New,
Counselor

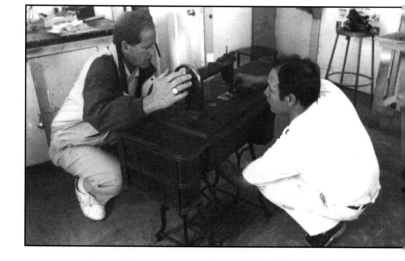

Bill Kronemeyer,
Coordinator

Fred Carter,
Counselor

Jack Jacob, Counselor

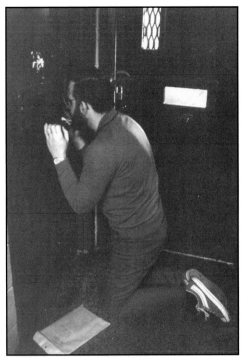

Gary Hinkle, Coordinator

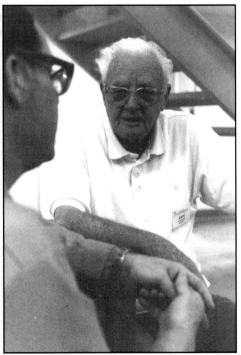

John Simons, Counselor

Pastor Kent Reynolds

Coordinator Dick Dunham helps an inmate in his garden.

Ed McNeil, Counselor

Perry Bodin, (c) Coordinator, is given this model boat by two grateful inmates.

Roger Hoss,
Chairman of
Hospitality

Nieves Ramirez (l.)
and Carlos Chavez
(r.) pose with Rick
after their incredible
meeting in San
Diego.

Joe Danielly,
Counselor

Mark Williams, Coordinator

Fred Spencer, Counselor

George Joslin, Counselor

Frank Green, Coordinator

Tom Stone,
Counselor

Dick and Colleen
Rohrer, Bill Glass
staff

Jim and Bonnie
Lang, Bill Glass
staff

Harmon "The Great" Oates, Counselor

Albert McMakin, Counselor

Counselors Carl and Mabel Hamlin with Rick

Frank Daniely, Coordinator

Gene Ellerbee, CEO of Bill Glass Ministries

"Hello...I'm Lamar W. Lundy...I'm a volunteer with the prison ministry...I'm here to witness to you fellows...I'm new...I'm going to throw up..."

Ted ("Doc") Monnier, Counselor

Don Lykins,
Control Room and
Transportation
Director

Coordinator Larry
Cowart (center)
prays with inmates
who are scheduled
to be released from
prison later that
day.

A group from
Meredith Drive
Reformed Church,
including Denny
Lillard (bottom
right), George
McVicker (top left),
and Buck
Groenendyke (2nd
in from top right).

Kris Parlee, Counselor, and Northwest Airlines Customer Service Agent.

Lois Spees, Counselor

Emmit Solomon, Head Prison Chaplain in Texas.

Jack Wilcox (r.) served as a Bill Glass counselor before becoming a chaplain in the Texas prison system.

Strongman Paul Wrenn compares his muscles with Warden Lansom Newsome at a Georgia weekend.

Commissioner Morris Thigpen visits with a death row inmate.

Commissioner Larry Meachum greets Bill Glass before a weekend in Oklahoma.

Don Smarto is the Director of the Institute For Prison Ministries which headquarters at the Billy Graham Center on the Wheaton College Campus. Don is one of the leading authorities on prison ministry and has written a number of books on the subject.

Chaplain Ray of the International Prison Ministry in Dallas, Texas.

Earl Smith, chaplain of San Quentin Prison in California, discusses an upcoming weekend with Bill Glass.

The sign and the armed officer say it all.

Coordinator Ted Farrar prays with an officer.

An officer keeps an eye on our program in San Quentin.

Paul Pedrick, prison chaplain from New Jersey, receives his prison cross.

An officer distributes toilet paper on the SHU Unit in Corcoran, California.

A counselor praying with an officer.

Reminder board for inmates.

Counselors check in with officers in Corcoran, California.

Ron with Warden Craig at the Mountain View Unit in Gatesville, Texas.

Warden Craig and the women on death row in her unit pose with dolls the inmates made while incarcerated.

An officer leads these Texas inmates out to the program area.

Sign on an officer's desk on death row at Sante Fe, New Mexico.

Ron with Warden Tom Jones.

Roscoe Plowman, circuit rider preacher, prison chaplain, and Bill Glass counselor.

Kitten Murphy chats with an inmate in front of her cell.

At one time evangelist Charlie Pratt was locked up in a prison for the criminally insane.

Bill Corum was destined to spend the rest of his life in prison until he gave his life to the Lord.

Dick Hanley, Program Director at Central Prison in Raleigh, North Carolina.

Colson scholarship recipient and ex-offender Don Holt.

Bob Erler, the "Catch Me Killer," now speaks in prisons all over the world.

Jerry Graham (r)and Mark Maciel, (l) Chaplain at the Los Angeles jail, team up with Rick for programs in San Quentin.

Ron and Jack "Murf the Surf" Murphy at Florida State Prison in the early 70's.

This inmate is reading the follow-up booklet which is given to inmates who make decisions.

Jerry Graham rides back into San Quentin, the prison where he gave his life to Christ.

Having served over seventeen years in prison, Harold Thompson has the answers to change lives.

Jack Murphy now works full time with the Bill Glass team and has a powerful, life-changing message for inmates.

Harold Morris (l.) with Randy Gradishar (r.), former Denver Broncos linebacker.

Bob Van Buskirk with his Messerschmidt airplane.

Harold and Mary Thompson work for Campus Crusade for Christ and direct all the follow-up with the Weekend of Champions.

Preparing to enter a death row cell block.

Don Lykins leads
South Carolina
death row inmates
in prayer on the
yard.

Bill Glass
counselors working
the cells on Texas
death row at the
Ellis I Unit.

A counselor and an
Alabama death row
inmate walk arm in
arm back to the
death row wing
after a program in
the yard.

While Alabama death row inmates look on, Tanya Crevier closes her show by spinning ten basketballs all at once.

Every cell is covered by Glass counselors on death row at the Holman Unit in Alabama.

Captain Bill Treadwell thanks Jack Murphy for visiting Georgia's death row.

Donald "Pee Wee" Gaskin admires cartoon characters he drew and mounted on the wall in his death row cell in South Carolina.

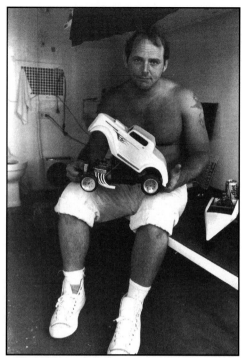

Robert Black, an inmate on death row in Texas, shows Ron a couple of his toys. He was eventually executed.

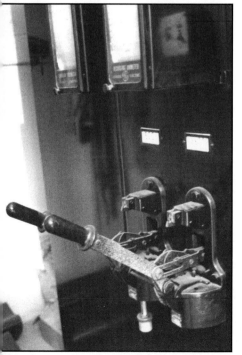

This lever controls the electric chair at Michigan City, Indiana.

The electric chair at Michigan City, Indiana.

Rick does card tricks for the first inmate he ever talked to on death row at H-Block in Jackson, Georgia.

A happy moment on death row at Central Prison in Raleigh, North Carolina when Michael Pinch accepts Christ while Ron is there.

Ron and friend David Huffstetler on death row at Central Prison in Raleigh, North Carolina.

Jack Murphy and Rick lead North Carolina death row inmates in prayer after a program.

Bunny Martin, World's Yo-Yo Champion, lights a match with his yo-yo for an inmate on death row in Santa Fe, New Mexico.

Warden Lamar Mothershed shows Rick a display of every style of license plate ever made in Alabama prisons.

Officers guard the gate at the entrance to Oklahoma's death row.

Counselors work the cells on Oklahoma's death row at McAllister.

Bill Glass and teammates wait for death row gate to open.

Some assistance from an inmate in a lockdown cell.

The women on death row in Texas enjoy Rick's card tricks while Chaplain Tim Crosby looks on.

Karla, Betty, Pam and Frances perform one of their favorite Christian songs in sign language.

Ron and the Glass counselors enjoy a special meal prepared for them by the women on death row in Texas.

Hazel Wilson (l.) and Helen Kilby admire the dolls the inmates made.

Ron with (l. to r.) Betty, Karla, Frances, and Pam on death row in Texas.

Renowned ventriloquist David Pendleton and his friend, Otis, entertain inmates.

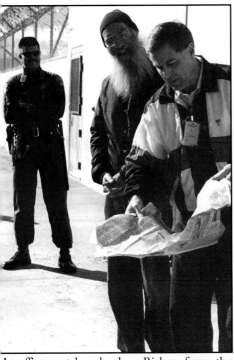

An officer watches closely as Rick performs the famous newspaper trick with a bearded assistant.

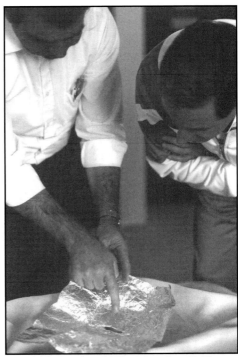

Dr. Carl Baugh of The Creation Evidences Museum shows Rick a piece of wood from Noah's ark that atheists tried to burn.

Rick performs through the food tray slot on a lockdown wing in Texas.

Joel Jeffries, counselor from Des Moines, uses the Braille *Four Spiritual Laws* booklet.

Rick waits to enter death row in Louisiana, where he had a divine appointment with an inmate named Glen.

Dave Nielsen, counselor from Nebraska, participated in an Indian pow-wow in a Montgomery, Alabama prison.

Dave Washington played 11 years in the NFL and was three times All-Pro for Denver, San Francisco, and Buffalo.

Bill Michael's song "Where Have You Gone?" opened the door for a divine appointment in Oklahoma.

A divine appointment took place in Sugarland, Texas in 1993 when Shawn Pardue suddenly spotted his grandfather, James Chambers, a Bill Glass counselor. The two had not seen each other for years, and Chambers didn't know Shawn was in prison. Pardue has a twin brother, Shane, who is also serving time. Counselor James Chambers hugs his grandson.

Rick and Ron visit with former death row inmate Bobby Joe Williams. When five Bill Glass counselors worked death row in McAllister while Williams was on death row, he intended to harm one of the counselors. But when Bud Hitt visited his cell, he couldn't go through with his plans. Bobby Joe was saved months later as a verse of Scripture that Hitt left haunted him to the point of conversion.

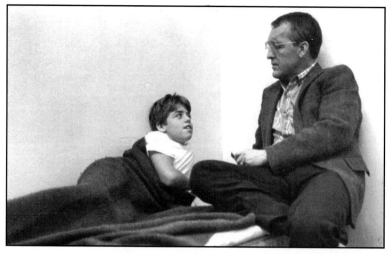

Bunny Martin shares with David Silva after David's attempted escape from a youth prison in California.

Rick visits with the inmate he met on death row at Angola prison in Louisiana.

Clyde Caylor, shown here sharing with an inmate, later helped lead an officers family to the Lord on a Washington weekend.

Ron with Larry
Plymesser on the
Wisconsin weekend
in 1984.

Most cells have two
inmates in them,
sometimes three.

Tanya Crevier
draws a huge
crowd inside a cell
block in Jackson,
Michigan in 1983.

A Santa Fe, New Mexico death row inmate watches with his mirror as Bunny Martin does coin tricks.

To prove the strength of his stomach, Paul Wrenn lets the largest inmate in the prison jump off a bench onto his flexed stomach.

This inmate comes up for a closer look during one of Rick's shows.

An inmate reads his Bible in the solitude of his cell.

Inmates cook burritos for a counselor in their cell.

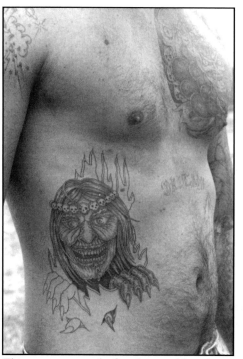

This tattoo was only four hours old and was done in prison.

Inmates who are locked in their cells often communicate with each other using these small mirrors.

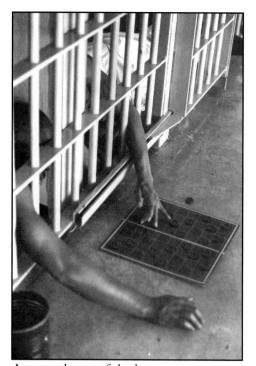

An unusual game of checkers.

This picture was made by an inmate who tore socks apart by the threads, sorted the colors, and knit them back into a piece of cloth.

These boot camp inmates march to a Weekend of Champions program.

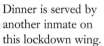

Dinner is served by another inmate on this lockdown wing.

You haven't heard music until you've listened to a prison choir.

Rattlesnake warning in San Diego.

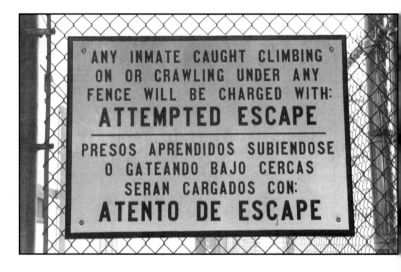

Escape sign in English and Spanish.

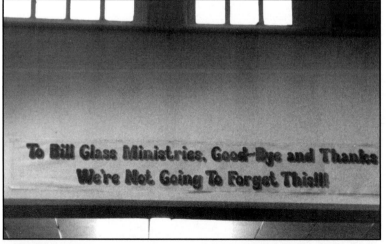

Inmates at Tracy-Deuel Correctional in Tracy, California knew how to say thanks for coming.

Peek-a-boo.

This inmate rolls back his mattress to create a makeshift work bench for a craft project.

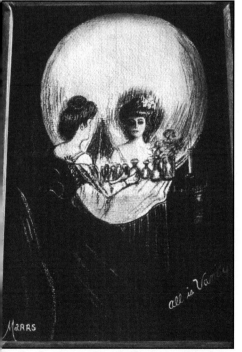

Look closely at this skull picture found on death row in Texas. It's not what it appears to be.

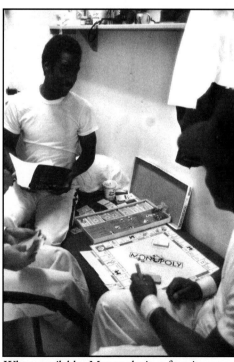

When available, Monopoly is a favorite game with inmates.

Art and Sue Gardner with Ron and Rick on the first weekend they met in 1990.

Joe Mason gives Ron a painting lesson.

Joe Mason, surrounded by some of his paintings, presented Rick this clown picture after they first met in December 1987.

Paul Wrenn always challenges any inmate to a contest in the squat lift.

An inmate throws his best punch at Paul Wrenn's large, solid stomach.

Ron and Earl "Cowboy" Taylor.

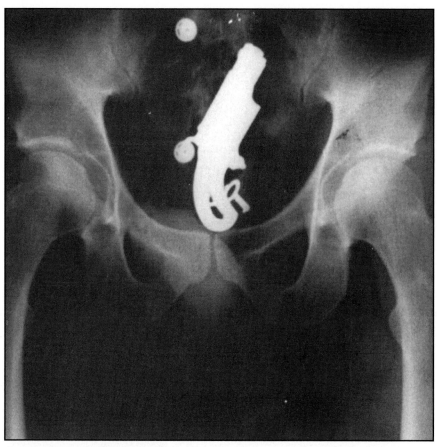

A close-up of the infamous Alabama X-ray picture.

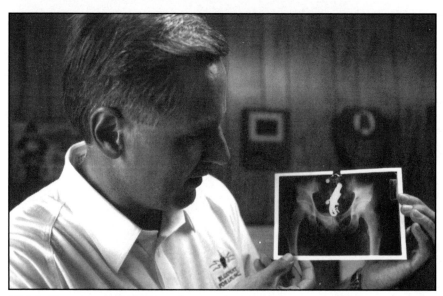

Rick holds a picture of the X-ray showing the gun an inmate smuggled into prison up his rectum

Dallas DeLay shows Rick the grandfather clocks he built in prison.

Ron Smart serves his sentence "one day at a time."

Paul Wrenn and Rick in front of a cell built in 1867. Paul couldn't fit through the door.

An officer in Alabama hooks Rick up to one of the old ball and chain locks.

Pablo's "family."

Boot Hill cemetery overlooking the bay at San Quentin. Tombstones are for inmates whose bodies are unclaimed, and graves are marked with numbers rather than names.

Earl "Cowboy" Taylor (l.) returns to a Bill Glass Weekend of Champions banquet to share how the ministry changed his life forever while in prison in St. Clair, Alabama. With him is Harold Thompson, who did time with Cowboy. Cowboy served 49 years in prison.

One of Ron's favorite paintings from Durham Stokes, an inmate he never met.

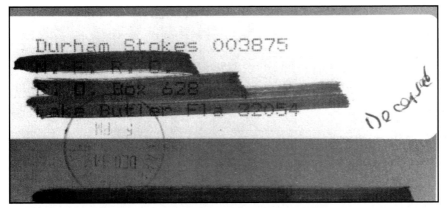

The returned postcard letting Ron know Durham Stokes had died.

Long hours are spent in front of inmates' cells sharing the Gospel.

Ron's famous Aussie hat is recognized by inmates all over America.

When weights aren't available, Paul Wrenn does a push-up with an inmate resting on his back.

Some inmates have pets for friends, much like the story of the "Birdman From Alcatraz."

Kevin Hamilton, a Texas inmate, painted this clown picture for Ron's son Joshua, after Ron told him Josh loved clowns.

These weapons were confiscated in this officer's prison and placed on display in the warden's office.

(l. to r.) Joe Mason, Ron, Hubert Tyson, and Rick in the paint shop at Ramsey I Unit in Rosharon, Texas.

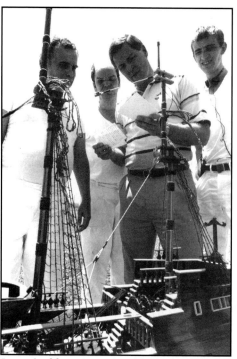

It took fifteen months for these Alabama inmates to build this beautiful model boat.

Entertaining correctional officers has always been a fun part of the weekends.

Weightlifting is very popular in prison. It helps relieve tension and stress and builds self-confidence.

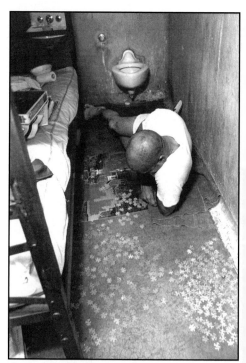

An inmate works on a jigsaw puzzle on the floor of his cell.

A game of dominoes helps pass the time.

Signs like these became necessary after an inmate escaped in a helicopter that landed on the prison yard.

Rick shares a simple message of hope at the conclusion of his program.

A tattoo like this is a great conversation starter.

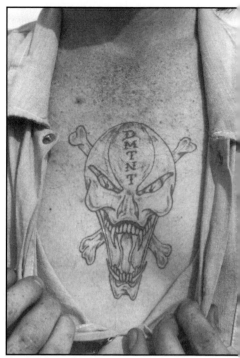
An inmate who claims to be an atheist shows off his tattoo. The letters DMTNT mean "dead men tell no tales."

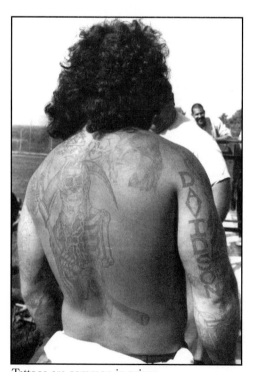
Tattoos are common in prison.

Spider Man and his cellmate show off their tattoos.

Rick visits with an inmate on death row in Connecticut.

Inmates in the medical wing of this prison enjoy a bit of Rick's magic outside their hospital unit.

Rick warms up the crowd before his program.

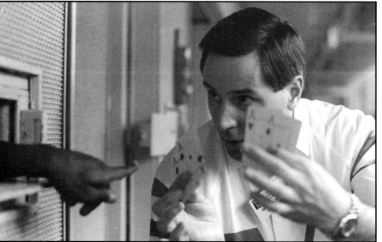

A four-ace card trick with assistance from an inmate on Alabama's death row.

The smiles appear
as the cards vanish.

Two inmates assist
Rick on stage in
this Texas prison.

Officers enjoy being
entertained as much
as the inmates do.

Inmates love to be on stage and help with the programs.

Mike Baldassin (dark shirt) played with the San Francisco 49ers and then became a policeman. The first four inmates he met on his first weekend were men he had busted on the streets.

Inmates like the close-up magic because they can participate.

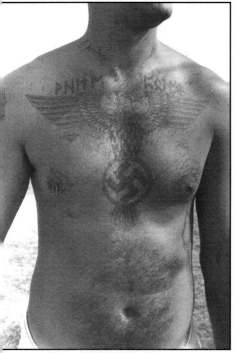

A tattoo like this provides information on an inmate's various interests.

Two officers lend me a hand with some card magic.

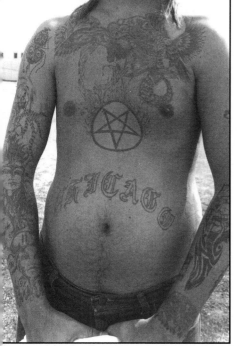

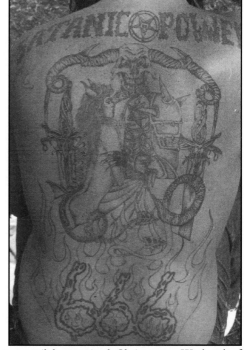

Front and back of an inmate who worshiped Satan until he received Christ on a Weekend of Champions.

"Another day at the office" for Rick in this New Mexico prison.

# CHAPTER 7

# EX-OFFENDERS
# INVOLVED

$O$ne of the most gratifying aspects of the Weekend of Champions is to see the change in men and women who have been released from prison and have returned to work as counselors or platform guests on Bill's team. It goes without saying that they have an established rapport with the inmates, sharing the common bond of incarceration. I'm amazed when inmates meet our counselors who have spent time behind bars, and without the counselors ever mentioning anything about their pasts, inmates invariably ask how much time they did. Inmates just seem to know. Counselors who have been incarcerated have walked in the same shoes as the inmates with whom they're talking. Consequently, inmates feel that they truly understand their dilemma. And they do. They've been there. This comraderie opens the door for counselors to share their faith and how a Christian commitment has made a positive difference in their lives while in prison and also after being released. I might add that counselors who have done time offer their own brand of hope to inmates. It's very encouraging to men and women who are locked up to meet people who have done something positive with their lives, despite their scarred and ugly histories.

It would be impossible for Ron and me to tell you the stories of every former inmate we've worked with through this ministry. However, there are a few we would like to recognize for their contributions to the Bill Glass team over the years. Two of the more prominent individuals are Jack Murphy and Harold Thompson.

Jack, better known as Murf the Surf, did twenty-one years; Harold, or Big Tom, did seventeen years. Jack is presently working full-time on the Bill Glass staff; Harold and his wife, Mary, serve full-time with the Campus Crusade for Christ Prison Ministry but still offer a great deal of their time and services to the Weekend of Champions program.

## Jack Murphy

Jack's background is best summed up through the introduction in his book, *Jewels For the Journey*, which was published by Chaplain Ray of the International Prison Ministry in Dallas, Texas:

> Jack "Murf the Surf" Murphy has often been a role model. As a youth, he was an overachiever. He excelled in sports, music, and scholastics. As a young businessman, Jack worked in south Florida real estate, and the resort hotel business. In the late 1950's he was a pioneer in the East Coast surfboard industry, the sport that gave him the nickname "Murf the Surf."
>
> Jack was always the center of interest and attention. His home was the "in place" to party with the fast crowd. Then, because of his hedonistic life style and lack of Christian morals or ethics, it was but a short surf ride to crime.
>
> In 1964, Jack and a partner were arrested after a daring robbery at the New York City Museum of Natural History, stealing a number of valuable gems from the J.P. Morgan collection, including the fabulous Star of India Sapphire. After that, his name was often in the news. He was the ideal criminal, a talented and daring jewel thief.
>
> When he received a double life sentence plus twenty years in the Florida prison system for a capital crime, he soon became the "main man" in the prison. He was a respected convict.
>
> But God was on his trail. Through the influence of Chaplain Max Jones, Jack Murphy became an outstanding Christian who stood up boldly for Christ.
>
> Now, out of prison, he has become an ideal role model for paroled prisoners. It is evident that Chaplain Max Jones spoke a great truth when he said, "Jack, God has a better plan for your life."

I was on the first Bill Glass weekend Murf ever attended after his release from prison. It was in the Atlanta, Georgia area in 1986. I had already heard a lot about him and the unbelievable change in his life after his conversion experience in the Florida State Prison in Starke,

Florida. On previous Weekend of Champions visits, many members of our team had helped Jack to come to faith in Christ and had encouraged him and helped him grow after that. Ron Kuntz was one of these individuals. Murf was a dedicated Christian for nearly eight years when the impossible happened. The front door of the prison opened and he was released. This was a miracle because Jack had been told when he entered prison, "Take one last look at the outside world. You'll never see it again, Murphy."

I suppose the last place I'd want to go after being released from prison would be back to prison, especially after spending twenty-one years of my life there. But Jack Murphy was a man on a mission and knew that with his background, plus his top-notch skills as a communicator and leader, the Lord could use him in a powerful way to touch the lives of thousands of inmates with the Good News of the Gospel of Jesus Christ. And he has done just that, sharing his incredible story with inmates all over the world.

As Jack began to serve as a platform guest with the ministry, it became apparent to Bill Glass that he was more than just a good speaker. Murf knew about prisons and prison ministry, and he knew the best way to effectively reach those who are incarcerated. He was hired in 1991 to work full-time and is now a regular on all of the weekends. With seemingly endless energy, Murf labors between prison weekends to help organize future events and to drum up additional support in the way of finances, counselors, churches, etc. He is recognized by many inmates in every prison we visit. They have read his book and heard his story, and he represents hope, especially to those who are serving lengthy sentences and were also told, "You'll never get out." Jack Murphy has undoubtedly made a positive difference in many lives through his involvement in prison ministry.

Jack's wife, **Kitten**, is also a dedicated volunteer who supports many families of inmates. She developed a sensitivity to the needs of inmates' families as a result of visiting Jack for over twelve years while he was in prison. She now works directly with Jack on many of his projects and also helps out in a variety of ways on the weekends. I especially admire Kitten's commitment to faithfully send post cards and letters all over America to inmates whom Jack and Kitten have met and continue to encourage through regular correspondence.

## Harold Thompson

At one point in his life, Harold Thompson was sentenced to serve 105 years in Alcatraz. He ended up serving sixteen years in the Atlanta Federal Penitentiary for bank robbery. He was also on the FBI's Ten Most Wanted List, and was considered one of the toughest inmates at Atlanta Federal. It was during his incarceration, however, that Harold invited Christ into his heart and, like Murf, spent a number of years as a Christian, still locked up, but growing and faithfully taking a strong stand with his newly-found faith. Like Jack Murphy, Harold had a heart for those who were incarcerated and knew that the same Jesus who had transformed his life could transform theirs and bring about lasting change. After his release from prison and eventually receiving a presidential pardon from President Richard Milhous Nixon, Harold joined the staff of Campus Crusade for Christ. The job role with Campus Crusade for Christ's Prison Ministry has been an excellent fit for Harold and his wife, **Mary**, whom he met while serving his sentence. Together they help Bill Glass with the follow-up aspect of the Weekend of Champions. This is one of the most critical parts of the weekend as many decisions for Christ are made, and these men and women need a steady diet of Bible study, encouragement, and teaching to solidify and maintain their Christian commitment. Many will have questions, and all will be tested and challenged by their peers in prison.

Harold and Mary work with many individuals to provide the most quality follow-up as possible, but the main players are the prison chaplain and the local Bill Glass prison counselors who volunteer to teach the follow-up course for about eight weeks. As decision lists are compiled after a weekend, every effort possible is made to get the inmates involved in the class.

A starting point is the distribution of a Weekend of Champions study guide that is placed in the hands of every inmate who makes a decision. This easy-to-read little booklet helps answer many of the initial questions a new believer usually asks and gives the inmate a chance to start looking into the Scriptures to better explain what has happened in his or her life through this important decision. It explains how to know God personally and begin growing as a Christian. I like what Bill Glass has written on the introductory page of this little book:

Dear Teammate,

In almost every game there is a turning point when it becomes obvious that one team is going to win. There may be much time left to play and there may be a genuine struggle yet ahead, but it has become obvious to both teams and to every spectator that one team has the victory.

You have just passed that turning point and it is obvious that you are going to win. You now have Christ as your coach and you are going to win in this game of life.

The worst thing that can be said about a player is that he is uncoachable. This simply means that he won't pay attention to what the coach tells him. A player must be able to take coaching and listen to instruction. And when the going gets tough, he must be even more careful about taking the signals of the coach.

You are now a Christian, so "get in the game." It is my feeling that too many Christians are still on the bench. Christians are too often spectators and aren't participants in the thick of the battle. I pray that this book will help in showing you a whole new way of life.

The inmates can do the lessons before the follow-up classes, and then discuss them with the leaders at their meetings. These sessions help build a firm foundation in their Christian walk.

In addition to putting the entire follow-up booklet together, Harold and Mary have made an unbelievable commitment to provide video resources for the chaplains at every prison that participates in a Weekend of Champions. Bill Bright, the founder and leader of Campus Crusade for Christ, has produced a fantastic ten-tape video series called *The Transferable Concepts*. A "transferable concept" is an idea or a truth which can be transferred or communicated from one person to another, and then to another, spiritual generation after generation, without distorting or diluting its original meaning. Topics include:

How You Can Introduce Others to Christ
How You Can be Sure You Are a Christian
How You Can Experience God's Love and Forgiveness
How You Can Help Fulfill the Great Commission

How You Can Love by Faith
How You Can be Filled With the Holy Spirit
How You Can Pray With Confidence
How You Can Experience the Adventure of Giving
How You Can Walk in the Spirit
How You Can be a Fruitful Witness

As these basic truths or "transferable concepts" of the Christian life are made available through the printed word, films, video tapes, and audio cassettes in every major language of the world, they could well be used by God to help transform the lives of tens of millions of people. These video tapes help educate the inmates and teach them many of the basic truths that Jesus and His disciples taught. They also give the chaplain some solid teaching material that can be used over and over with many inmates in the future.

In addition to the "how to" tapes, two outstanding films, *Jesus* (in English and Spanish) and *A Man Without Equal*, are also included on video tape and as part of the package delivered to the prisons. As you know, videos are expensive, and this entire set of tapes isn't cheap. What's remarkable is that the Thompsons have raised the finances necessary to provide this at no cost to every prison we visit, plus any others they work in outside of the Weekend of Champions. Their goal is to see these tapes in every prison in America before they retire from Campus Crusade. This project has involved much time and many miles of hard travel, but Harold and Mary Thompson are extraordinary people who have a passion for serving Christ and others. They deserve a big "high five" from Ron and me for their tireless efforts to share the hope Harold found in prison through faith in Christ with those who are locked up and still searching for answers.

## Jerry Graham

I first met Jerry Graham on a San Quentin prison weekend. Jack Murphy had lined him up as one of our platform guests, and Jerry had even done part of his seventeen years in prison at San Quentin. Jerry was, as he calls it, "state raised." Constantly in and out of prison, his life was bound by drugs, booze, and crime. He hated it, but couldn't seem to free himself from these horrible addictions. Eventually he was charged as a habitual criminal. If the charge stuck, he'd never see the outside of prison again. Only a miracle could set him free, and that miracle came in the form of a commitment to Christ that totally transformed this rogue into a saint. In his book, *Where Flies Don't Land*, Jerry tells the story of his supernaturally transformed life and the series of miracles that find him today serving as the director of His Farm, a ranch for abused children near Sacramento, California.

Jerry attends many of our Weekend of Champions programs in California and also shares his story in other settings that give him a chance to testify first-hand what can happen to an inmate who sincerely makes a commitment to Christ and stays obedient and faithful to that decision. Jerry had a strong ministry in prison as well, as is evidenced by a poem an inmate named Don Major slipped into Jerry's hand on the day Don was released. This poem is one of my favorite parts of Jerry's book because it speaks volumes of the sincerity and genuineness of Jerry's faith, and the positive influence he had on other inmates:

> Today I went into a prison
> where I looked upon anguish and strife.
> But the message I learned from a convict there
> I'll remember the rest of my life.
> The prisoner said he was contented
> in paying society's due.
> It's easy to render to Caesar," he said,
> "When you have the Master with you."
> Oh I've seen his anger fly out of hand
> for he was just human, you see,
> then ask both offended and God to forgive
> unashamed—when bending his knee.
> Many long years it has been
> since I had the faith that this convict has shown,
> and tho' I was with him for only a while
> his message has pointed me home.
> Yes, today I went into a prison
> and saw there, to my disbelief,
> the face of our Savior Lord Jesus
> worn on the face of a thief.

I love to work with Jerry Graham and marvel at his ability to speak to men and women in prison. He is another ex-offender who is a living testimony of what can happen to even the vilest of people who experience the love and forgiveness that comes with a relationship with Jesus Christ.

### Eddie Ronquillo

Another ex-offender from California who has given a great deal of time to this ministry is Eddie Ronquillo. Eddie's large family was raised in poverty. He hardly knew his alcoholic father, and his crime career began at age seven. He was also state raised and became a drug addict at an early age.

Through the faithful efforts of prison ministry volunteers, Eddie eventually trusted Christ and has devoted his life to helping those in prison or those just getting out. He and his wife, Evangelina, run After Care Homes which exist to help ex-offenders ease back into society after doing time. His experiences as an inmate, along with his ability to speak Spanish, are tremendous assets to us on our weekends, as many inmates only speak Spanish.

### Bill Corum

For much of his life, Bill Corum was involved in crime and addicted to drugs and alcohol. As a teenager, he began an incarceration process that placed him in prisons and jails in ten different states. He traveled more than 2,500 miles in handcuffs, waist chains, and leg irons. At age eighteen, he was suddenly exposed to the harsh life behind prison walls, and like many others, he found himself becoming hardened and accustomed to the violence and pain of prison life. Hitting the weight pile to help ease the boredom and take his mind off being locked up, Bill grew stronger physically, and with each repetition of the weights, his heart also became hardened, like stone.

Soon after his release from prison Bill married and started a family. He got a job in construction, but he had learned so many burglarizing skills while doing time that he hated to see them go to waste, and he continued to steal in the evenings after work. He would tell his wife he was going to help a friend on another construction project, and then go out and burglarize. He continued this routine successfully for almost ten years, only getting caught once and he beat that rap with a good lawyer.

After ten years and three children, his marriage ended. Bill had been involved in pornography since he was twelve years old, and with prostitutes at age fifteen. These earlier lifestyle activities took their toll on his marriage. Nonchalantly shrugging off the divorce and quickly putting it behind him, he rejoiced in the fact that now as a free man he could concentrate fully on pursuing a dream he'd had since he was a teenager–to become a gangster.

At age thirty, Bill began to associate with some drug dealers who hired him as an enforcer. His time on the weight pile in prison had made him big and strong. He had boxed Golden Gloves and hung around gyms through his married years, even receiving a $5,000 bonus to sign a pro contract, so he certainly had the right credentials to be an enforcer.

Bill loved enforcing but was soon attracted to something that was even more appealing–he wanted to be *the man* in the city and run the drug show. While pursuing that goal for the next seven or eight years, he watched many of his friends die or be sent to prison. Bill, however, became one of the leading cocaine dealers in Kansas City, achieving the three things he told himself he'd always wanted–money, power, and influence. He was selling $6,000 to $7,000 worth of cocaine daily, and it wasn't uncommon at certain times for him to be carrying as much as $50,000 cash with him. He stayed in expensive motel rooms, rode in limos, and threw parties on a regular basis, giving no thought to the cost.

Bill also had the power he craved. With just one phone call he could have someone killed in less than twenty-four hours. He carried two pistols everywhere he went and kept an Uzi in his briefcase. He was arrested on an attempted murder charge but was out of jail the next day. Bill Corum decided about all he didn't have was peace of mind, and that was something he desperately wanted and needed.

As is usually the case with this type of lifestyle, the trail of crime eventually starts to catch up with a person. Bill's lawyer got the attempted murder charge dropped to first degree assault with intent to kill, but the twenty-page statement his victim had given the State Narcotics Division placed Bill in a precarious position with them. He became a man on the run, ducking and dodging his partners, and eventually leaving Kansas City.

While hiding in an old farmhouse, miles from Kansas City, Bill wrestled with a thousand thoughts and asked himself some serious questions about his immediate future. He had attained the money, power, and influence he had so desperately wanted, yet he still felt empty and unsatisfied. The gangster lifestyle was also getting less and less exciting.

As he reflected, Bill thought of the many times he could have been killed. He was involved in over twenty-five car or motorcycle wrecks, had several close calls from drug overdoses, and was even shot at while in prison during several race riots. Why was he still alive? He remembered his faithful mother who constantly prayed for him. She always said, "Bill, don't you see God has his hand on you?" But Bill shrugged it off and said, "God has nothing to do with it."

However, one night in the old barn, Bill had to deal with reality. All those close calls were more than luck. He knew all too well he could have easily been killed on over a dozen occasions, and he wondered if perhaps his mother was right. Maybe God *had* been watching over him. Finally surrendering, he bowed his head and said a simple prayer, "God, if you're real and you can change me, I'll live for you." Tired, worn out, and scared, Bill fell asleep.

He woke up the next morning and, although he didn't feel that much different, he knew something had happened. Second Corinthians 5:17 says, "If any man be in Christ, he is a new creature, old things are passed away, behold all things become new."

Eager to flush this unusual feeling, he tried to get high but couldn't. He noticed that he could now go places without carrying his gun and not be afraid. For the first time in a long time, he slept peacefully at night. There was no denying these changes, and the obvious conclusion was that the Lord had heard his prayer and had come to his rescue. Now it was Bill's turn to live up to his end of the deal–to live for God.

A second marriage proved to be helpful to Bill. Shortly after the wedding, his new wife became a Christian and began praying for a change in her husband's life. Her prayers were answered, and Bill started waking up in the morning in a good mood. Bill also took some steps to begin growing spiritually, and contacted an old friend, Ray Hildebrand, a singer and songwriter in Kansas City. Ray was thrilled that Bill had given his life to Christ and gave him some advice he's never forgotten. Ray said, "Big Bill, if you want to grow, here's what you need to do. Your head is so full of trash, you need to force it out by filling it full of God. If you want to watch television, watch Christian television. If you want to listen to the radio, listen to Christian radio. If you want to read a book, read the Bible. If you need to talk to someone, talk to another Christian."

Bill heeded Ray's advice and has never looked back. As he began to read his Bible, one verse in particular caught his attention. Mark 8:36 reads, "What does it profit a man to gain the whole world and lose his soul?" Bill realizes he almost lost his life trying to gain all he could, and thankfully he found out that even when he had all he wanted, he still felt empty. He knows now that living the Christian life is so much easier and more rewarding than living in sin. He went from making $1,500 a day to a job working for a landscaping company, planting flowers and mowing lawns for five dollars an hour, but the contentment and peace he felt inside was worth more than any high-paying job. It didn't make sense until he read a verse in Philippians that says, "God will give us a peace that passes our own understanding." This was certainly true for Bill Corum.

Bill is now actively involved in prison ministry and participates regularly with the Weekends of Champions. As he shares his story with inmates, many can relate to his past and find hope in the marvelous way the Lord has changed his life and given him a new direction and purpose. He recruits friends from his church to go on prison ministry weekends and shares his testimony whenever possible. The man who had a heart of stone now has a heart of love—for God and others.

### Tony Ortiz

Tony Ortiz, an ex-offender and ex-addict, lives in San Jose, California, where he and his wife, Liz, work with ex-offenders and youth groups. Tony is now recognized as a community leader and authority on gang intervention. Like Eddie, he also brings a message in Spanish and English, and his years of incarceration have now become his ally in bringing the Gospel into prisons.

### Harold Morris

Harold Morris may be one of the country's most well-known

ex-offenders through his book, *Twice Pardoned*, and his powerful message captured on video and produced by James Dobson and *Focus on the Family*. Harold served a long, hard prison sentence for a crime he never committed and learned the hard way that you'd better watch the company you keep and the type of friends you hang around with. When Harold took part in the Weekends of Champions, he was always well received by inmates. However, he also drew thousands of teenagers into arenas across America to talk to them about teen issues and the importance of giving their lives to Jesus Christ. His graphic description of the harshness of prison life served as a sobering reminder to these youth that if they made poor choices in their lives and weren't careful to select the right kind of friends, they, too, could end up in trouble—or even in prison. Health problems eventually forced Harold to drastically cut back on his personal appearances, but his books and videos continue to touch lives around the world.

### Bob Erler

One of the more fascinating ex-offenders who has worked with Bill and with other prison ministries is Bob Erler, better known as the "Catch Me Killer." This ex-policeman received a ninety-nine-year prison sentence through a series of bizarre events. With a background in the Golden Gloves, black belt in karate, and as a former Green Beret, supercop Bob Erler had earned the colors of manhood. But would he survive prison life? His powerful story is featured in a book called *They Call Me the Catch Me Killer*, which was Campus Life magazine's book of the year. Bob's conversion to Christ in prison and his background, along with his incredible story, have given him many opportunities to speak in prisons; whenever it's possible, he joins us.

### Bob Van Buskirk

Bob Van Buskirk's background is similar to Bob Erler's. A former Green Beret and pilot, Bob got sucked into some escapades that turned sour. He found himself in one of Germany's toughest prisons. His incarceration, along with time spent serving in Vietnam, gives Bob some real ammunition as a speaker, especially relating to war veterans, who often attribute the war and its effects to their landing in prison. After his programs, many inmates who experienced a variety of personal problems from fighting in Vietnam looked to Bob for help, answers, and support. This opened the door for him to relate how his faith in Christ gave him strength to overcome his prison experience, as well as the ill effects of Vietnam.

Bob loves to fly and sometimes brought his Messerschmidt plane on weekends to buzz the prison yard with a couple of low fly-bys, before landing and eventually sharing from the platform. On one occasion, he and Bunny Martin pulled off one of the most amazing performances ever accomplished on a Weekend of Champions. Bunny had reconstructed a small scale model replica of Bob's plane, and at the end of his program vanished it right under the inmates' noses. With perfect timing, the moment Bunny's miniature plane disappeared, Bob came screaming over the prison yard in his Messerschmidt. The place went crazy, and I doubt the inmates who were in that prison yard that day will ever forget what happened.

Bob's amazing life story was eventually captured in a book called *Tailwind*, and hundreds of copies were distributed on weekends that Bob attended. I still meet inmates today who show me the book and ask about Bob Van Buskirk.

### Charlie Pratt

Maybe one of the most remarkable stories of the changed life of an inmate is that of Charlie Pratt. At one time, Charlie was locked up in a ward for the criminally insane and was considered hopeless and beyond help. Officers were afraid to even get near him because of his violent temper and the fact that he was so large and strong. Once again, however, through the faithfulness of volunteers who understood that Christ can change the heart of even the most violent offenders, they eventually reached Charlie. The man they said was hopeless is now an evangelist dispensing hope to others in prison.

Charlie spoke at one of our Spiritual Enrichment meetings, and I could have listened to him for hours. The one thing I'll never forget him saying is that no one is beyond help and Christ can work miracles in anyone's life. Certainly Charlie Pratt is living proof of that, and I've thought of him many times when I was dealing with extremely tough, hostile, angry inmates.

## Colson Scholars

Ron and I meet ex-offenders quite often who join us as counselors while attending Wheaton College as Colson scholars. Don Smarto, the Director of the Institute For Prison Ministries, oversees this program, which offers scholarships to ex-offenders who wish to pursue a degree that would eventually place them in Christian ministry. Organized by Prison Fellowship founder Chuck Colson, this is an outstanding opportunity for those who are screened and selected to participate. Don Smarto is a great friend of Bill Glass and a staunch supporter of the ministry, so he frequently encourages these men and women to join us as counselors because he feels that the experience enhances their ministry studies. He also knows these people can bring a lot to the table as far as contributing to a successful weekend. One ex-offender, Don Holt, worked in Bill's office as an intern to complete requirements for one of his classes. He, too, had a remarkable conversion experience after receiving a prison sentence of five hundred years.

## Don Holt

Don Holt was born and raised in Oklahoma. He enjoyed a normal childhood, but began to use drugs at age sixteen. Don and his friends discovered they could get high with a nose inhaler that could be purchased for sixty-nine cents at drug stores. This inhaler contained 250 milligrams of methyl amphetamine, one of the strongest amphetamines. Initially, they took amphetamine-soaked cotton orally by cutting it into smaller pieces and washing it down with soda pop. It wasn't long, however, before they were injecting it into their veins with a homemade syringe.

The next twenty-one years of Don's life were filled with heavy drug use. He was in and out of prison four times for crimes ranging from possession of narcotics, possession of stolen property, and burglary to armed robbery. He thought with each new stretch of incarceration that it would be his last, but after trying to hold down a job and straighten out his life, he always ended up in trouble again.

In 1974, after stealing a car with two other men and robbing a pharmacy, Don and his partners were captured with all the evidence in their car. Because his past was so saturated with previous offenses and prison time, Don was sentenced to five hundred years in the state prison at Mcalester, Oklahoma. He was in more trouble than he'd been in his whole life, and felt a pain that even the stiffest narcotic couldn't wash away.

Looking at the possibility of spending the rest of his life in prison, all Don could think about was escaping, and before even serving one year of his sentence, he escaped one night by climbing up a tug with a scaffold on top and jumping over the wall. Don's glove caught on the barbed wire on the way down, throwing him off balance, and as he awkwardly hit the ground he broke his leg. Limping off into the woods, he heard one shot. He later learned that in the excitement the tower guard dropped all of his shells except the one in the gun chamber. Although Don didn't realize it at the time, this unusual mishap probably saved his life. The broken leg slowed him down, and he was captured the next day. He later understood that God preserved his life and allowed him to be captured for His own ultimate plans.

After his leg was placed in a cast, Don was put in a maximum security cell, and it was during this time that he realized his best efforts to solve the problems of his life failed miserably. The guilt and pain were almost unbearable, and Don knew he was hopelessly lost and felt he deserved to die.

It was then that the Lord began to reveal Himself to Don. He had an unexpected visit from a pastor who had met Don's brother on an airplane and felt led to help Don. Through this man's letters and visits, Don eventually trusted Christ as his Savior.

He spent the next five years in prison witnessing for the Lord and, in spite of stiff opposition from doubtful prison officials, he was released on parole in 1982. After spending ten months at a community treatment center, the governor signed his parole and Don Holt became a free man on January 19, 1982.

Don has never looked back and has devoted his life to Christian service, including his enrollment at Wheaton through the Colson Scholarship to study specifically for the ministry. I have had the pleasure of working with Don and am always motivated and inspired with the sincerity of his Christian commitment. He continues to touch lives in prisons since his release.

## In Closing

Some ex-offenders I've mentioned in this chapter have such remarkable life stories that books have been written about them and how they came to know Christ while in prison. If the little bit I've written intrigues you enough, you may want to contact Chaplain Ray, Director of The International Prison Ministry, P.O. Box 63, Dallas, Texas 75221. He has a brochure listing all the books he has written about inmates who found Christ while in prison. His ministry is to distribute the books to prisons all over America.

Although I've written about just a few ex-offenders who have worked with us on the Weekend of Champions, my hat goes off to each one who makes a commitment to return to that place which they grew to hate and despise and holds such horrible memories. And in serving they put "shoe leather" on a verse that most likely helped change their lives: "I was in prison and you visited me." And because someone did, they will never be the same. They now find it easy to obey the Lord's command to "go into all the world and make disciples."

# CHAPTER 8

# DEATH ROW
# EXPERIENCES

*R*on and I consider it a great privilege to be given the opportunity to work with inmates incarcerated on death rows all over America. It is a testimony to the Bill Glass Ministry's reputation when we are granted access to more secured areas of prisons, some of which have never otherwise welcomed visitors from the outside. Ron has worked in more of them than I have, but each of us has had many incredible experiences, and occasionally we have been able to share them together.

One of the rules of our prison ministry, with which I am in strong agreement, is that we are never to discuss the death penalty with an inmate. It's a "no win" situation, especially on death row. Our job is to share our faith and hope in Jesus Christ with inmates—not to influence the prison system.

Death row is often one of the easiest places within a prison to share our faith as those inmates have been forced to address questions about their own life after death. "Is there really a heaven and a hell?" and "Where will I go?" are two of the most common. Also, visits are limited, and most of the incarceration time is spent inside a cell, so when we can come right to a death row cell, we are usually enthusiastically received and welcomed.

### What I Learned on "H-Block"
### Jackson, Georgia

I don't think I'll ever forget my first visit to a death row cell block in Jackson, Georgia in 1987. I was a rookie in terms of prison ministry when I attended the Atlanta, Georgia area weekend, and went with the sole intent of serving as a counselor. I was assigned to the Jackson Diagnostic and Classification Center and discovered at the Friday morning coordinator meeting that this would be the largest prison complex I had worked in up to this point. The facility housed three thousand men. We broke it into a number of smaller areas to work it more effectively. I remember being in awe at the size and impressed by the cleanliness. This was my first taste of the Georgia system, and in addition to neat, clean prisons, the inmates wore uniforms and their appearance was closely monitored, ensuring they were all somewhat disciplined in their dress and hygiene. It *was* impressive and seemed to create happier and more friendly inmates.

The most memorable part of that Friday in Jackson was meeting Wayne Williams for the first time. He was convicted of the murders of twenty-three children in and around the city of Atlanta. I enjoyed an approximate one-hour visit with him in the chaplain's office and found him to be quite cordial, friendly, and receptive to the Christian faith. I was surprised to learn that he had attended seminary prior to his arrest and incarceration.

Later that evening I was relaxing in my motel room when the phone rang. It was Bunny Martin, and he wanted to stop by to ask me a favor. I thought maybe he needed a little help with a magic trick, but I was wrong. He told me the officials at Jackson had agreed to let five men work all day Saturday in an area of the prison called H-Block, and he wondered if I might like to be a part of the team.

"What's H-Block?" I asked him.

"Death row."

I thought maybe I had misunderstood, so I asked, "What did you say?"

"Death row," Bunny repeated. They've got over a hundred men in there, Rick, and they need our help."

I wondered aloud, "What does that have to do with me?"

Bunny continued, "Rick, these men don't get to attend any programs, so if you'll take your magic up there, you could provide a little bit of fun to help open the doors for you and the other counselors to witness. I think you'll be surprised at how receptive these men will be to our message."

I just stared at him blankly until he finally asked me what was wrong.

I explained I'd heard from some of the other counselors about those kinds of places—lockdowns, segregation units, "the hole," solitary, and death row. They housed hostile, violent men, and I'd heard war stories of their rude behavior–cursing at counselors, throwing their food, spitting, or even storing up urine and tossing it into the eyes of those who approached their cell. I wasn't sure I was ready to deal with these types of individuals. I had to be honest; I already had preconceived images of these areas of prisons.

I finally told Bunny, "We've been friends for a long time so I'll do it as a favor to you, but I think you know I'm a little uneasy about it. I'm not sure I'll be able to come up with the right words to say to them."

He assured me, "Rick, the message we bring in doesn't change, and neither does the need of the inmates. Share with these men like you've been sharing with other inmates on your previous prison weekends. You'll do great! See you in the morning."

I didn't sleep very well that night because I was thinking about my "opportunity" in H-Block the next day. Part of me was excited, but another part of me was concerned and worried.

We left early that morning, and on the hour-long ride to Jackson I was wishing it was only a bad dream and I'd wake up soon. But I knew better, and when we began the long security check to work in H-Block, it was too late to turn back. I remember this check was a little more extensive than most, and it got so bad I was expecting an officer to put on a rubber glove. I can promise you if that had happened, I *would* have found the exit–and fast! Fortunately, there were no rubber gloves. We were told to wait by a specific cell door for the security captain.

A few minutes later, Captain Bill Treadwell greeted and welcomed us to H-Block. He had been the captain there for seven years. Treadwell thanked us for coming and informed us he was there to serve and make our visit to death row as productive as possible. He was a Christian and therefore was eager for us to share with as many men as possible, realizing that we offered the only hope many of them would ever know.

Treadwell went over a few brief rules with us and then began to brag about "his men" incarcerated in H-Block. He assured us that he didn't condone what any of them had done–they had murdered people, been found guilty, and would probably pay for their crime by execution in Georgia's electric chair. But, he told us to relax because "his men" would be well behaved, would treat us with respect, and would be grateful we had come. Yeah, sure. I thought maybe Treadwell had worked too many years on death row, and perhaps his elevator wasn't going to the top. The last thing I expected these inmates to be was well behaved, respectful, and grateful we had come. If anything, they would be the exact opposite. Again, I thought of all the stories veteran counselors had told me about death rows and the types of individuals who were incarcerated there.

After giving us one last dose of encouragement and affirmation, Treadwell took out a large key and unlocked the huge door that led to the cell blocks. The population in H-Block was 116, and as we moved into the area, the first thing I noticed was the quietness. I expected lots of noise—inmates hollering and screaming. But the only sounds came from old black and white televisions that were strategically positioned in front of the cells across the catwalk so that inmates in about every eight cells or so could watch television. I was later told the televisions only picked up a few channels, and the reception on them wasn't very good.

Once we were all inside, Treadwell locked the door behind us and reminded us once again that he was there to serve, and to let him know if we needed anything. Suddenly, one of the guys in our group suggested that if we split up we could cover more ground and talk to more inmates. What a genius this guy was! As if it wasn't bad enough to be in H-Block, now I was going to have to work by myself! Treadwell smiled and applauded the counselor's excellent suggestion, and then said, "Rick, you come with me. I'll get you started on "D" tier. I've got some fine men up there, and you'll enjoy working with them. They tell me you're a pretty good magician. Be sure and share your talents with my men. They don't get many special programs like this."

He directed me to a narrow set of steps that led up to a long row of cells. He shook my hand again and thanked me for coming. Then he told me to go ahead and get started on my visits and he'd come back a little later to check on me. He left me there and went to assign the other counselors to their designated areas of H-Block.

There I was. I vividly remember that moment—looking up those steps and on down the long row of cells, and praying a simple prayer: "Lord, protect me, ease my anxiety and fear, give me a bold witness, and teach me something today."

As I reached the top of the stairs, the first cell I came to housed a sleeping inmate. I'd already learned to leave men like him alone. In the second cell, there was another man asleep. Then in the third cell a middle-aged man was just sitting on the end of his bed staring at the gray concrete wall. Feeling most comfortable entertaining with cards in my hands, I grabbed a deck out of my briefcase, took them quickly out of the box, fanned them, placed them next to the bars, and said, "Pick a card, sir, any card." And he looked at me like my elevator didn't go all the way to the top!

He leaped off his bed and began yelling at me, "What's going on in here? Who are you? Where's Treadwell? I want some answers!"

In that quiet cell block, his sudden movements toward me and his loud voice scared me to death. I dropped my cards all over the floor and immediately jumped back away from his cell. (I had heard about inmates who would pull a shank out of their socks or the back of their pants and stick someone who approached their cell, and I thought this guy was going to stick me.) As I jumped backwards, I was fortunate to hit a railing on the back of the catwalk, and it's a good thing it was there because behind it was nothing but a two-story drop to the concrete below.

"I'm sorry, man, I didn't mean to startle you," I tried to explain. "I'm here with the Bill Glass Prison Ministry, and a few of us are going to be spending the day here in H-Block with you guys, but we don't want to bother you. I'll get my cards picked up and be right out of here. I'm really sorry. I didn't mean to upset you. As soon as I pick up this mess I'll move on to some other cells."

With that I slowly knelt down to pick up the playing cards, carefully watching out of the corner of my eye to make sure I was safe. As I did, however, the inmate surprisingly bent down on one knee and began to help me clean up the mess, handing me the cards.

"Buddy," I said, "you scared me to death. I thought you were going to stick me."

"No," he said, "and funny you should say that, because you really took *me* by surprise and startled *me*. I've been in here a little over ten years and you're the first visitor I've seen in about eight. I guess when you stopped at my cell, I assumed the worst—that I was in trouble or there was some kind of problem in H-Block."

Although it's difficult to believe, Ron and I meet hundreds of inmates every year who are doing time and never receive any visits. This includes many juvenile facilities. Can you imagine going through one of the darkest moments of your life and not even having one friend to walk through the valley with you?

We introduced ourselves. I explained to Ken about the Weekend of Champions going on in the institution that weekend, and that a few of us were allowed to work in H-Block for the entire day. Slowly, we both began to relax, and I was especially relieved that Ken didn't plan to stick me. Instead of telling me to leave him alone and mind my own business, he now seemed deeply interested and enthused about my being there. It became obvious I posed no harm to him, and not having talked to anyone from the outside in eight years, he was excited about the chance to visit, even with a complete stranger.

Ken was curious about the playing cards, and when I told him I was a magician, his interest in me piqued. "Are you really a magician?" he asked. I told him I was and that I'd show him a card trick. He could decide for himself how good a magician he was looking at. He pulled the pillow off his bed, set it in front of the cell, plopped down, and excitedly said, "Let's get to it. I ain't goin' nowhere. Show me your stuff!"

I put my close up mat down on the catwalk in front of Ken's cell, opened my case, and began to entertain. For the next thirty minutes or so, I performed magic for him, and with each trick, he smiled a little bit more, began to relax and respond positively to my visit.

After entertaining, I began to talk to Ken, trying to get to know him a little better, and, more importantly, finding out if he had any kind of spiritual direction in his life. Not surprisingly, his childhood was a nightmare with many of the problems that are typically found in death row inmates. I listened attentively as he painfully told about the horrible trail of misfortune and mistakes that eventually led to his incarceration on death row. When he finished, he then asked me what I did for a living. I told him about my company, Blueprint For Life, that I was a professional speaker and entertainer in all kinds of settings, and that one of my favorite "jobs" was volunteering about a hundred days a year with the Bill Glass Prison Ministry, sharing my Christian faith in prisons all over the country.

"Do you try to help people be more successful through your message?" Ken asked.

"Yes, and I use entertainment as a vehicle to deliver it. The magic, humor, and juggling are especially helpful in working with students who are usually skeptical that a drug speaker could actually be interesting. Wouldn't you agree? Card tricks certainly helped open the door for me to share with you–that is, after we picked them up off the floor. I think laughter and fun *always* helps build a rapport between a speaker and his audience and makes the audience more receptive to the speaker's message. I want my message to make a positive difference in people's lives."

Ken appreciated my desire to help others through my work and was a little bit surprised that there were actually people who lived out that philosophy of life. Almost everyone he was exposed to as he grew up was a "taker" whose motto in life was: "I'm gonna get mine, and I don't care who I have to step on to get it!"

Suddenly, with a gleam in his eye, Ken looked at me and said, "Rick, you know, I think I could tell people how to be successful. Wouldn't it be great if we could change places?"

I quickly nixed that idea but asked, "What do you mean–trade places? What would you tell people to do to become successful?"

He then proceeded to tell me about a dream he had where the officers brought his meal, but instead of food on the tray, there was a magic vase–the kind you rub and a genie appears to grant you a wish. He said, "Do you know what I'd wish for?"

I said, "That's easy. To get out of this prison."

"No," he said, "I spent a lot of time thinking about it and decided my wish would be to go back to a place called the "Land of Beginning Again." He said he got the idea from an old poem he'd heard as a young boy. He recited the poem for me.

### Land of Beginning Again

I wish there were some wonderful place
called the Land of Beginning Again,
Where all my heartaches
and all my poor, selfish griefs
could be cast out the door
Like some tired, old coat
and never be put on again.

"If I could start my life over, Rick, I would change four of the bad choices I made that I *know* would make me successful." And I'll never forget what he told me.

The first choice that he would make differently would be to get a better education. Ken had dropped out of school in the third grade and could not read or write. (Prison officials tell me the average grade level for inmates in America today is about the sixth grade.) I had to agree with this choice, for I had already seen in my early years of prison ministry how a lack of education, especially dropping out of school, was the first step on the road to doing time in prison. When young people aren't in school, they have a lot of idle time on their hands. Idle time is used either constructively or destructively. Unfortunately, most drop-outs end up in destructive activities that eventually lead to arrest and imprisonment. Once the cycle of being in and out of prison begins, it is difficult to break. I admire those inmates who use their incarceration time to further their education or even complete their GED through courses offered at the facility or by correspondence. It can only help an inmate in the long run. I tell students and inmates that the best mindset is that education is a lifelong process, and we're never really out of school.

The second choice Ken would make differently would be to totally avoid the drug and alcohol scene. He said that if I asked every man on Jackson's death row, they would all admit that drugs and alcohol played a major role in their eventual incarceration. What many didn't understand is that the "kicks" or good times they were after always have "kickbacks." Eventually, the bottle wins the game, and they lose. It's just that simple. In listening to the sad stories of inmates during the years I've worked in prison ministry, I can certainly attest to the fact that drugs and alcohol played a predominant role in the life of many who are doing time. Even while incarcerated, addiction is one of the most difficult habits a person will ever attempt to overcome.

Choice number three that Ken said he make differently if he could go back to the "Land of Beginning Again" would be to learn to respect authority and live by the Golden Rule. Growing up with attitudes of "having all the answers" and "nobody's gonna tell me how to live my life" always leads to problems. Ken was right. This rebellious approach, especially in the home at an early age with parents, stepparents, or guardians, almost inevitably spells disaster. Usually authority is placed in our life for a good purpose and, although it isn't always right, we are always right to be obedient to it, especially with parents. Obedience to their authority helps build trust, which eventually leads to what most young people want–freedom. And establishing an attitude of respect for authority will ultimately pay large dividends when we enter the workforce, as a majority of the jobs in this country are set up with a pecking order or chain of command.

Although Ken had very little Biblical education, he did know what the Golden Rule was and strongly believed that if people lived by it, America's crime problem could almost be eliminated. He put it best when he said, "If folks would just treat other folks and their stuff like they'd like folks to treat them and their stuff, we'd all have a Merry Christmas." Not bad insight for a man with a third grade education.

I asked Ken what the other choice was that he'd make differently, and his answer surprised me. He said, "I'd be more grateful. When I was growing up, I'd get up every day and look at everything I *didn't* have, instead of focusing on all I *did* have. I realized too late that great people are always grateful people. They convey an attitude of thankfulness in every area of their lives, concentrating on the positive, not the negative. You know, spending ten years in a 5' x 7' cell on death row makes people appreciate a lot of things in life, especially their freedom. Rick, our society today has become very selfish, and it seems we are never satisfied. A greedy, self-serving attitude will cause a lot of problems in your life, and thinking everyone owes you something will not do much to build strong friendships and relationships, which are critical to surviving the hard knocks of life."

Ken was a smart guy. I told him that people often ask me if I know any magic words, and I always tell them, "Yes, and they're the most powerful words in the world. I learned them as a boy when I watched Captain Kangaroo and Mr. Green Jeans on television. They would always close their popular children's show by reminding me not to forget the magic words–*please* and *thank you*. It seems we've removed them from our vocabulary today. We've forgotten how and when to use them. However, people who do always seem to have a positive, winning attitude in life and are successful in whatever they do. I read an interesting statistic that stated for every one hundred people who intend to write a thank you note, only one person actually will. Using the magic words coincides with a grateful attitude and appreciative heart."

Reflecting on what Ken had just told me, I thanked him for his insights and said I agreed with his philosophy. As a matter of fact, I was so impressed with what he had said, I asked him if I could share his "formula for success" with my audiences. My speaking on his behalf seemed like a far better idea than "trading places" which he had previously suggested. Ken was genuinely pleased that I was so impressed with his thinking, and he was obviously enjoying this visit with a person from the "free world" for the first time in eight years.

Eager to bring the conversation back to spiritual matters, I casually mentioned that I felt there was one other choice he'd left out that would help ensure ultimate success.

"What's that, Rick?" Ken asked.

I answered, "You must have a faith. I believe a person needs to make a commitment to Jesus Christ and embrace the Christian faith."

"Oh, Rick," he sighed. "I wish I could, but I'm not sure even God could forgive me for the horrible things I've done."

Ken then went on and on about his horrible crime spree, which eventually ended with the murders that saddled him with the death penalty. He was convinced that if the bad deeds in his life outnumbered the good ones, he could never go to heaven and he'd be destined to hell. It was obvious to me that it was going to take a little more time to share with this man about God's free gift of salvation, so maybe I could come back later in the day to tackle the challenge.

I told him I wanted to try to share with as many inmates as possible that day and probably ought to be moving on. Realizing that I was about to leave, he asked if I'd like a cup of coffee. In that cold, damp cell block, the thought of a hot cup of coffee sounded terrific. I offered to find Captain Treadwell and see if he could get us some. Ken chuckled and reminded me that this was death row.

"Rick, there aren't any vending machines here, and luxuries like coffee are rare. As a matter of fact, about the only thing I look forward to is the cold Pepsi they give us once a month. The coffee will be my treat."

For the next few minutes I watched inmate ingenuity at its very best. Ken pulled out a Pepsi can that he'd cut in half and set it on the floor. He took out another Pepsi can, which had the lid cut out of the top. Next he tied a long nylon shoestring to the two sides of the top of the can, forming a long string handle. Then he filled the can with water from his sink. As if he hadn't aroused my curiosity enough, what he did next almost blew my mind. Ken took out a roll of toilet paper and began to methodically unroll it around his hand, carefully counting each revolution of the paper. Once he reached a certain number, he folded the paper inward to halve it, and then folding the first tier of folds once again, he formed a cone-shaped, compressed pack of toilet paper that fit exactly in the half Pepsi can. He took the can of water and hooked the long string handle over a faucet handle in the sink, suspending it toward the floor, where it hung almost touching the half can with the compressed toilet paper. Grabbing a pack of matches, he lit the toilet paper in the can, and as it slowly burned, it created an effect much like a burner on a gas stove. The heat boiled the water in the full can hanging over it from the sink handle. While the water was heating, Ken removed from his storage area a plastic bag filled with instant coffee crystals. By the time he poured some crystals into an old dirty cup, the toilet paper had finished burning and the water was hot. Grabbing an old sock to prevent burning his hands on the hot can, he unhooked it and poured the water into the cup with the coffee crystals, and, believe it or not, took his finger and stirred it to dissolve the coffee. Handing it to me, Ken apologized that he had no cream or sugar! As I waited for the coffee to cool down, he began the entire procedure again to make himself a cup of coffee, and I was as fascinated watching him do it the second time.

As we sat there drinking our coffee, Ken told me that one of the things he missed the most since his incarceration was enjoying a good visit with a friend over a hot cup of coffee. He said that his limited supply of instant coffee was used only for special occasions, and my being the first visitor he'd seen in eight years deserved breaking it out.

I knew that the reason Ken made the coffee was to keep me from leaving his cell, and I also believed that deep down he wanted to explore the faith issues I had brought up earlier. So as we continued to drink our coffee, I asked him again if he'd like to talk about his relationship with Christ. I was not at all surprised that he did, and for the next hour I answered questions and shared with him how to become a Christian. A little while later I had the privilege of watching this man trust Christ as his Savior, invite Him into his heart, and accept His love and forgiveness. This was really special to me because Ken was the first person on death row that I ever helped lead to the Lord, and once he realized that he could be forgiven for his sins and spend eternity in heaven, he simply broke down in tears of gratitude. It was as if a huge weight had been lifted from his shoulders. The cup of coffee he made may not have been the best-tasting coffee I'd ever had, but it certainly was the most meaningful.

After Ken prayed to receive the Lord, I prayed for him, and when I finished, I noticed Captain Treadwell was standing beside me.

"Captain," I said, "Ken just accepted Christ."

"That's fantastic, Rick! Best decision he's ever made." And Treadwell shook Ken's hand and congratulated him. Then Treadwell told me to take my magic and come with him. He said, "Rick, we've got a lot of fine men up here, and I want all of them to see a card trick, and for you to share with each one. You have the only hope for these men, and we must get busy if we're going to get to everyone before supper."

I grabbed my case, said goodbye to Ken, and followed Treadwell down to the next cell. As we walked, I told him how Ken made coffee for me. Treadwell's eyes welled up with tears.

"Captain, what's wrong?" I asked.

He explained, "Rick, toilet paper is a rare commodity here on death row. These men only get so much each month. For Ken to share his toilet paper and coffee with you like that, why, it would be like me giving you $500. He must have thought you were very special for him to do that." That was the most valuable coffee I had ever been served.

For the next nine hours, Treadwell led me through H-Block. Late Saturday afternoon as I was sharing with one particular inmate, I felt comfortable enough to ask if he often thinks about that day he will be executed and if it scares him. He said that ending up on death row was probably the best thing that ever happened to him, because it was in H-Block that he made a commitment to Christ through the efforts of some faithful volunteers who shared the Gospel with him. As a result, he knew he would spend eternity in heaven with the Lord. He said that it was a miracle he wasn't killed before being locked up, considering his former lifestyle. If he had been killed, he'd have gone to hell not knowing Christ. He assured me that now he *knew* his future. "When they execute me, it will be justice, not necessarily a tragedy. Oddly enough, *everyone* has been given the death penalty. We're all going to die someday. However, I know *when* I'm going to die and I'm ready. The real tragedy is that many people who don't know when they'll die never do trust Christ and prepare themselves for eternity. That's much worse than my impending execution." I couldn't help but agree with him, and our conversation served as a timely reminder of the importance of my work with Blueprint For Life.

By the end of the day, I had shared with all 116 men there and had done some magic for each inmate. I was exhausted. The most inspiring part of my day was watching the interaction between Treadwell and the inmates. As Captain Treadwell approached each cell, the inmate jumped to the cell door to greet him and shake his hand. Their love and respect for him was quite obvious.

"Captain," they asked, "who's your friend? Any friend of Captain Treadwell's is a friend of ours!"

Bill Treadwell then told me something positive about each inmate. "Rick, this is Fred. He's a great artist. Fred, show Rick some of those pictures you painted. Aren't those fantastic, Rick?" At another cell, "Rick, this is my friend Billy. He's a poet. He even wrote a poem about me—and rhymed every word. Hey, Billy, read that poem you wrote about me to our friend, Rick." At every cell that day, Treadwell said something great about each inmate, and they beamed with pride when he bragged about them.

At supper time when we were getting ready to leave the unit, an amazing thought occurred to me. All of the men on death row were well-behaved, courteous, polite, and treated me with respect. And they were all grateful I'd come; many shook my hand and with tears in their eyes, thanked me for visiting them, praying for them, and showing them a special time. I had expected the worst, yet these men were exactly what Captain Treadwell had said they would be. The way he spoke to them altered their behaviors and attitudes. It was hard to believe, but this one man changed them through the power of the spoken word. Treadwell's motto, "Fairness, Firmness, and Respect," paid large dividends in the lives of the inmates on H-Block.

Before we checked out, I hugged Captain Bill Treadwell and thanked him for everything, but especially for teaching me such a valuable lesson that day about the powerful effect our words and speech have on others. "These men were exactly what you said they'd be, Captain—well behaved, respectful, and grateful. They have become what you told them they would be. Unfortunately, for many of them it may be too late."

And Treadwell said, "Rick, you're right, but it isn't too late for the thousands of individuals you speak to every year. If just a few could grasp this idea of being a builder and an encourager through the way they talk to others, we could make a positive difference in this hurting old world, one life at a time."

I agreed with him and made a personal commitment to share the lesson he taught me that day with everyone I could. I've kept that promise, and through my programs all over the country I've spoken about Captain Bill Treadwell and the story of being a builder. I was so intrigued by the idea of the power of the spoken word that I began to research the subject and eventually produced my first audio-cassette entitled, "Words We Speak," which tells the story of my first visit to death row in Georgia. Wanting to do something special for Bill Treadwell, I dedicated the tape to him. Shortly after my visit there, I learned that he retired and had to undergo open heart surgery. I was told by some correctional officers in Georgia that on Captain Treadwell's last day on the job, he shook the hand of each inmate and said goodbye, and when the door clanged shut, signifying his final departure, inmates could be heard weeping in the cell blocks.

As I drove to the Atlanta airport at the conclusion of that weekend, all I could think of was Captain Treadwell and my incredible experience in H-Block. I reflected on the powerful principle of the impact our speech has on others, and I thought if this idea will work on death row, it will surely work in our homes and communities if we will just put it into practice. Since my visit to H-Block, I've tried my best to live out this principle in my own life–with my family, flight attendants, waiters, clerks, and the many individuals with whom I come in contact through my work. I find that as I practice being a talent scout–looking for the good in others–and sharing it with them, I seem to be the one who benefits the most. For as I lift others up, I tend to lift myself up, too. There's a poem I recite when concluding my message on this that seems to sum it all up best.

### Builder or Wrecker

I watched them tearing a building down,
A gang of men in a busy town.
With a ho-heave-ho and a lusty yell
They swung a beam and a sidewall fell.
I asked the foreman, "Are these men skilled . . .
The men you'd hire if you had to build?"
He gave me a laugh and said, "No, indeed.
Just common labor is all I need.

For I can easily wreck in a day or two
What builders have taken years to do."
And I thought to myself as I went my way,
"Which of these roles have I tried to play?
Am I a builder who works with care,
Measuring life by the rule and square?
Shaping my deeds to a well made plan,
Carefully doing the best I can?
Or am I a wrecker walking the town,
Content with the labor of tearing down?"

We all need to learn to picture people wearing a tattoo that says MMFI. The letters stand for Make Me Feel Important. If we develop that attitude and share it with others through the spoken word, we can change hurting lives and have a positive impact on our society, just as Captain Treadwell did on H-Block.

### Nine Years of Persistence Pays Off
### Central Prison - Raleigh, North Carolina

Ron's first visit to death row at Central Prison in Raleigh, North Carolina was in 1983. He hit it off with an inmate named Michael Pinch who was a big boxing fan, especially of "Boom Boom" Mancini. Ron had covered a number of Mancini's fights and sent Michael some photographs of the boxer, along with some pictures from other big fights and sporting events. Ron realized how special this was to Michael when we visited Central's death row again in 1992 and saw Ron's pictures plastered all over Pinch's cell.

Ron wasn't really sure where Michael stood in his faith, although Ron had written letters, sent pictures, and presented the Gospel to Michael since their first meeting. Michael never gave him any indication he had invited Christ into his life, so Ron assumed he hadn't been able to really reach him. However, late one afternoon after Jack Murphy spoke to the population, Jack gave an invitation as counselors and inmates circled and held hands for prayer. While Jack was praying, Ron kept a close eye on Michael and noticed he was praying. Afterwards, Ron asked Michael if he'd prayed to invite Christ as his Savior, and Michael grinned and said he had.

It took about nine years of persistent correspondence and a couple of personal visits, but finally Michael had established a relationship with Christ, and Ron was especially pleased he could be there during this wonderful moment in Michael's life.

### Photograph an Execution?
### Central Prison - Raleigh, North Carolina

Ron also met David Huffstetler in 1983 and introduced him to me in 1992. As Ron did with Michael, Ron began corresponding with David years ago. David is a Christian and asked Ron to witness his execution and take pictures of it, but Ron has no interest in doing this. As a matter of fact, Ron has no desire to even witness an execution.

### Central Prison
### Raleigh, North Carolina

Although I've now worked on many death rows, one of the most unique ones is at Central Prison in Raleigh, North Carolina. On my first visit there, I was the weekend coordinator for Central Prison and worked directly with one of the program directors, Dick Hanley. I could tell immediately I was going to enjoy working with Dick, and we quickly developed a friendship. Dick Hanley is a special man and a real servant. He loves the Lord and cares deeply about his work and serving others. He is humble, kind, and a true professional.

Dick, Chaplain Skip Pike, and I mapped out a very good game plan for covering every area of the prison, which housed a large number of inmates in an unbelievable variety of areas including death row, a hospital, a mental health ward, and a receiving unit. Making sure we had counselors and programs in all of these areas was no small task, and it took some creative planning and preparation. Fortunately, Dick and Chaplain Pike were familiar with our program and had already done most of the groundwork for us. We had done a Weekend of Champions at Central a few years earlier, and they were employed there at the time.

An official told me that on our very first visit to Central, we hadn't been cleared on death row and that our program had been scrutinized by a number of the officials there. The good news was that they were so impressed with what they had seen, they said it had been a terrible mistake not to open the death row to us, and vowed if we ever came back they would insist we provide enough counselors and programming for all death row inmates. With that mandate, we treated death row at Central as a separate unit and scheduled programs with platform guests and counselors to work the blocks for the entire weekend. My job, of course, was to coordinate death row, as well as the rest of the facility.

The most unique aspect of working on North Carolina's death row was the fact that they let all of the inmates out of their cells and into the cell pods for our programs. This is unusual, as most of our death row work is done one on one, cell to cell, and without platform guests and programs. This decision enhanced our efforts to reach these men, as the programs allowed them to laugh and have a good time; it also freed up our counselors to visit on a more personal basis, rather than through the cell bars.

We had an outstanding experience on death row and throughout all of Central Prison that weekend. Dick and Skip were with us the entire time and went the "second mile" to create opportunities for us to share. Before we left on Sunday, Dick told me to let him know if I was ever going to be in the Raleigh area again and that he'd love to get together. From that day on, whenever we had a prison weekend in North Carolina, I called ahead and offered to share a program for the men on death row at Central.

Ron also got to know a lot of men on death row that weekend, so he has usually joined me for the programs, coming in a day early to serve. John Lotz, the Assistant Athletic Director at North Carolina University, has worked with us several times. The inmates love to hear John speak and get the inside scoop on Tar Heel athletics, especially the basketball program. I've made five visits to Central's death row and am scheduled to speak there again. Unfortunately, because of health problems, Dick Hanley retired in August of 1995, after many faithful years of service at Central. The prison will miss him. Ron and I will too.

### Michael's Timely Commitment
### Central Prison - Raleigh, North Carolina

John Lotz, Ron, and I were on death row at Central just two weeks prior to the scheduled execution date of an inmate named Michael

McDougal. I did my program, John spoke, and Ron showed slides of some of his best photos. Ron did have a chance to visit briefly with Michael and discovered they had come from similar religious backgrounds. Ron tried to stress that heaven or hell wasn't going to be determined by what church we attended, but by what we did with Jesus Christ.

I can recall Ron being very disturbed that day as we left the prison because he felt that Michael had not accepted Christ, despite a strong possibility he would be executed within a few weeks. We prayed for Michael, and oddly enough I was back in Raleigh doing a program for North Carolina State University on the day Michael was executed. It was an eerie feeling as I had just been there and talked to him. I called Ron to let him know about the execution, and neither one of us still knew whether or not Michael had made a decision about the Lord. It was a week or so later when another of Ron's inmate friends on death row, Anson Maynard, wrote to tell him that right before Michael was executed, he made a commitment and was baptized. Chaplain Pike later confirmed this for us, and we were thankful for this victory in Michael's life.

A letter I received from Chaplain Pike meant a lot because it reminded me of just how important our ministry in prisons is, and the positive impact we can have for eternity in the lives of many inmates.

Rick,

I deeply appreciate your willingness to spend time with our men on death row at Central Prison ... Your presence could not have come at a better, more needful time. Your timely message was extremely helpful as two weeks later we had to confront the valley of the shadow with one of our inmates who was executed. How grateful I am that you have not only heard but responded to God's call to visit those in prison. Your unselfish spirit brings honor to the Kingdom of God.

Rev. Luther M. Pike
Senior Staff Chaplain
Central Prison

### Our Friends on "Life Row"
### Mountain View Unit - Gatesville, Texas

There are four very special women residing on death row at the Mountain View Unit in Gatesville, Texas. Karla Faye Tucker, Betty Beets, Pam Perillo and Frances Newton have all been given the death penalty for their crimes and are incarcerated in a special, modified housing unit at Mountain View. Through the efforts of many faithful Christian volunteers, all of these women have trusted Christ and are now deeply committed Christians. Although this will not eliminate the possibility of their deaths by execution, their relationship with the Lord does play an important role in their lives together on death row. Being with these women truly has been one of the most unique scenarios Ron and I have experienced in our many years of prison ministry. Ron met them in 1986 and has developed strong friendships. I have just made one visit, and Karla Tucker, who is probably the most dynamic Christian of the group, corresponds with me occasionally.

It all started in 1986 when Ron joined Hazel Wilson and Helen Kilby, two veteran Glass counselors who were friends of the inmates, at the Mountain View Unit. They enjoyed a delicious meal prepared especially for them by the three women incarcerated there. (The fourth inmate, Frances Newton, arrived later.) Watching them prepare the food is what Ron remembers most from that day because they had learned innovative ways to cook, such as using can lids as knives. Ron's first visit opened the door for many subsequent visits. He began corresponding faithfully, sending them photos of his visits to their cell block, which they call "Life Row."

By the time Ron returned in 1989, all four of the inmates had made commitments to Christ and had grown close to the Lord and to each other. Ron was able to show the women some of his photography on slides, including his trip to the South Pole. During the four-hour visit, the inmates also gave Ron and the counselors a tour of a little workshop next to their cells where they made dolls.

In 1992, Ron had a special surprise for the women at Mountain View. He had invited Dr. Carl Baugh to come to our Weekend of Champions in Gatesville. Dr. Baugh is the Director of the Creation Evidences Museum located in Glen Rose, Texas, and is one of the most brilliant scientists in the world. Dr. Baugh shared at our Friday morning

Spiritual Enrichment time and then with the women on death row.

Dr. Baugh talked about his negotiations with officials in Turkey to gain permission to dig Noah's ark out of Mount Ararat. A fascinating man, Dr. Baugh grew up as an atheist, but when a friend challenged him to explore the Christian faith so he could be sure his views were correct, he couldn't dispute the evidence he found and realized he was wrong. He became a Christian and has continued to be a great witness for Christ through his museum which serves as a vehicle to prove the Creation story. I specifically recall him showing me a small piece of wood with burned edges. He kept it sealed in special paper, which was then covered with aluminum foil. This wood was an actual sliver from Noah's ark. Atheists had tried to burn and destroy the wood. They obviously don't want the ark discovered as it would certainly prove the scriptures to be true.

After Dr. Baugh shared with the women on death row, Ron introduced the inmates to Jack Murphy and me. Ron had cleared our visit with security through his good friend, Chaplain Tim Crosby. Several of our veteran female counselors were also spending the entire weekend with the women. These counselors were friends of the four women and corresponded regularly with them, so this was a special reunion for everyone. The love these inmates had for our counselors, and vice versa, was incredible.

Upon entering the death row housing unit, I was greeted with smiles and hugs from the inmates, as Ron proudly introduced me as his "friend with all the neat magic tricks." It was as if we'd been lifelong friends the way they embraced me and welcomed me into their home. The unit itself was unique in that there was a large day room area next to the individual cells where the inmates could be locked up. A large area near the entrance was occupied by officers who could survey the housing units from their posts. The women had decorated this room as best they could on their limited budget and resources, and it was cozy, despite being a cell block. The plants and flowers scattered about seemed almost out of place, but certainly added to the homey atmosphere. Adjacent was another small room that was filled with dolls. Ron had told me that the women made dolls as part of their work. The room was full of them, and I remember how beautifully crafted they were. So far, this place wasn't anything at all like other death rows I had seen.

They ate their meals together at a large kitchen table in the middle of the room. My time was limited, so Ron told everyone to gather around the table to watch me do card tricks. He positioned himself in a prime spot for taking pictures, and I was off and running. For the next forty-five minutes I had the time of my life entertaining these women. They were one of the most enthusiastic and appreciative audiences I've ever worked with and absolutely loved each trick. Ron enjoyed the women's laughter while I was entertaining, and I think he was proud to be able to help provide this special opportunity for them. Moments like these were extremely rare for them, and they savored each minute we were there.

A feeling of disbelief swept over me as I reminded myself that we were inside a death row cell block, yet enjoying our time just as much as if we were at home grilling out on a Saturday night. It was also amazing to me how quickly friendships were formed; this was obviously because of the Christian commitments we all shared.

After I had entertained the women, they winked at each other and announced that now it was their turn to entertain us. We all sat down and one of them put a cassette in a tape player. As a beautiful Christian song played, the four of them signed the words to the music. They had learned sign language to some of their favorite songs and enjoyed performing. I was inspired and amazed and fought back tears as they thanked us in this very special way for our visit. Each of us were touched by this moment, and when they were finished their faces beamed with pride and joy.

As we struggled to control our emotions, Chaplain Crosby reminded us that it was almost time to leave because Ron and I had evening programs starting soon in a couple of units nearby. We circled around the large table to close in prayer, and as we joined hands Jack Murphy asked Betty to pray. Suddenly the room became very quiet as we waited for her to begin. I looked at Betty and could see she was shocked that Jack had asked her to pray, and I think for a moment she hoped maybe I would intercede and rescue her from this dilemma. Then all of a sudden, she began to pray. "Lord, you know I have never led a group in prayer, and I'm scared to death." She went on to communicate with God from the bottom of her heart in a way that was so honest and sincere, and we felt the overwhelming presence of the Lord as never before. I had goose bumps as Betty prayed and thanked the Lord for our time together. This wasn't some eloquent prayer that had been written out and rehearsed. It was straight from the heart and soul of a woman who was truly thankful to God for the miracles He had worked in her life since her incarceration. I had not been moved like this for a long time.

When Betty finished and we all regained our composure, we hugged each other again and said goodbye, thanking each of the women and Chaplain Crosby for the opportunity to be together. I have to admit, it was difficult to leave them and anticlimactic to go on to another unit for my next program. This was an experience I would never forget. That evening, Ron and I stayed up late to talk about our day; we shook our heads in amazement at what had taken place.

In 1993, we had a prison weekend in another area of Texas, and Ron and his wife, Nancy, made a special trip to Gatesville so Ron could introduce Nancy to his friends on death row. Ron's years of involvement in prison ministry had always been encouraged by Nancy, but their five children at home in Cleveland kept her hopping and she'd never had the opportunity to literally be a part of it all.

The initial terror of the fences and razor wire wore off quickly once Nancy met the women on death row. She was warmly welcomed, and their two-hour visit went by quickly. Nancy was astonished at the love and warmth these women shared. She experienced first-hand the uniqueness of the death row wing and the inmates at Mountain View, and understood more fully why Ron and I had such strong feelings for our friends there. Ron was able to capture much of the visit on film, and the women were glad to receive pictures a few weeks later.

The last time Ron visited Mountain View was in 1994, shortly after he and I had gone on a missions trip to Kiev, Ukraine, and he was permitted to show slides and share about our trip. It was difficult for him to leave the women because two of them had execution dates coming up soon, and the possibility of their death was becoming more of a reality with each stay of execution. Of course, when dealing with inmates on death row, this is an ever-present issue.

All of our friends at Mountain View know that their lives may end in the execution chamber in Texas, but their faith gives them a sense of purpose and hope. Sharing the same destiny, they lean on each other for strength and are determined to do all they can to minister to others through the mail, including prison ministry visitors like Ron and me.

Receiving a letter from Karla is like getting money from home. She knows how to inspire and encourage and is a dedicated prayer warrior. I know she prays for Ron and me as we serve the Lord, especially in prison ministry, and Ron and I will continue to pray for and encourage each of the women on death row in Texas and trust their futures to the Lord, which is exactly what they have done.

### Stay of Execution Leads to Miracle
### Atmore, Alabama

An early recollection Ron has of a death row experience occurred in 1979 on a prison weekend at the Holman Unit near Atmore, Alabama. About a week prior to the weekend, an inmate by the name of Johnny Evans was scheduled to be executed. However, Johnny's mother had fought hard for a stay of execution and won. When Ron arrived at the Holman Unit, there was a great deal of tension at the institution, especially on the death row wing. Because of this, they didn't allow any counselors or platform guests to visit death row, even though we normally worked that area. However, by Friday evening the officials sensed a calmness among the population, and after the evening program they allowed five members of the team into the death row cell block. Ron was included in that group, as was platform guest Bob Cole. Ron and Bob were both aware of Johnny's stay of execution and of his case, and they found his cell to meet him and share. Because he had just come so close to being executed, they thought the timing might be just right. Bob and Ron eventually helped him to make a decision for Christ. After praying to invite Christ into his life, Johnny looked at Bob and said, "This really was a miracle. If I had been executed last week, I would have died without Christ and spent eternity in hell." His commitment was legitimate because for the next few months, Ron received many tremendous letters from Johnny, and he stood tall in his Christian commitment, even conducting Bible studies for the other inmates on death row.

It was about two years after Ron's visit that Johnny was finally executed, but he had a fantastic testimony of his strong faith prior to being put to death. Although it was a difficult time for Ron, it was a lot easier knowing Johnny was now in heaven.

## Commissioner Says, "Everybody Out"
## Atmore, Alabama

Alabama's death row is at the Holman Unit located near Atmore, Alabama. At the time that I coordinated that unit and worked on death row, there were ninety-one men incarcerated there. Warden Lamar Mothershed was in charge of the entire facility. He was an extremely laid back, easy-going man. I enjoyed working with him, and he was very cooperative and helpful. In addition to housing the death row inmates, Holman was also where the Alabama license plates were manufactured. Warden Mothershed was eager to show me this large operation, and I asked if he could give me a tour of that area later when Ron came to the facility, explaining that Ron might like to take some pictures. He agreed, and later in the weekend Warden Mothershed gave Ron and me a tour of the entire process from start to finish. We both enjoyed it and were astonished at the number of plates that they could crank out in one work day. It was fun to watch.

Little did we know we were in for a memorable death row experience on Saturday afternoon when Tanya Crevier, the basketball handler, came to Holman for her program. Commissioner Morris Thigpen drove her to the facility, and in typical Thigpen style carried all of Tanya's equipment inside for her show. After finishing on the main yard at Holman, Commissioner Thigpen asked Tanya if she would mind doing another program for the death row inmates. Of course, Tanya, being familiar with death rows, said she'd be glad to, as long as there was enough room in front of each cell to do a few ball-handling tricks. Thigpen then told her that his plan was to bring the entire death row population together on the yard by the basketball court to watch her entertain. He happened to mention this idea right in front of Warden Mothershed, who stopped dead in his tracks and looked at Thigpen as if he'd lost his mind.

"Commissioner," he said, "we've never brought all of the death row inmates together at one time. That could spell trouble, and if there is any, we could both lose our jobs." And Thigpen replied, "Warden, there *won't* be any trouble. And besides, if there is, I'll lose *my* job; *yours* is safe. I'll take full responsibility for the entire situation."

Even with that I'm sure Mothershed thought the Commissioner had lost his mind, but he cooperated fully. Within fifteen minutes the concrete area by the basketball goal was surrounded by ninety-one death row inmates, all staring at each other, wondering what in the world was going on. Whatever it was, it must be pretty special because they all had never been out in the yard at the same time, and the Commissioner of Prisons for the State of Alabama was standing right in the middle of them.

Once Mothershed gave the signal that everyone was present and accounted for and security officers were in place, Commissioner Thigpen explained to the inmates why they were assembled in the yard and informed them that they were about to see an incredible program that he didn't want any of them to miss. He expressed his confidence that there wouldn't be any problems, and then asked me to introduce Tanya.

As I was introducing Tanya, I watched the faces of these men, glad to be out of their cells, but wide-eyed with skepticism and wondering how some girl dribbling basketballs could be all that great. I smiled inside because I had observed this so many times in other institutions and then had watched Tanya begin her show and totally change the complexion and spirit of tough inmates, turning their hardened expressions into laughter and smiles as they were mesmerized by her skills. After I built Tanya up with an enthusiastic and exciting introduction, she turned on the upbeat music she plays while performing and began demonstrating the skills that won her the title of the World's Finest Basketball Handler. Within minutes the entire death row population was clapping their hands and giving "high fives" to each other, to Tanya, and to me. And, as usual, within minutes, they were all smiles as Tanya's infectious grin and dazzling skills transformed a crowd of hardened convicts into a circle of grown men acting like five-year-olds at a birthday party. It didn't take long for the inmates to see why Commissioner Thigpen insisted on all of them seeing Tanya's performance. This was a moment they would never forget. They would talk about it for years to come.

After the program and an invitation to which a number of inmates responded, our counselors worked with the inmates who made decisions for Christ. Many of the men also had an opportunity to meet Tanya and get her autograph. It was heart warming to see many inmates go to Morris Thigpen, shake his hand, and thank him for providing this very special opportunity for them. As they visited with him, I realized that eventually, Morris was the same man who might have to return to their facility to orchestrate another program–the execution of any one of these inmates on death row. I talked to Morris about this part of his job, and it was hard for him to speak about it without his eyes welling up with tears. An execution is a gut-wrenching, soul-searching time for him, and he never looks forward to an appointment in the room that houses "Big Yellow Mama," the inmates' nickname for the electric chair. This day, however, being on Alabama's death row was fun, and because a few men on the row had made a commitment to Christ, Thigpen knew that it would make his difficult job at least a little bit easier if execution day arrived for those particular men. He had been able to provide something special for the inmates, truly risking his job to be able to share the Gospel through Tanya's program out in the yard. By the way, once the yard had been cleared and the inmates were back in their cells, Warden Mothershed was also all smiles, obviously thankful there were no incidents.

## Gallows
### Walla Walla, Washington

Walla Walla, Washington has a unique death row setting and at the time I visited, only seven men were incarcerated there. Although most Washington executions are carried out by lethal injection, the state still has a gallows where inmates given the death penalty may be hung. Recently the gallows was used for an inmate who requested it since he had killed his victim by hanging. I was curious to see the gallows but was informed it was a highly secured area and very few people were permitted there.

However, I have been in execution chambers on other death rows, and believe me, it is an eerie feeling. I've been in those with an electric chair as well as those with a gurney for a lethal injection. A holding cell is usually next to the chamber, and that is where the inmate spends the last twenty-four hours of his life, unless a stay is issued. I can recall sitting in a holding cell like that trying to imagine what it would be like to know my life was almost over. Many inmates on death row have told me that experiencing that last twenty-four-hour process, preparing themselves to die, and then receiving a stay is almost worse than actually being executed. The mental strain and anguish of saying goodbye to loved ones for the last time and preparing for what's beyond the grave, and then finding out they'll have to do it all again later, is very difficult and often leaves permanent psychological scars.

### From the Death Watch Cell to Freedom
### Jackson, Georgia

On one of Ron's first visits to Georgia's death row, he met an inmate named Billy Moore. Although their visit was brief, Ron got to know Billy better by corresponding with him. A few years later, Ron was scheduled to attend a prison weekend in Jackson, Georgia, so he arranged his flights and activities around a visit with Billy. When Ron entered the visiting area, he was surprised to see a Glass counselor and friend, Jerry Morris from Missouri. Seeing Jerry reminded Ron of the faithfulness of many of the counselors who make special trips to visit inmates they've met on previous weekends. He also recalled what ex-offender Jack Murphy had told him. Jack said that Christians are usually the only people who visit inmates, other than their immediate family. Jerry Morris had the same idea as Ron—he came to the prison weekend early to see a man he was corresponding with and offer him some personal encouragement.

Billy Moore's 1983 stay of execution was quite an experience, and he shared some of the details with Ron. Billy was escorted from his cell to fill out some paperwork regarding the distribution of his personal effects, and then he was placed under close surveillance in the death watch cell. (This is a cell near the execution chamber where inmates spend their last twenty-four hours before the scheduled execution. Inmates have their last meal, last visits, and last rites. Officers are assigned to keep a close eye on the cell and are required to record everything the inmate says and does while under the death watch.) Normally an inmate is allowed to bring one book to the death watch cell, but Billy was given special permission from the warden to bring two books—his address book and his Bible.

When Billy laid down to get some sleep prior to his execution the next morning, one of the officers asked him, "How can you go to sleep knowing you'll probably be executed in a few hours?" And Billy, who had come to know the Lord, told the officer he had complete peace about it. He then requested that the officer awaken him at three o'clock in the morning, and said that he would be very upset if they forgot to get him up. Curious, the officer asked him why it was so important that he be awakened in the middle of the night, and Billy explained that for the past year or so, he had gotten up at three o'clock every morning to pray for everyone in his address book—starting with A and praying right through to Z—and it took nearly two hours. The list of people were many friends whom he'd come to know after accepting the Lord.

When Ron heard Billy tell this story, he was ashamed of his own prayer life and how some days he found it difficult to pray for two minutes, let alone for two hours. And Ron wondered what it must have been like to concentrate and pray during what might be the last few hours of Billy's life. Billy's prayers were always for others, and this really touched Ron; but Billy must have worded at least one prayer for himself during that lengthy prayer vigil because he was granted a stay.

The victim's family forgave Billy and fought his execution, pleading for his sentence to be changed. Their efforts were not in vain as Billy's sentence was eventually changed to life, and he was transferred from death row to a prison in Reidsville. After serving more time there, Billy sent Ron a letter saying he had been released and was getting married. Billy is now doing well and living in Michigan.

## Murderous Logic
### Ellis I Unit, Huntsville, Texas

One Texas death row inmate was memorable, but not for his fine qualities. Because James was so violent, he was kept in a special cell that was covered with very thin, wire mesh screen so there was no light in the cell. Ron said he never did see James' face when he was talking with him, and all James talked about was killing. He had already killed three inmates on death row and told Ron he'd take out an officer, too, when they transferred him to the Walls Unit for his impending execution. His logic behind these senseless killings was that with each murder he'd have to go through an additional trial, consequently adding continuous delays to his actual execution date. He was eventually executed.

## Donald H. "Pee Wee" Gaskin
## South Carolina

Probably the most fascinating death row inmate Ron ever met and became acquainted with was Donald H. "Pee Wee" Gaskin, whom he first met on South Carolina's death row in 1979. Pee Wee Gaskin stood 4' 11" tall. He was fascinated with Ron's photography abilities and experiences. On that initial visit in 1979, Pee Wee told Ron he had made a commitment to Christ, so Ron wrote him for a couple of years, until the mail from Pee Wee suddenly stopped.

Years later, in 1991 we were involved in a huge weekend in the Columbia, South Carolina area, and Broad River Prison was on our schedule. South Carolina's death row was now located there, having been moved from a prison called Central, which was in the heart of downtown Columbia. We were allowed to bring some programs and counselors into death row, and during one of the Friday programs which Ron was covering, he noticed Pee Wee observing from the small window in his cell door. He seemed content to watch from there rather than come out.

Ron asked the warden if he could visit Pee Wee, and the warden was curious to know why. Ron then explained how the two of them had met in 1979 and corresponded regularly for some time later. The warden gave Ron permission, but also told Ron that the following Monday morning there was a strong possibility Pee Wee would be receiving some bad news. It wasn't too difficult to figure out what the bad news was, and after visiting with Pee Wee, Ron knew Pee Wee had already gotten the drift that he was going to be executed.

After visiting for about forty-five minutes, Pee Wee confessed to Ron that he was planning to take his own life before they could execute him. He told Ron he had a couple of ways of doing it without pain. It made Ron very uncomfortable talking about it, and deep down he probably wished Pee Wee wouldn't have brought it up. Changing the subject at the first chance possible, Ron asked Pee Wee to tell him again about when he trusted Christ into his life. All Pee Wee said was, "I read my Bible and pray." It wasn't the answer Ron was looking for.

That evening Ron felt obligated to tell Bill Glass about Pee Wee's confession, but Bill felt it wasn't any of our business to say or do anything about it. Upon arriving home, however, Ron, still troubled by what he'd heard, talked to his pastor, who encouraged him to talk to the prison authorities. Ron just didn't seem to feel totally confident that this was the right thing to do, so he decided to focus his energy back on Pee Wee and his problem.

Bothered with the possibilities that Pee Wee hadn't really ever made a sincere profession of faith and that he would be executed soon, Ron wrote him a long letter and got it in the mail right away. He shared about Johnny Evans on Alabama's death row, and how he came to know the Lord just in the nick of time. Ron expressed his uneasiness about Pee Wee's answers when asked about his relationship with Christ, and Ron explained again as clearly as possible how to become a Christian by accepting Jesus Christ as Lord and Savior, and claiming the forgiveness He provided us through His shed blood on Calvary's cross. Certainly Ron emphasized the urgency of settling this matter immediately because the scriptures plainly state that when we die we will stand in judgment before God, and our only hope for spending eternity in heaven is through faith in Christ.

Ron continued to pray for Pee Wee. Then one night Pee Wee telephoned to tell Ron that prison officials had scheduled his execution for September 6, 1991. Apparently some of the officers had gotten word that Pee Wee had contemplated suicide before his execution because Pee Wee told Ron they had moved him into a new cell, given him a new uniform, and not allowed him to bring anything out of his old cell into the new one. He was also under twenty-four-hour surveillance.

When Ron brought up the letter he'd sent and confronted Pee Wee again about his relationship with Christ, Pee Wee simply said, "You know, Ron, I was good all my life." This really bothered Ron for a couple of reasons. First, he knew Pee Wee was one of the most notorious serial killers in the United States. And secondly, he knew that Pee Wee didn't know the Lord. Unfortunately, when September 6th came, Pee Wee was finally executed after spending over twenty years on death row.

Ron was astonished when he read a newspaper clipping about the execution, which described Pee Wee's attempt to commit suicide just before the execution. While back in his old cell, he had somehow swallowed a single-edged razor. Then without eating or drinking for over a week, in the middle of the night right before his execution, he coughed it back up and slit his wrists. With twenty-four-hour surveillance on his cell, officers saw the blood and rushed him immediately to the infirmary. He received eighteen stitches and was executed several hours later. What a bizarre ending to the life of one of the more fascinating individuals Ron has ever met on death row. Ron does not know if Pee Wee Gaskin ever trusted Christ and made a commitment.

## We Thank the Lord for Every Opportunity

Ron and I will continue to visit death row cell blocks and meet many more individuals who have been sentenced to the death penalty. Our message won't change, and we will thank the Lord for every opportunity we have to share our faith with these men and women. We know that a commitment to Christ gives them hope in a situation that delivers very little of it. Tracy Housel, a death row inmate in Jackson, Georgia, gave me a poem after my first visit there in 1986. It reminds me of the positive difference faith in God makes in the life of a death row inmate and the importance of our continued work in this area of prison ministry.

## God Shares Every Mile

People often wonder as days go passing by
why I keep on smiling when it seems that I should cry.
And people often ask me why I'm never down
and how I keep my head up when miseries abound.

But people only look as far as people want to see.
They just don't take the time to see God inside of me.
They do not know God's in my heart and on my mind each day.
Why else would I be acting and doing things this way?

But my reply to them is prompt and always with a smile:
"My burdens aren't too heavy–God shares every mile.
He lifts the load that I can't bear, and helps me make it through.
And that's why I can raise my head and share a smile with you."

# CHAPTER 9

# DIVINE APPOINTMENTS

*T*hroughout the years, team members with the Bill Glass weekends have been in many situations that were, without a doubt, divinely ordained. They can't be explained any other way. These experiences always remind us that, although we may plan the weekends, God is the one who orchestrates every move by placing just the right people in just the right locations at just the right times to accomplish His perfect will. These are what Ron and I like to call divine appointments. Miracles. They take place every weekend, and they keep us coming back. Ron and I want to share a few of these miracles with you.

### Desperate Inmate Meets Understanding Counselor

During an afternoon program at a women's unit in Oklahoma City, platform guest Bill Michaels had begun singing a song entitled "Where Have You Gone?" which is a touching story of how quickly our children grow up and suddenly they are gone, all grown up and on their own. As he was singing to the eight hundred-plus inmates, one of our counselors noticed that the inmate seated next to her was having a very difficult time controlling her emotions. What began as gentle crying turned into weeping, and the counselor gently took her by the arm and led her out of the program area to comfort her. With her arm around the inmate's shoulder, she let the woman cry. Once she had calmed down, the counselor asked her why she was having such a difficult time. The inmate told our counselor it was something she wouldn't understand in a million years, and couldn't do anything about it anyway.

"Try me," the counselor urged.

The woman proceeded to explain that she was doing time for

murdering her two children, and Bill's song had resurrected the horrible memories of what she had done. The inmate recounted the awful details of the murders but was certain that the counselor couldn't possibly understand what it was like having to live day to day with the knowledge that her children were gone and that she was responsible for their deaths. Nothing she could do would ever bring them back, and the rest of her life would be spent in prison, leaving her with no hope. She admitted to the counselor that she had serious thoughts about committing suicide because she had nothing left to live for and she would carry the pain of this crime to her grave.

When the counselor sympathized with her by saying, "I know how you must feel," the woman snapped harshly, "How could you possibly know how I feel?" The counselor then related an incident in her life that had left her burdened with guilt and pain for many years. She told the inmate that as a teenager she had gotten pregnant by her first love, and he insisted she get an abortion. Not really knowing much about abortion, she agreed and the arrangements were made. Being young and naive, she believed there was just a blob of tissue inside her. She didn't realize until the day of the procedure that the fetus was sucked out of her by a vacuum cleaner-type machine. As if that wasn't enough anguish, while she was recovering, she saw in a jar not one, but two heads and realized she had aborted twins.

As the counselor shared her story, the inmate stopped crying and listened intently. The counselor told her she had carried the guilt of this for many years and, although she didn't pull the trigger of a gun to kill her children, she felt she could empathize with the pain the inmate was experiencing. The counselor said she had thought her life was ruined and had wondered how she could go on living. And she, too, had dealt with thoughts of suicide. But her guilt was finally removed when she accepted Jesus Christ as her Lord and Savior and claimed His forgiveness in her life. "He'll forgive you, too," she said, "and heal your pain and guilt." The counselor was able to lead this woman to faith in Christ and help her begin her road to recovery. The Lord used a horrible experience from the counselor's past to bring something positive into the inmate's life.

After talking for a while, the inmate asked the counselor if she had any children since the abortion, and she pulled out a photograph and said, "Aren't these the best looking twelve-year-old twin boys you've ever seen?" In an audience of eight hundred, God placed these two women right next to each other so that the counselor who could best understand the inmate's unique needs could be right there to help. It was certainly a divine appointment.

### Blind Compassion

Joel Jeffries, a blind friend from Des Moines, Iowa, has found a niche serving on the Bill Glass team. His wife, Colleen, is also involved, and they attend several weekends annually.

Joel's blindness became an ally on his first weekend in Missouri. He was on my team, and together we worked out all of the extra little details that were involved to take a blind counselor into the prison. I hadn't encountered this type of situation before but remained optimistic that there would be no problems and Joel would get along fine. He enjoyed the training, the spiritual enrichment, and meeting the other counselors on his team, and Joel was fired up to begin sharing his faith with the inmates. To be honest, I had no idea how they would react to Joel, but I quickly discovered that his blindness had no bearing on his effectiveness in the prison. Joel brought with him the *Four Spiritual Laws* booklet written in Braille and knew how to present it very effectively.

In the particular prison we were working that weekend, there was a blatant homosexual who bore so much resemblance to a woman that we had to do a double take to be sure he wasn't a female. The inmate was very difficult to talk to, and frankly, most of our counselors headed the other direction when he approached them. Nobody really wanted to deal with him.

The inmate attended all of the programs and listened attentively to the messages of the platform guests. Then after our Saturday evening program, he sat right down next to Joel on a picnic bench and introduced himself. Joel, thankful for another opportunity to visit, began to challenge the young man to make a commitment to Christ. Of course, the inmate's appearance wasn't a factor to Joel, who only looked into his needy soul and saw the pain of his past. Eventually, Joel led the man to faith in Christ.

It was remarkable to see the same inmate the next day wearing no makeup or female attire. In fact, we almost didn't recognize him. He told several of our counselors that he had thrown away his female clothing and was eager to be the man God called him to be. Through the messages from the platform and the compassion of a counselor who could look beyond the physical appearance of a person, this man's life was changed that day in Missouri.

### Pow-Wow in Alabama

Dave Nielsen, my good friend, was divinely appointed on his first prison weekend with me. About one month prior to the weekend, Dave and his family were on vacation in the Black Hills of South Dakota. During a side trip through the Badlands, Dave became hopelessly lost on back roads and was forced to seek shelter at a park service outpost during a severe thunderstorm. While waiting for the storm to break, the ranger showed Dave a book on the life of Crazy Horse and Native American culture. Having an interest in a broad range of subjects, Dave decided it might be interesting reading. He bought the book and read it prior to attending the Weekend of Champions. Oddly enough, what makes this story so unusual is that his newly acquired knowledge of Native American culture came in handy in a prison in Montgomery, Alabama–the last place you'd expect to encounter an Indian pow-wow.

I had been in a number of prisons that had special "holy ground" reserved for Native American inmates, so I was somewhat familiar with the rituals practiced in those areas. One thing I knew for sure was that a person shouldn't wander onto this sacred ground without an invitation, and invitations were rarely extended. I was aware that there was a "holy ground" area reserved at this Montgomery facility because I had seen it on the Thursday check-out. Also, the security officers had reminded me to warn our counselors not to wander there. Therefore, I was surprised to see Dave, apparently ignoring my warning, and sitting cross-legged in a circle within the designated "holy ground" visiting with the inmates. I was concerned for his safety and his adherence to the rules.

It seems Dave was invited to join the circle, and as they visited, the inmates were impressed with his knowledge of their culture and religious beliefs, extended their friendship and made him their guest for the day. The information Dave learned from the book was fresh in his mind. Dave was the perfect counselor to befriend these inmates and converse about faith issues with them. Because he had read the book, a door was opened to communicate the Gospel to inmates who would have been the most difficult to reach.

Dave swears God led him over one hundred miles of gravel roads on the south side of the Badlands in the heat of July and whipped up the biggest thunderstorm he ever saw just so he'd meet that ranger and buy that book. I believe He did.

### A Grateful Heart Brings Healing

A particularly meaningful experience for Ron occurred in 1980 and also falls under the category of divine appointments. While Ron was in Moscow covering the Olympic games, his wife, Nancy, delivered their son, Josh, on July 22nd. Ron was in Moscow for three weeks; then he spent another three weeks in France and London visiting relatives. Eventually returning home, he was able to see Josh for the first time and, although he didn't see anything drastically wrong, he sensed there was a problem. Finally, Nancy broke the news to him. Josh was a Down's Syndrome child. The news crushed Ron. He hadn't been excited about having another child in the first place, as he and Nancy already had four children. And then to have a handicapped son was more than he could handle. His pastor told him, "God gives special children to special parents." But Ron's reply to that was simply, "I don't feel that special. Why didn't God give him to somebody else?" Ron carried the pain for almost a year, constantly struggling with having a child like Josh. However, a prison weekend in Millville, New Jersey changed his attitude forever.

Bill Glass's message during the spiritual enrichment time concluded with a challenge to the counselors to thank God for something they had never been able to thank Him for. Mustering up every bit of courage he had, Ron stood before the team, expressed his bitterness about having a Down's Syndrome child, and thanked God for Josh. Later that afternoon, the Lord honored his prayer and attitude through a unique experience at one of the prisons.

After shooting pictures of a program featuring Pat Williams, General Manager of the Philadelphia 76'ers, Tanya Crevier, and Bill Glass, Ron was preparing to leave the institution with them. On his way toward the gate, one of the counselors invited Ron to stay and talk with some of the inmates. Since he hadn't taken any shots of the counselors at this particular unit, he thought it would be a good idea. Ironically, as he headed to one of the dorms to shoot pictures of counselors, he discovered there were only a few at this unit, so he spent more time talking to inmates. Two of them were particularly interested in Ron's work and invited him to join them for lunch.

After lunch as the three were talking, Ron asked them if they had enjoyed the program earlier in the day. Both of them said it was great, and an inmate named Nick said he especially enjoyed the part in Bill's message when he talked about his Down's Syndrome grandson. That caught Ron's attention, and he asked Nick why that was so meaningful.

Nick responded, "Because I have a child like that." Ron's chin dropped to the ground. He reached in his pocket for his wallet, pulled out a picture of Josh, and showed it to Nick. Upon seeing the picture, Nick broke down in tears and confessed his struggle with his child, only to learn that just that very morning Ron had finally been able to thank God for Josh. Sharing a kindred spirit because of their special children, Ron and Nick visited for quite some time. Ron eventually was able to help Nick trust Christ as his Savior and also to thank God for his Down's Syndrome son. Ron recalls that as they were praying, he completely lost it and began to cry because that very morning he had given this troubling matter to the Lord. In return, God honored Ron by introducing him to an inmate who needed the same healing touch.

This story was certainly a memorable and meaningful one for Ron. However, another experience he had in California would rank right up there with the story of Nick and Nick's Down's Syndrome boy. Also, this experience allowed Ron to capture one of his most prized photographs throughout all his years of prison ministry.

### The Boy With the Tear in His Eye

Stockton, California has a number of juvenile facilities, and Ron and Bunny Martin were assigned to participate in a Sunday morning program in a facility called O.H. Close. While Ron and Bunny were waiting for the last dormitory's residents to arrive, they were visiting with an officer when suddenly there was a great deal of commotion in the gym, and a number of security officers rushed out of the building. It was obvious something was wrong, and they discovered that one of the young inmates was trying to escape. The whole situation was rectified very quickly, and within ten minutes the escapee was caught.

During the ordeal, Ron felt a real burden for this young person and asked the prison chaplain if it might be possible to visit the inmate. The chaplain was skeptical and told Ron the escapee would probably be sent right to lockdown to be grilled by the officers. About that time, security granted permission to go on with the scheduled program, which Ron and Bunny did.

After the program, however, Ron went back to the chaplain and asked once again if he could visit the young man who had tried to escape. Ron's persistence and genuine concern paid off, and the chaplain eventually cleared a visit through one of the prison officials. Ron and Bunny wasted little time and were immediately escorted to the lockdown area to meet the boy named David.

Ron wasn't at all prepared for what he saw when the officer opened the cell door. A very young boy, shaking with fear, was sitting on a bunk, tears streaming down his face. When he saw Ron and Bunny, the boy grabbed a blanket, pulled it up completely over himself, and continued to weep. Bunny and Ron entered the small cell, and Ron gently began to speak to David, introducing Bunny and explaining why they were at the institution that morning. Ron's gentle, loving approach convinced the boy to slowly lower the blanket off his head. David peeked through a small opening to make eye contact with his guests.

Ron told David he was sorry that David had missed seeing Bunny's show because Bunny was the World's Yo-Yo Champion, but Bunny was here for a special show just for David. And as Bunny began to twirl the yo-yos, David slowly eased the blanket off himself and stopped crying. By the time Bunny struck two matches with his yo-yo as David held them in his hand, Bunny and Ron had won his complete attention and trust.

Bunny put his yo-yos away and began to tell David about the message he had given to the other inmates at the Sunday morning program. The subject was the prodigal son, and Bunny ended the story by saying to David, "I understand you were trying to run away, too." David nodded and listened intently to Bunny as he continued. Up to this point, Ron hadn't snapped one picture, but just then he took a memorable photo exactly at the moment a tear was welling up in David's eye as Bunny was talking.

Bunny continued to share with David and eventually asked him if he had ever received Jesus Christ as his Lord and Savior. David told him he hadn't, but wanted to. As Bunny invited him to pray, David looked into Bunny's eyes and said, "I've never prayed in my whole life."

So Bunny led David in the sinner's prayer and, at the conclusion, Bunny asked him, "Where is Jesus?"

David pointed to his heart and responded, "Right here!"

Bunny and Ron affirmed his answer and his decision, and encouraged him to start reading the Bible and to get involved in the follow-up study group. By now this frightened little boy was smiling with his two new friends, and feeling very special.

When it was time to leave, David jumped off the bed and hugged Ron tightly, refusing to let go. Eventually, the officers pulled David away, and Ron and Bunny left his cell. Ron said David's hug disturbed him for several weeks because it was the first time he'd dealt with a young inmate like David. All Ron wanted to do at that moment was take David out of the cell and home with him. He found out later that David had no father, and David's mom was raising him. He was locked up for stealing a car and, of course, the escape attempt would add time to his sentence.

A week later, Ron called the chaplain at David's facility to check on how he was doing, and was told that David had shared his testimony at one of the Sunday morning services and was doing great.

As the years passed, Ron lost touch with David, until he met an inmate in San Quentin who had also done time at the O.H. Close facility in Stockton. He remembered Ron sharing that morning and knew David. At that point David was still incarcerated there. He would have been about sixteen at the time. Then several years later, Ron was attending a prison ministry conference in Chicago with Don Smarto, the director of the Institute for Prison Ministries. During one of the sessions a film was being shown on the Match Two Ministry and, much to Ron's surprise, a portion of the film showed David, now nineteen years old, giving his testimony. What a thrill for Ron to know David was standing firm with his Christian commitment.

By the way, the picture Ron shot of a tearful David now hangs in the Bill Glass office in Cedar Hill, Texas. Ron feels it is one of the most powerful photographs he's ever taken, and many of our prison counselors have requested reprints to display in homes, offices, and churches around the country. It seems to really capture what this ministry is all about.

### "I'm From There, Too!"

The name tags we wear while on the weekends have produced some interesting encounters. They bear our name and state, and many times an inmate will notice where we're from and a relationship gets started because he or she is also from that state. Being from the same state is one thing, but often as a counselor and inmate visit, they discover they are also from the same city and even have a friend or two in common. A majority of the time this situation seems so unusual to the inmate that he or she almost senses the Lord has set up this bizarre meeting in their prison yard or cell, and quite often a conversion experience takes place.

I recall serving as a coordinator at Walla Walla, Washington. I'm guessing there were close to eight hundred inmates in the yard after one of our programs, and an inmate spotted Iowa on my name tag. "What town you from in Iowa?" he asked.

I told him, "Algona, a very small town in the north central part of the state." You'd have thought I just hit him between the eyes with a two-by-four.

He said, "Algona? That's where I'm from!"

And as we began to visit, I discovered that he was younger than I, but he knew me because I was on the basketball team that finished 22-3 in 1971 and placed fourth in the state tournament. (Yeah, I was a great outside shooter. Then they moved the game indoors!) He also remembered that I had been very active in the Fellowship of Christian Athletes, and he wasn't surprised that I was involved in a program like the Weekend of Champions which has a Christian outreach. This meant a lot to me, and it was an important reminder that people *do* notice our commitment, even though they may never say anything to us about it.

There we were, shaking our heads in amazement at meeting each other in a prison yard of eight hundred inmates in Walla Walla, Washington years later and far from the corn fields of Iowa. I finally said to him, "I don't believe it's an accident that we've been brought together here like this. I believe it's a divine appointment." And I began to steer our conversation to spiritual concerns, inquiring about his faith. We had a fantastic visit, and I discovered that he had made a profession of faith years ago but his Christian walk had really gotten off track. I was able to encourage him, and eventually he rededicated his life to Christ and was motivated again to grow. The connection that started it all was being from the same hometown.

## Divine Seating Assignments

Not all of our divine appointments occur on prison weekends. A number of years ago on an airplane leaving Cleveland, Ron was seated next to a beautiful girl. The typical conversation ensued, and they shared their destinations with each other–the girl was on her way to Las Vegas, and Ron was headed to prison in St. Louis. Naturally, she was taken aback and asked what crime he had committed. After allaying her fears and describing a Weekend of Champions, Ron had a chance to share the Gospel with the girl. They learned they were from similar religious backgrounds. Ron explained that she couldn't be saved by being a good person or because of her good deeds, but by what God had already done for her by sending His son, Jesus, to take her place on the cross.

Later in their conversation, Ron learned that the girl was from Boardman, Ohio, so he asked if she knew Dave Dravecky. She looked at Ron in amazement and told him that just before she boarded the plane, Dave's wife, Jan, gave her some Gospel tracts to read. Ron looked at her and replied, "It was no accident that we were seated together."

Although she didn't make a decision for Christ at that time, Ron is certain that because of Jan Dravecky's thoughtfulness and the chance Ron had to share what the Lord had done for him, there will someday be meaningful results in the girl's life.

## Journalism Soul Mates

Ron had a similar experience, except the connection was working in the newspaper business. On his second prison weekend in Waupun, Wisconsin, an inmate named Larry Plymesser approached Ron and introduced himself as the editor of the *Waupun World*, which was the prison newspaper. Because of their mutual interest in journalism, they quickly became friends. Ron shared the Gospel with Larry before leaving the prison early to cover Hank Aaron's game in Cincinnati, where Aaron was close to breaking Babe Ruth's home run record.

Several weeks later, Ron received a letter from Larry, in which he told Ron that he had decided before the Weekend of Champions that he wasn't going to associate with any Christians; therefore, he would avoid our team and our programs. Of course, he discovered Ron was a Christian, and Ron didn't fit the stereotype that Larry had expected. He was almost embarrassed that his goal was to avoid us, yet he ended up spending a great deal of time with Ron–a Christian. Because of their involvement in journalism and Ron's gentle and loving presence, seeds were planted in Larry's life, and at the conclusion of the weekend, one of the counselors led Larry to the Lord. This experience early in Ron's involvement in the ministry reminded him that our job is to be faithful to simply share our faith with others and, although we may not see a life change, we can be confident that we played a small role in that person's conversion experience.

### An Officer's Family Meets Clyde–and the Lord

Sometimes the results of divine appointments occur outside the confines of prison walls, as was the case with Clyde Caylor, a veteran counselor and good friend of ours. We were all together on a weekend at a large prison in Walla Walla, Washington (the same weekend I met the Iowan), and Clyde was counseling on death row. Clyde had spent quite a while with one of the inmates, and when he finished his visit and left the cell to go to another wing, an officer stopped him. He told Clyde that he had been monitoring his conversation with the inmate and wondered if Clyde would be willing to come to his house that evening and tell his family what he had told the inmate. Of course, Clyde was very happy to accommodate the officer, and after dinner that evening he led the officer's entire family to faith in Christ.

### Prayer Paves the Way for a Visit on Death Row

In August 1990, I was speaking in Conway, Arkansas at a week-long camp for senior high youth from Methodist churches across Arkansas. I had asked the young people to write their prayer requests on slips of paper for me so I could pray for them. A young counselor named Jana handed me a prayer request. When I opened it later in my room, I read her request to pray for an inmate named Glenn on death row at the Louisiana State Prison in Angola, Louisiana. Not only did her request surprise me, but "coincidentally" I was headed to the Baton Rouge area (which included Angola) three weeks later for a prison weekend. I prayed for Glenn and looked forward to visiting with Jana the next morning.

I learned that Jana had been writing to Glenn for over a year and that he was a Christian. They had established a pen pal relationship due to a lack of visitors at his institution, and the two had formed a strong friendship. Jana was shocked when I told her I was going to Angola in three weeks, and she wondered if there was any way that I could visit her friend. I said I wasn't sure about the death row situation in Angola, but that we often had the opportunity to visit death rows and I would do my best to try to see him. I wrote down his name and cell number and eagerly anticipated the upcoming Baton Rouge trip.

Between the camp and my Baton Rouge visit, Jana wrote the inmate to inform him of our conversation and that I would try to see him during the Bill Glass weekend. After receiving the letter, Glenn wrote back and told Jana he appreciated her thoughtfulness but that it would be *impossible* for me to see him as there had never been any visitors allowed on death row. Jana continued praying for a miracle.

Upon arriving in Baton Rouge, I discovered that I would be doing several programs at Angola, but it didn't look like there would be any time to visit death row, and I wasn't absolutely sure it would be open to us for counseling. Then after my Friday afternoon program, Emory Wilson, the coordinator for the area of Angola including death row, asked Ron and me to join him on death row. The prison officials had given us one hour. Because of some last-minute scheduling changes, my next program was also at Angola later that evening, so the door had been miraculously opened. Ron and I jumped into a state vehicle and headed for a brief visit on death row.

After checking through security, I headed straight for Glenn's cell, and when I stood in front of his cell, he stared at me and said, "You can't be Rick Nielsen!" Glenn was astonished that I had been able to get into the death row wing to visit and, although our time was limited, I knew it meant a lot to him—I was his first visitor since his incarceration at

Angola eight years earlier. He had no idea where his family or any relatives lived, and his only contact from the outside was through his pen pal correspondence.

I had an opportunity to do a few card tricks and chat a little while about Jana and how surprised she would be that I had been able to visit. Then I prayed for Glenn and his situation. With tears in his eyes, he thanked me. He commented again about how amazed he was that I got in to see him and that my visit affirmed to him that we serve a God of miracles. I thanked him for reminding me once again of the importance of my ministry and how the Lord is constantly at work in our lives.

I received a letter several weeks later from Jana, who enclosed a copy of a letter Glenn had sent to her. It was exciting to know how much my visit had meant to each of them. Here is part of Jana's letter:

Dear Rick,

There are so many things that I would like to say to you, beginning with how glad I am that I got to know you at Senior High Assembly in Conway, Arkansas. I know that you have touched many lives in a very special way and I just want you to know that you have also touched my life.

I have said many, many prayers with the hope that you would be able to visit with my friend, Glenn, at Angola. I recently received a letter from him and I am so happy to hear that my prayers were answered! Rick, I cannot thank you enough for spending time with Glenn. You certainly came into his life when he was really needing a little extra lift. In his letter he speaks very highly of you. In fact, half of his letter is about your visit! I thought you might like to see just how much your visit meant to Glenn so I am sending you a copy of his letter. It really astonishes me how many "little" details about things he remembers, like your card trick. (That's something he won't forget for a very long time!)

I want to do anything I can to help him. Right now all I can do is pray that God will help him to stay strong in his faith. Thank you again for taking time to talk with him!

And here is an excerpt from Glenn's letter to Jana:

Now for the good news . . . I had just come back into my cell . . . and this free person was in front of the cell next to mine, and he said my name. By the time I looked up, he (Rick) was in front of my cell. Right away I knew who he was, before he introduced himself. That moment was wonderfully strange. I knew it was Rick Nielsen! It really was a beautiful surprise! . . . Rick even did a card trick for me. . . That amazed me. But it amazes me even more that Rick and the rest of his group were allowed to come on this tier! These people as a rule don't let any visitors on death row. For sure, the Lord moves in strange and wonderful ways.

### Angel on Death Row

After a prison weekend at San Quentin in California, one of the counselors in my group sent me a story he wrote of an amazing experience he had while there, and he encouraged me to share it with others. After reading it, I was convinced that it belonged in this particular chapter on divine appointments. Here's Ted's story:

Four-and-a-half years ago, I learned that a man I once worked with was convicted of first degree murder with special circumstances and sentenced to die in the gas chamber at San Quentin. When the sentence was handed down, I felt a strong desire to talk to or write Bill. It had been seven years since I last talked to Bill. I wondered how I could tell him that I understood and cared. I had no desire to ever visit a prison, let alone talk to inmates about Christ. However, while Bill was in the process of settling in to life at San Quentin, the Lord was already in the process of showing me how to reach out to him with the love of Jesus.

The process started when one Sunday morning in church the pastor preached a sermon from Matthew 25:31-46, including Jesus' familiar words, "...and when I was in prison you came to Me." When I heard that, I knew who the Lord was speaking to, who He was speaking about, and where I was to go. Yet I still struggled with the idea of going into prison. But as hard as I tried, I could not argue with Matthew

25, and one day it became clear to me in no uncertain terms that I needed to go to Bill's cell, re-establish our friendship, and share my faith with him. And over the years, I've learned a simple lesson–that when God asks me to do something, the sooner I do it the better off I'll be. There was only one problem–how in the world would I ever get into San Quentin to see Bill?

About that time, however, an active Weekend of Champions counselor from Texas started a new job in Yorba Linda, California and began attending my church. From day one, all Jeff ever talked about was how exciting these prison weekends were and how eager he was to take a number of our church members on one of the upcoming outreaches in California. I couldn't help but wonder if the Lord specifically sent Jeff to our church to help open the doors for me to re-introduce myself to Bill and get into San Quentin. But when Jeff asked me to go on the weekend, I told him I had other plans. As a matter of fact, I turned him down a number of times before finally making a commitment to attend my first weekend in 1986. My obedience was rewarded as the experience as a prison counselor changed my life and strengthened my faith. It also prompted me to finally write a letter to Bill and tell him how my life had drastically changed since I had last seen him eight years ago. I explained how I had returned to the God of my youth–abandoning a lifestyle that had almost cost me my wife, two children, and a baby boy that never would have been born had we divorced.

Bill and I corresponded briefly, but after several of my letters went unanswered, I quit writing him, and for two years wondered why Bill didn't respond. Was it because I shared my faith, or did he just misunderstand my motive for writing? "Did I move ahead of your plan, Lord? Was I not listening to you?" These questions haunted me for a long time.

In 1989, I had a renewed interest in getting back on a prison weekend, and told the Lord that I would try to go to all the prison weekends in California that year. What a sense of humor the Lord has! The 1989 Bill Glass schedule was the most aggressive California prison outreach in their history, with three trips planned, and, believe it or not, the second trip in September of 1989 was scheduled for–you guessed it –San Quentin!

As September grew closer, the excitement grew inside of me and I solicited prayer from everyone I knew. I even went so far as to ask Jeff if he would call the Glass office and request that I be placed on the team visiting death row. (I knew that only a few experienced counselors were usually allowed in these heavily secured areas.) On the flight to San Francisco International, I asked Jeff if he called the office with my request, and he replied, "No, I'm sorry, I forgot. But don't worry. Those little details are the Lord's responsibility."

Upon arriving at San Quentin, I entered the facility with Jack Murphy, one of our platform guests, and mentioned that I had a friend I wanted to see on death row. My heart sank when Murf informed me that no one would be allowed on death row that weekend. Murf went on to explain that one of the death row inmates had prepared a legal writ complaining of religious discrimination, and the warden and chaplain were faced with letting everyone in or closing the door to all. They chose the latter. Although discouraged but not defeated, I decided my next best bet would be to go to the prison chaplain with my request. Surely he would understand how important it was that I see Bill. I introduced myself, pleaded my case, and asked him if he could make arrangements for me to see my friend. Unfortunately, he replied in no uncertain terms, "No!" Okay. I learned my lesson. "I'll wait on you, Lord, to open the door."

That afternoon we split up into five groups to begin visiting the various buildings which overflowed with more than four thousand inmates. My group was led to an area between two of the largest buildings in the entire complex. The huge, five-story cell blocks looked just like scenes from old prison movies. The block was so large our coordinator split us up into two groups, assigning part of us to the north block and part of us to the east block. I was assigned to the latter. As we entered the east block, we were told it was also separated into two sides and that we were not allowed on the side facing San Francisco Bay as that was where the death row inmates were incarcerated. (Quietly I prayed, "Thank you, Lord, this is getting interesting again.")

Upon entering the east block, I was astonished at the large number of security officers on duty in this particular area. I could tell this was a very highly secured area, and also a dangerous place to work. A memorial sign at the entrance confirmed my suspicions as it listed names of correctional officers who had been murdered in the line of duty at San Quentin. There were almost three in each decade for the past thirty years. Also, I couldn't help but notice the officers armed with automatic rifles on the catwalks across from the tiers of cells. With all of this security, plus remembering what Murphy said, and striking out with the chaplain, I began to wonder how in the world the Lord would allow me to see Bill.

Not to be denied, however, I decided to approach one of the officers standing by the entrance gate to death row, and I asked him if it would be possible for me to visit a former fellow employee on the row. The officer replied, "I'm sorry, no one is allowed on this side."

"Can I give you a note to give to him?" I asked.

"Yes. He's on this level. I'll deliver it for you."

I quickly wrote on the back of a *Four Spiritual Laws* book, "Bill, I'm here trying to get a chance to see you this weekend. Ted." I wondered if the note I wrote on a Christian tract would even make it to Bill considering the religious discrimination charges which had closed death row to visitors. However, as the officer left to deliver my message, I was encouraged thinking of the stories of Brother Andrew and how God blinded the eyes of the Iron Curtain border guards as they looked into a trunk full of Bibles. I spent the rest of the afternoon counseling on the opposite side of death row.

The following morning as we entered the prison, we discovered the east block was closed. We were all assigned to the north block, and I was afraid we might never get back to the east block where I knew God wanted me to be. However, after lunch, east block was opened to us again, and as we began to walk toward the unit, Jeff said, "I wonder how God is going to open the door for you to see Bill." Within minutes of that statement, we arrived at the security entrance to the two areas of east block and looked at each other in astonishment because although there were four or five officers at the security door leading to death row, the door was left wide open! Shock quickly gave way to a rush of excitement and laughter, only to be deflated as we learned that the door was only open because a cell by cell shakedown was under way. In addition, they were in the process of relocating a number of inmates to some newly remodeled cells. We were really tempted to walk right through that door into death row, but we knew we'd better work the areas we were assigned and left to report to the opposite block.

We had only taken a few steps when Jeff grabbed me by the arm and said, "That open door is too clear of a sign. You have to go back and beg them to let you in to see Bill." I agreed with Jeff and turned around and headed back for the still open door, but when I arrived something was strangely different. Instead of the four to five officers who were there only seconds ago, only one remained at the open door. I quickly approached the officer and politely asked if it would be possible for me to visit my friend who I used to work with. The officer asked, "What's his name?" And when I told him, he said, "Let me check my file." A minute later, the officer came back and said, "He's on the fifth level, second cell in. You can go on in, but only to talk to your friend. Don't bother any of the other inmates."

With that, I thanked him and moved as quickly as I could to level five. As I raced up the stairs, so many feelings were running through me. I thought of Peter and Paul and how the Lord opened prison doors and loosened chains. I felt like jumping and screaming with joy, but subdued myself as I noticed the officers on the catwalks with the automatic rifles.

Finally I reached level five, only to find another security guard standing at the entrance to the catwalk that led to the cells. Out of breath, I explained to him that the officer on level one gave me permission to see my friend, Bill, who I used to work with, and he let me pass. (I should add that I was carrying a heavy coat and a large brown envelope, yet was virtually unchallenged all the way up five levels of cells on death row to Bill's front door.)

When I got to Bill's cell, he was sitting on the end of his bunk and was shocked to see me standing there. He was also a bit embarrassed as he had been in lock down for four days without a shower or a shave. Bill exclaimed, "How did you get in here? No one has been up here for two months!"

I replied, "Jesus opened the door down below and let me in. God told me four-and-a-half years ago that I would be standing in front of your cell, and here I am."

About this time, another officer supervising the movement of inmates on the blocks overheard me and wondered who approved my being on death row. Furthermore, I'm certain he was sure there was no officer by the name of Jesus on duty down below. He called me over and told me I would have to get his sergeant's permission to stay and visit Bill. I told him I already had *his* permission, and *he* let me in here. The officer, with a puzzled look on his face, asked, "*HE* did?"

"Yes," I replied. "He did."

"Well, that's funny because my sergeant is a woman, and *she*'s responsible for the security entrance to death row. You need to go back and get *her* permission."

By this time I was absolutely convinced that my meeting with Bill was divinely ordained and that a divine appointment would certainly have to last longer than one minute. Under my breath, I quietly asked the Lord to forgive me for telling a little, white lie and said to the officer, "The female officer you're referring to *was* down there, but the male officer I talked to gave me permission to enter the block." Still not satisfied, the officer insisted I return to the security entrance to be cleared by his sergeant.

"Oh Lord," I prayed, "I'm in trouble again. How about another hand?" All of a sudden, as I'm almost resigned to going back down to the security entrance, the officer leaned over the railing, and from five stories below a male voice simply says, "The civilian's been cleared. He's okay."

The officer then turned to me, shrugged his shoulders, and said, "I'm sorry. I guess you're okay." And for the next hour Bill and I had a great visit. We were both candid in our discussions about his crime, his punishment, the past, and our respective faiths. Bill told me that he quit writing because he didn't know how to respond to my questions and experiences relating to my faith in Christ. He told me that his faith was private and that it was the only thing he had left that the State didn't own, and he wanted to keep it private.

We agreed to start corresponding again, and I told Bill that Jesus Christ was such an important part of my life that I would continue to write about my faith in my letters, but that he shouldn't feel threatened or obligated to have to reply to that part of my letters. Leaving the cell, I was optimistic that our meeting had finally opened the doors for me to possibly help lead Bill to the Lord someday.

As I hurried down the stairs, I couldn't wait to thank the officer who let me in to see Bill and explain to him the important role he had played in allowing me to fulfill the vision I had four-and-a-half years ago. However, as I reached level one, I saw the female sergeant and three other officers, but the special officer that let me on death row was nowhere in sight. As a matter of fact, I didn't see him anywhere the remainder of the weekend. An officer unlocked the now secured gate, and without exchanging a single word I was let out.

I couldn't help but believe that the fact that I was able to enter a cell block that was totally off limits to civilians would have a profound impact on Bill. Only God could have conquered the insurmountable obstacles that stood in the way of my visiting him. Only time will tell when Bill gives his heart to Christ. In the meantime, I will continue to pray for my friend.

Reminiscing, it's exciting to look back on that San Quentin weekend where for one brief period a tightly locked door was suddenly opened. And I'll always wonder. Was it opened by a correctional officer . . . or by an angel?

## Conclusion

These are only a few of the many incredible divine appointment experiences that have occurred throughout the history of the Weekends of Champions. And, of course, Ron and I aren't even aware of many others that happened. While writing the stories for this particular chapter, I often caught myself grinning. Only God could conduct the symphony of these unusual encounters in prisons all over America. I will always be amazed at how He works through the lives of His faithful followers to bring people into a relationship with Him, often in ways that are so unexplainable that the only explanation is His deep desire for us to know Him.

# CHAPTER 10

# PERSONAL
# ENCOUNTERS

*R*on and I have had so many memorable experiences on prison weekends that it would be impossible to write about all of them, so we have chosen a few of the highlights, including some we have been through together.

### Magic and Manson

Mike Baldassin and I shared an incredible experience in prison when we were working at a facility called Corcoran in Corcoran, California. You might remember from the chapter about counselors, my friend "Baldy" was the former University of Washington football stand-out who later went on to play pro ball with the San Francisco 49-ers, and eventually became a police officer in Oakland, California. Bill Pruitt (one of the team coordinators) and I were assigned to work a unique area of the prison called the SHU (Security Housing Unit). This is a heavy duty lockdown for level four inmates and is the most tightly secured prison area I have ever visited. Bill and I each selected four counselors to work with, and the ten of us were the first civilians ever to enter this highly secured wing of the prison. These cells housed 1,500 of California's most difficult and hostile inmates.

The security captain of the SHU block was a little reluctant about our visit, sensing that none of the men would even want to talk to us. However, other prison officials who were familiar with our program encouraged him to allow us to work the blocks and even suggested that if things didn't work out on Friday, he could always cancel our visit on Saturday. Then we could join the rest of the counselors in the main yard the remainder of the weekend. That suggestion seemed to satisfy the captain, and on Friday afternoon shortly after lunch, Bill and I, along with the eight counselors we had selected, showed up for duty at the SHU unit. Mike Baldassin was one of the members of my team. His years of service as an Oakland police officer, combined with his strong faith and ability to communicate it with others, made him an ideal candidate for dealing with difficult individuals like these men.

Upon checking into the SHU unit, I knew immediately that the next couple of days would be very different from most of the prison weekends with which I'd been involved. First of all, there would be no programs, only counseling. Since the programs help break the ice and allow the inmates to have a good time, this would make our approaching them more of a challenge. Also, since there were only ten of us and 1,500 of them, we agreed that we ought to set a maximum amount of time spent in each pod and then move on to a new area of cells. This meant getting right down to business as far as addressing spiritual issues. This would prove to be difficult for me as I'm a firm believer that building a relationship first always creates a better opportunity to share. Nonetheless, we had to use our time wisely, and we knew this might be the only time these men might ever hear the Gospel message. Fortunately, I was allowed to bring in some of my magic, which was a real asset in getting the inmates' attention and opening the door for our visits.

The security captain briefed us on the specific conditions of the unit and gave us some security restrictions to follow. He assigned several officers to escort us the entire weekend, following our every move and never letting us out of their sight. He then proceeded to distribute twelve-pound flak jackets to all of us, which we were required to wear while in the cell blocks. The officers had no problem with our plan to try to spend twenty minutes on each tier, and then move on to another block of cells. One interesting restriction they enforced was that we were ordered to pull out all of the staples from the *Four Spiritual Laws* booklets that we used to present the plan of salvation. Each little book only has one staple, but we couldn't give an inmate a book with a staple in it. That gives you a little idea of how tight security was. I recall Bill Pruitt and I spent an hour or two the evening before our visit pulling staples from the books. This unit also was full of guns, which is a little bit unusual. Normally the guns are kept in the tower away from the inmate population or checked out to officers from a weapons closet at times when they are necessary.

In front of each cell there was a white line approximately eighteen inches from the cell door. We were instructed to stay behind that line while sharing with the inmates. A few of the cells had a television or radio, but there were no electrical outlets. The electrical cord ran through a small hole in the wall of the cell, and officers plugged it into the electrical outlet from the outside. These inmates remained in their cells constantly, except for a couple of showers and three blocks of yard time, three hours long every week. The yard looked basically like a racquetball court, and about all they could do was get some fresh air and sunshine.

After going through all of the debriefing, I began to wonder if maybe that security captain was right in that these guys may not give us the time of day. I would soon find out, as our escort officers introduced themselves and then took Bill and me and our teams through the many security check points to begin counseling in our first assigned areas. It was unbelievable how many locked doors we went through before finally entering the first cell block. I was already sweating from the flak jacket plus the lack of air conditioning in the cell blocks, and upon entering the first pod of cells, I could see this was not going to be a picnic.

The cell doors themselves were the regular cylindrical steel bars, but they were covered by a very tightly meshed screen wire, making them difficult to see through. Consequently, the officers required that the inmates turn on the light in the cell if they wanted to visit with us. This made it a lot easier to see them. Oddly enough, the light switch was even unusual. It looked like a nickel stuck on the wall, and when it was touched, the light went on and off. No chance here of getting to any wiring. The catwalks were concrete, which meant we would be on our feet all day on the hard surface as we moved from cell to cell. There was no doubt this was going to be difficult. Each cell had just a large enough opening by the lock on the door to slip a *Four Spiritual Laws* booklet through a tiny crack. I wondered what type of magic to use since there was no way an inmate could assist me in picking a card or using his hands to help me with a trick or two. If anybody was to pick a card, it was going to have to be an officer who was escorting us.

As we climbed the small set of steps to begin working our first set of cells, I reminded my team that we were only going to spend about twenty minutes in this area and then move to a new set of cells.

The minute we entered the cellhouse and were visible to the inmates, the place came alive. And thus began one of the most challenging and interesting prison weekends I've ever been on. The escort officers instructed the inmates to turn on their lights if they wanted to visit with us. Their curiosity was instantly aroused as they stared at these unfamiliar civilians intruding in their houses. As we spread out and approached the cells of inmates whose lights were on, their first question was obviously, "Who are you, and what are you doing in here?" They knew something unusual was happening and demanded some quick answers.

We worked hard all Friday afternoon, and the response was very favorable. Actually, the fact that these men were so tightly confined and had such a shortage of visits made for ideal conditions to share our faith, and the response was incredible, considering we were working such short shifts at each group of cells. The escort officers were astonished with the results, and by Friday evening when we finished for the day, they told the security captain it would be a terrible mistake not to invite us back for all day Saturday. The officers told him they saw extremely hostile men wiping back tears and hanging on every word we spoke, and that the response toward our visits was fantastic. They gathered up our flak jackets, thanked us for our efforts, and told us to report for duty the next morning around nine o'clock. We closed in prayer before we left and found our vehicles to attend the Friday night dinner. Mike and I finally had a chance to visit on the way back to Visalia, and he told me that he recognized a number of inmates in the SHU Unit that he had arrested while serving on the Oakland police force.

Saturday morning shortly before nine o'clock, we donned our flak jackets, loaded our pockets with materials, and headed into the next building of cells, picking up where we had finished Friday evening. The response continued to be favorable, and we were also building great relationships with our escort officers. As a matter of fact, each time we entered a new building to work, the officers asked our escorts if we would be all right, and they'd respond, "Are you kidding? These guys are pros. You won't believe how the inmates will respond to their visit." It was almost comical to go from being told we would waste our time to hearing officers bragging about us and our efforts.

After a successful Saturday morning, we took a break for a brown bag lunch. Just taking off the flak jacket for a little while felt good, as did being able to sit down and relax. As we finished lunch, something unusual occurred. Bill's team had already left to begin working in a new pod, and most of my team had assembled outside the break room, preparing themselves for the long afternoon. I was waiting in line to use the restroom when I saw my escort officer suddenly reach into my flak jacket pocket, grab a *Four Spiritual Laws* booklet, and quickly stuff it into his pocket. He did this, not realizing I was watching, and I'm sure he didn't want me to see him. I grinned as I realized that listening to our visits made this officer eager to see just exactly what was in the little gold book and perhaps consider taking a closer look at the spiritual conditions of his own life.

After using the restroom, I put on my flak jacket and told the officer we were ready to get back to work, but he grabbed my arm and said, "Rick, could I ask you a favor?"

I said, "Sure, what can I do for you, Officer?"

He replied, "You know that trick you've been doing with the four aces?"

"Yes, it's called McDonald's Aces, and it's a great one."

"Rick, I wonder if you'd do that for Charles Manson and a couple of my officer buddies in his cell block. I think Manson might like the magic. At the rate we're moving, we'll never get to his housing unit, but if we skip the next building, we could go visit him. There are also a number of tougher inmates in that block, if you and your team are up for it."

"Officer, you're in charge," I answered. "We'll go wherever you lead us, and I'll be glad to share the trick with Mr. Manson and your friends." The officer was happy with my willingness to work with him and called the other cell block to let them know we were coming.

I informed my team of the officer's request, and we followed him down the sidewalk into the building he'd asked us to work. This pod was no different than the rest, other than we would be visiting a new group of inmates, including Charles Manson. The escort officer introduced me to his officer friends, and they told me they were really looking forward to seeing the trick with the aces. They warned me to expect anything when we got to this tier of cells, but that we shouldn't worry; we'd be very safe. Of course, my escort officer immediately bragged about us, again reminding them that we would be fine and they shouldn't worry about us. It was amazing how he had gradually become our greatest advocate.

We climbed the stairs at the end of the pod to work level two, and

Manson's cell was the second one in from the end. As we settled in on the catwalk, I positioned myself between his cell and the cell at the end. The two inmates in that cell immediately jumped off their beds and responded like the others, questioning the officers about who we were and why we were there. The officer said, "I brought this man up to show you a great card trick. He works with the Bill Glass Prison Ministry."

They were excited, and so was I. I laid my close-up mat down on the concrete and started the trick, using one of the duty officers as my assistant. At this point, the light was still off in Manson's cell, but about a minute into the trick, he came to the front of the cell to see what was happening. The officers informed Manson that if he wanted to visit he would have to turn his light on, which he did.

I introduced myself to him and said, "Mr. Manson, I'm a magician and I'm showing a pretty good card trick to the officers and your cell mates. You're welcome to watch, too."

"I'm a magician, too," he replied. I invented every card trick ever invented."

I responded, "Well, watch me closely, then, to make sure I do the trick correctly." I knew he was aware that we were with a prison ministry, and I suspect this is why he really never did show any interest in the card trick or in us, stopping intermittently to observe, but then retreating quietly to the back of his cell.

I finished the card trick and the inmates in the cell next to the wall gave each other high fives, while the officers laughed and showed their appreciation. My escort officer seemed proud that he could share something special with his officer buddies, and that I had blown their minds with the trick.

As we were all enjoying the moment, most of us had forgotten about Manson. However, he hadn't forgotten about us, and all of a sudden he got on his soap box and began to let us know how he felt about the whole deal. In a nutshell, he blasted our faith and reminded us of some of our fallen leaders like Jimmy Swaggart and Jim and Tammy Faye Baker. At one point he even tossed me into the ring as a loser for having playing cards. This tirade went on and on and, although it was fascinating to watch, I knew we were losing valuable time that we could be using to share our faith with inmates who would be more receptive.

Consequently, I interrupted him and simply said, "Time out, Charlie. We didn't come in here to bother you. We simply came in to share our faith in Jesus Christ and try to offer some hope through faith in Him. We've shared this message with thousands of inmates across America and have observed the miraculous changes in people's lives when they have gotten serious about making a commitment to the Lord. If you'd like to discuss the Christian faith, I'll be glad to stay here and talk to you and send the rest of the team on. I'm going to visit the rest of the cells on this tier and then come back by your cell before we leave this area and move to another cell block. If you'd like me to stay and visit, just let me know. It's been a pleasure meeting you."

I walked away, and Mike Baldassin and I just looked at each other for several minutes, reflecting on this bizarre encounter, and then Mike asked me if I was okay. I told him I was and returned the question to him. He said he was fine, but this visit would have to rate near the top of the many unusual experiences he'd had serving in prison ministry or even on the police force in Oakland. We were both glad that we went through this together because odds are people would think we were crazy, and at least one could verify the other's story.

Most of the men on the rest of this tier were sleeping, so we moved back to the end of the cells and to the stairs to leave. As we passed Manson's cell, he showed no interest in visiting any further, so we left.

The duty officers apologized for Manson's behavior and the scene he made. We told them not to worry; it certainly wasn't their fault. We thanked them at least for the opportunity to share and showed our admiration for the tough job they had working in the SHU facility. One of the officers told me that he was part of a group of staff who had to monitor Manson's mail. He said Manson receives a huge amount of mail, and it must be scrutinized very carefully. The officer also said that someone from the media shows up at least once a week to request an interview with Manson, especially around his parole hearing dates. Because he is a high profile inmate, the officers have to be extra careful with him as he does present additional security concerns for them. However, a majority of the men in the SHU unit require special security and constant monitoring.

The rest of the afternoon went well, and by Saturday night, ten weary counselors turned in their flak jackets for the last time and gathered in the break room to check out of the prison. We thanked our escort officers for their good help and for their mother hen approach toward our safety. Bill Pruitt and I collected the decision cards from the counselors. The cards served as a reminder that our labors were not in vain as a large number of decisions were recorded, despite only ten of us working the blocks for merely a day and a half.

To conclude our time in the SHU unit, we formed a circle, joined hands, and prayed. We were all exhausted, but this was the kind of tired that felt good, knowing we had been faithful and obedient to share the Good News in an area far from our comfort zone, and with many men who desperately needed heart transplants.

When we got to the parking lot, I gave Mike a big hug and thanked him for helping. This was hard work and tough duty. He told me it was a privilege to work with me in the SHU, and hoped that we could work together again soon. And fortunately, we *have* been able to serve at several prison weekends together since that time, and we continue to stay in touch. After experiencing severe back problems a few years later, Mike was released from the police force and now teaches and coaches in a high school in Seattle, Washington.

### The Little Art Room in the Corner of the Gym

Ron and I met Joe Mason in December 1987 while I was a coordinator at our Bill Glass Weekend of Champions in Lake Jackson, Texas. Joe was serving a life sentence and had already been incarcerated twenty-eight years.

As I prepared to introduce our first program on Friday afternoon in the gymnasium of the Ramsey I Unit, my attention was diverted to a little room in the corner of the gym. From the doorway peered an inmate, curiously watching our team as we began to stir up interest for our program with Jack "Murf the Surf" Murphy and Tanya Crevier, the World's Finest Basketball Handler. Little did I know that most of my weekend would not be spent in the gym or in the cell blocks, but in that little room in the corner of the gym. You see, behind that inmate were a number of beautiful paintings that intrigued me.

After a fantastic program with Jack and Tanya and then sending our counselors throughout the institution, I wandered over to meet the man guarding the door and find out about the paintings. Thus began my friendship with Joe Mason, #235188.

After exchanging pleasantries, Joe sensed my curiosity about the artwork and invited me into his paint shop. Wow! Everywhere I looked, there were exceptional oil paintings of all types and sizes! I learned that Joe had painted all of them. He was self-taught, never having had the opportunity for lessons. In my eyes, this made each picture even more special.

He began to tell me about his life, the problems he had encountered that landed him in prison, and how painting had helped him begin putting the pieces of his life back together. As Joe later said, "At first, I went through a lot of supplies without any tangible results, yet the material and my efforts were not wasted. I found talent amidst the messy paint tubes and gaudy canvases. I found something I could share with others. You might say I found myself."

After developing a tremendous ability with a paint brush over the course of nine years, Joe's life began to fall apart again. He escaped from prison and spent a year looking back over his shoulder—unhappy, unfulfilled, and without a single moment's peace of mind. Joe remembered, "I didn't paint—I was never in one place long enough—and I felt guilty. I was actually glad to be caught and returned to prison even though I knew it was possible that I would never leave again."

Finally back at the canvas, Joe found satisfaction again. He enjoyed great artistic success, winning many awards for his work. Each painting was better than the one before, and through his art, Joe found fulfillment and recognition.

This man really captured my attention, and before I knew it, it was time for our evening program to close our visit on Friday. Just before leaving his paint shop, I asked Joe about the spiritual dimension of his life. He simply said there really wasn't much going on. He wasn't sure God could forgive him for what he'd done, let alone tolerate someone who professed to be a Christian when his lifestyle didn't back up the profession. I thanked him for his honesty and said I would look forward to seeing him again the next morning.

Ron joined me Saturday and met Joe. We spent a good portion of the afternoon taking pictures and enjoying Joe's company and artwork. In addition, many other counselors met Joe, and he sold a number of paintings that day.

As we concluded our Saturday evening dinner back at the hotel, Ron and I prayed for Joe. He was hesitant to make a decision for Christ until he was absolutely sure this was the direction he wanted his life to go.

Prior to leaving the institution on Sunday morning, Ron and I thanked Joe for such an enjoyable weekend and asked him again if he wanted to give his life over to the Lord. His answer was the same: "I'm not ready." We appreciated his honesty and promised to keep in touch.

For the next eight months, Ron and I sent notes of encouragement to Joe with reminders that we were praying for him. Joe always responded, relaying his honest feelings about this very important decision in his life. In addition, Ron and I began to order paintings from Joe to try to give him some business and exposure. It was through these purchases that we became acquainted with Art and Sue Gardner of Chattanooga, Tennessee.

Sue was Joe's only surviving sister, and she and her husband, Art, helped Joe by displaying his paintings at art shows and by handling his finances. In corresponding with the Gardners in order to purchase Joe's paintings, Ron and I discovered that they, too, were concerned about Joe's relationship with Christ. Art and Sue were Christians and were thankful that Ron and I had reminded Joe of his need for the Lord, and they continued their prayers for him.

With each letter from Joe, I could sense the Holy Spirit moving in his life. Then one day, almost eight months after Ron and I met him, I opened one of Joe's letters to read that he had invited Christ into his life. What a great day! James 5:16 is true: "The effective, fervent prayer of a righteous man avails much." We were so grateful for the decision Joe had made, especially after he had given it so much thought.

Ron and I have had several opportunities to visit Joe while on other prison weekends in his area. On our last visit, he mentioned to us that he feels his painting has improved since he accepted the Lord. Joe's attitude is an inspiration. He is simply trying to make the best of each day while doing his time, utilizing his artistic talents and growing in his newfound faith.

When Art and Sue eventually received word of Joe's salvation, they were thrilled with the news. In April 1990, they drove from Chattanooga to meet Ron and me. It was nice to finally put faces to so many letters and to spend time getting to know this faithful couple. They joined us for a prison banquet and became so excited about the Bill Glass Weekends of Champions that they expressed a desire to meet us the following month in Birmingham, Alabama. Art shared with us that he and Sue had been praying every day for thirty years for Joe to come to know the Lord. They always believed this miracle would someday occur in his life, even though the odds of a sixty-year-old man accepting Christ were slim, especially while he was incarcerated. They never gave up praying and never lost hope. What a tremendous reminder to Ron and me of the power of faithful, persistent prayer and that the Lord is never in a hurry–He's always on time.

After Joe's conversion, we participated in another Weekend of Champions that included the Ramsey I Unit, where Joe was still incarcerated. At that time we met another inmate, Hubert Tyson, who had become friends with Joe and was also an artist. When we met Hubert, he had already done sixteen years of a life sentence, so in addition to sharing their interest and talents in painting, they also had many years in prison in common. Joe and Hubert made a great team, combining their skills to work on paintings, often creating several at a time. Their art was displayed in the lobby of the prison, and they continued to sell many pictures to Ramsey I visitors. Art and Sue were also showing Joe and Hubert's work at art shows around the country.

On March 26, 1991, Joe Mason was released from prison after serving thirty years. Using some of the funds he'd saved while serving his sentence, he set up a shop to continue painting and to teach art lessons. Ron and I stayed in touch with Joe for several months as he began his adjustment back into society. Eventually, however, Joe quit returning our letters and we lost track of him. Eager to determine his whereabouts, Ron called the warden at Ramsey I to see if he knew where Joe was. Unfortunately, the warden delivered some bad news. Having been locked up for so many years, Joe had a difficult time adjusting to society and, although he never got into serious trouble, he left town after violating his parole by failing to check in with his parole officer. Ron then called Art and Sue to see if they had heard from Joe, but they hadn't either. Sue was worried that Joe might have left the country or could even be dead. At this point, all any of us could do for Joe was pray. And pray we did–for almost a year, still receiving no news as to Joe's whereabouts. It wasn't until Ron attended another Weekend of Champions in the Lake Jackson, Texas area that we learned exactly what had happened to Joe.

As Ron flew to Houston for the Lake Jackson weekend, he was

reminded of the first time we met Joe at his paint shop at Ramsey I Unit. This prompted Ron to again pray for Joe, as we still had no idea where he was or what had happened to him since Joe failed to report to his parole officer. On Friday morning Ron received his instructions to take pictures that afternoon at the Retrieve Unit in Angleton, Texas. As he drove into Angleton, Ron remembered that this little town was where Joe worked after he was released from prison. He prayed again that he might see Joe, possibly walking along a street somewhere in town, but there was no sign of Joe anywhere.

Upon arriving at the prison, Ron began shooting pictures of the counselors and visiting with a few of the inmates. As he peeked into one cell, Ron was intrigued by an elderly inmate working on an oil painting. Ron introduced himself and said, "Watching you paint reminds me of an inmate I met at Ramsey I Unit a number of years ago. He was an incredible artist."

"What's his name?" the inmate asked.

When Ron answered, "Joe Mason," the gentleman smiled and said, "Mason is here in D Wing." Ron couldn't believe it, and politely excused himself to head over to D Wing to look for Joe. Ron was so excited about the possibility of seeing Joe again that he did something he knew he should never do in a prison–RUN! Upon reaching D Wing (fortunately without being shot!), Ron asked the first inmate he saw if he knew where Joe Mason was. The inmate replied, "Sure. He's painting in the craft shop. He's in there every day." Ron raced to the craft shop and, sure enough, there was Joe–busy with his paint brush. Giving Joe a big hug, Ron exclaimed, "I can't believe I found you! I'm so glad you're alive! What happened? How did you end up back here?"

They had a great reunion. Joe explained how his struggle with adjusting to society and to working again resulted in his breaking parole and running away from his problems. Eventually, the law caught up with Joe in Arizona and sent him back to Texas to serve some additional time for the parole violation.

Later that evening, Ron called Art and Sue to let them know where Joe was and what had happened to him. Apparently Joe had been too embarrassed to call them. Ron also called me to update Joe's situation. Ron and I have continued corresponding with Joe, as well as with Art and Sue Gardner. All of us pray that when Joe finishes serving this short sentence he'll be able to make a more successful transition back into society, doing what he loves most–painting.

## Creating Time While Doing Time

Ron and I met another artistic inmate named Dallas DeLay, who is serving time at the state prison in Jefferson City, Missouri. Dallas had always dreamed of building a grandfather clock, but when he mentioned it to some of his inmate friends, they laughed at him and thought he was crazy to even think about it. However, taking a job repairing watches and jewelry for inmates, as well as many of the officers, Dallas slowly gained the confidence and trust of the warden. He also educated himself about the inner workings of a grandfather clock. Eventually he was given permission to build a clock while officers monitored his work, especially around the saws and other tools he needed to carve the wood. It became apparent to the officers that Dallas had no intention of using the equipment for anything other than building grandfather clocks and repairing watches.

When Ron and I met Dallas, he had his own little workshop where he could be by himself and report for work every day. By that time he had built sixty-nine clocks and had sold them all, mainly to officers and their friends. What little profit he made on each clock was used to purchase materials for the next project. His labors helped him do his time without getting into trouble and provided some self-satisfaction and pride in his accomplishments. Dallas was especially happy that I introduced him to Ron as he wanted some good pictures of himself with his clocks, and Ron was able to provide those for him.

## "One Day at a Time"

Ron Smart has been in prison for thirty-six years and is presently incarcerated at Kirkland Correctional in Columbia, South Carolina. Ron Kuntz and I both claim him as a close friend and brother in Christ. He is one of the most committed Christian inmates we've met in all our years of service with Bill Glass. He loves to give his testimony, witness to others, and teach Bible studies, all within the confines of prison walls. Ron Smart ministers to many folks outside of prison through letters, tapes, and interviews he has done for magazines and newspapers. His favorite saying, "I'll serve the Lord *one day at a time*," has provided his motivation through years of incarceration. We have corresponded faithfully at least once a month for quite some time. He has helped me in my ministry by writing letters of encouragement to first-time counselors I've invited on weekends. He has also dictated messages on cassette tapes for me to share with troubled and struggling teens I meet through my work in schools. He is especially good at challenging young people to stay away from alcohol and other drugs, as they greatly contributed to his problems and eventual prison sentences.

Steve Vinson, a staff writer for the *Christian News and Herald*, wrote an excellent article on Ron Smart in the June 1995 issue. I'd like to share some excerpts from the article that detail Ron's background and eventual conversion to Christ.

Ron's stay in South Carolina began in 1968 with a fifteen-year safe-cracking conviction; add three more years for escape. The Florida native was out of prison for only eight days before murdering two of his former inmates in a much publicized case in 1978. He received two death penalties. Upon hearing the judge's sentence, Ron stated, "Whoopee! We all gotta go sometime." When asked by a news reporter if he thought the electric chair was cruel and unusual punishment, Ron said, "What is cruel about it is having to wait."

Back then Ron was still tough, mean, and defiant on the outside. On the inside, however, there was a war being waged for his soul. On the way to his death row cell he prayed on the inside, "Almighty God, whether I live or whether I die, the rest of my life is yours. In Jesus' name I pray, Amen." From that moment on, Ron Smart was a free man.

Thus began six years on death row. While there he met and witnessed to some of South Carolina's most notorious criminals, like Pee Wee Gaskin and many more. It was there that he started to read, study, and memorize the Bible. He claimed Philippians 4:6-7 as his peace while he awaited his execution date: "Do not be anxious about anything, but in everything, by prayer and petition, with thanksgiving present your request to God. And the peace of God which transcends all understanding will guard your hearts and your minds in Christ Jesus." (NIV)

The automatic appeal process of the court system for death penalty cases brought Ron Smart back before a judge in

1984. "For three days I heard in great detail every crime I had committed. Hour after hour, everything bad I had ever done was told to the judge." But Ron held onto peace with his verses. That was all he had; that was all he needed.

Just prior to his final sentencing, a chaplain and another friend, without corroboration, gave him the same two verses he had claimed, but added verses 8 and 9. These two people had no idea Ron was hanging on to verses 6 and 7.

Ron was relieved to read Philippians 4:8-9. "Finally, brothers, whatever is true, whatever is noble, whatever is right, whatever is pure, whatever is lovely, whatever is admirable–if anything is excellent or praiseworthy–think about such things. Whatever you have learned or received or heard from me, or seen in me–put into practice. And the God of peace will be with you." (NIV)

Ron knew then that God had told him he would live, and *how* he was to live the remainder of his life. The next day, to many people's surprise, the judge changed Ron's two death penalties to two life sentences. Thus began a ministry behind bars that has reached hundreds for Christ.

"It is easy to say, 'lock 'em up and throw away the key,' but an almighty God in his wisdom and mercy has placed salt and light in prisons, too." Ron reminds us that God can even use murderers to do his will: King David, Moses, and the Apostle Paul, just to name a few. "A lot of people cannot accept the fact that I am a changed man, not by my hand but by Jesus."

There is much talk today in the media about prison reform and getting tough on crime. Ron states that many folks in society seem to think that prisoners have it too easy; therefore, they want prisoners to suffer harsher punishment. Speaking of what prisoners have (which isn't that much), it wouldn't matter if the state put in TV's, swimming pools, or even a Hardee's. It doesn't matter what "things" you give anyone in prison; they are still lacking the main ingredient in life–freedom! Of course, the only true freedom and peace is through a personal relationship with the Lord Jesus Christ. One does not have to be an inmate to realize that concept.

Ron says, "There is no freedom outside or inside prison without Jesus Christ."

Ron's greatest joy is witnessing for Christ and encouraging others in Christ. "You get closer to the Lord by serving Him. That is true happiness, no matter where you are."

When asked what he would like to see from other Christians, he reminds us of what Jesus said in Matthew 25 when He separates the sheep from the goats. "I was sick and in prison and you did not visit me." Prisoners must have been important to Jesus for him to mention them in this manner.

Ron said that the most difficult part of his ministry is keeping a positive attitude in a negative environment. He ministers to many lost and lonely people in prison and even some on the outside. Coping with the same trials as those around you can be very hard, especially when you must assume the role of the encourager. Perhaps that is why the condemnation Jesus gave to the "goats" in Matthew 25:43 was that the prisoners were not visited. Visitation is the greatest weapon against loneliness. How often we forget that!

Ministries like Ron's require much prayer. Ron faithfully calls a local Christian radio station every morning prior to his Bible study and solicits prayer. He has seen the results of faithful prayer in the lives of many around him, himself included. Ron said, "My mother prayed for me forty years of her life before I woke up. God honors faithful prayer."

In addition to his ministry at Kirkland, Ron has taken a stand on many issues, writing letters to editors, etc. I like what he wrote in a letter sent to a newspaper in response to an article that had been published expressing the need to be tougher on inmates in the South Carolina system:

In order for prisons to be truly effective, society must temper justice with mercy. You can send men and women to prison with longer sentences, but you must give them some kind of hope/incentive while they are in prison. If all society is interested in is using prison as an instrument of punishment, then all society will end up doing is creating an even more dangerous class of people. Whatever happened to love, even if it has to be "tough love"? I've spent most of my life in prison, and the only thing that changed me was love. (Please read I Corinthians 13.) It didn't happen overnight, but the love of my Lord and Savior, Jesus Christ, finally brought me to my senses. I was one of those people that society considered beyond redemption, but I thank God that He didn't view me with the same lack of compassion. What **hope** would any of us have it if wasn't for **God's Amazing Grace?**

If you truly desire to do something about the crime problem, implement programs that will reach the children in their formative years. Instilling spiritual and moral values through proper parenting is our only hope of curtailing the crime problem in society. It will be a long process, but it can be done **one day at a time**!

May God bless all of you.

Ron Smart hasn't let prison walls prohibit him from having an effective ministry and being a servant for Jesus Christ. He prays for Ron Kuntz and me and for all of our Bill Glass weekends. I admire Ron Smart and am thankful to know him as a friend and teammate in the Lord. Whenever I'm in South Carolina, I make it a point to go early or stay a day late to squeeze in a visit with Ron at Kirkland. I also pray regularly that he will be released someday. He has a lot to offer society, and I know he will continue to be a faithful follower of Christ.

### A Glove and a Feathered Earring

Kirkland Correctional in Columbia was also the site of an amazing experience Ron Kuntz had with another inmate.

After a Friday evening program, three Christian inmates approached Ron and asked him to pray with them for an inmate they had been trying to reach. Glad to help, Ron encouraged them to grab hands and circle up for a moment of prayer. But when Ron reached for the hand of the inmate next to him, suddenly a hand with a glove on it grabbed Ron's. Turning to see who the gloved hand belonged to, Ron saw an inmate wearing a bandanna around his head and an earring. He had joined the circle and started to pray aloud in spite of another inmate's taunting. At the conclusion of the prayer time, the gloved inmate was still there. Ron introduced himself and learned the inmate's name was Doyle.

"Are you a Christian, Doyle?" Ron asked.

"No!" the inmate responded abruptly.

That puzzled Ron because many times even professing Christians won't pray aloud, yet this man who denied knowing the Lord was eager to lead the group in prayer. Ron visited with Doyle the remaining few minutes before the Glass team left the yard to return to their hotel, but there was no real favorable response from him.

Ron's schedule on Saturday took him to death row at Broad River, which is located next to Kirkland. He got so busy and involved visiting with Pee Wee Gaskin (more about that visit in the death row chapter) that he never made it back to Kirkland that day. But at the Saturday night banquet, a counselor who had been assigned to Kirkland, approached Ron and placed a pair of gloves on the table.

"These gloves look familiar," Ron said. "Where did they come from?"

"They belonged to an inmate," the counselor told him.

"Was his name Doyle?"

"Yes," the counselor answered, "and, Ron, Doyle was going to kill another inmate Saturday morning. He had a knife planted somewhere in the compound and was wearing the gloves so he wouldn't mess up his hands. And, by the way, Ron, how did you know?"

Doyle had apparently thought about the things Ron had discussed with him on Friday evening and scratched the murder plan. The next day the counselor affirmed Ron's conversation and Doyle made a decision for Christ. Doyle took the gloves off, gave them to the counselor, and asked him to give the gloves to Ron and tell him what had happened.

On Sunday morning Ron attended the chapel program at Kirkland and spotted Doyle in the crowd. Ron asked him if what the counselor had told him was true, and Doyle confirmed that he had indeed trusted Christ. After the service as Ron was preparing to leave, Doyle came up to him to say good-bye. Then he took off a feathered earring he was wearing, handed it to Ron, and said, "I don't need this garbage anymore either!"

I remember Ron returning to the hotel that morning as I was packing to go to the airport. He showed me the earring and the gloves. We thanked the Lord for Doyle's conversion, and also that another inmate was still alive because of the sudden change in Doyle's life as a result of our visit.

## Powerlifting Challenge at Stateville

Powerlifter Paul Wrenn has provided some wonderful memories for Ron and me through his programs. On a large weekend in the Joliet, Illinois area, I was the coordinator at Stateville, a rough maximum security facility which also houses the Illinois death chamber. Paul was scheduled for the Saturday night program and, after visiting with several inmates on Friday at the weight pile, I could tell it was going to be a humdinger.

Part of Paul's program is to allow any inmate to challenge him in the squat lift, and there's always one inmate who takes on the challenge to compete against a world champion. Some of these contests have been very exciting and have really brought the inmates and our team together as they enjoy cheering for the contestants.

However, instead of one challenger at Stateville, on this particular weekend there were three extremely talented lifters. All were serving natural life sentences, which means they will never leave prison. This was their chance to be involved in world-class competition with Paul. An opportunity like this doesn't come very often, and they were primed and ready, having worked out rigorously to peak for the match.

On Friday I met each of these men. They were all very courteous and polite, and they thanked me for coordinating the Weekend of Champions and making the necessary arrangements for the contest. They had lined up some other lifters to spot and had talked the recreation director into having the competition in a large concrete area, which was surrounded by steep, grassy hills. This formed an amphitheater-type setting so inmates could sit around the concrete and see the event. One of the only drawbacks to the whole scenario was the temperature. Unfortunately, the weather had been very hot, and the mercury was expected to soar close to one hundred degrees that day.

On Friday night I advised Paul to be sure to eat his Wheaties Saturday morning because there were three world-class powerlifters at Stateville who were hungry and excited because this was their one chance to beat a world champion. The competitor that he is, Paul just grinned and thanked me for the warning. Paul thrives on a good competition, and he and I were both aware that contests like these draw huge crowds, which gives Paul a chance to share his faith with a lot of inmates. Paul is one of the best at challenging inmates to consider faith in Christ through his short, but very effective message.

Saturday was a fantastic day at Stateville. The early afternoon program featured Mike Singletary, the all-pro linebacker from the Chicago Bears. A huge crowd turned out to hear him, and it gave me a great opportunity to announce our evening program, featuring three of their own challenging Paul Wrenn in a powerlifting extravaganza. I assured them there would be plenty of room for everyone and asked them to bring a friend because this would be something to see. Of course, the inmates all knew the challengers and their abilities, so they were especially looking forward to cheering them on, well aware all three of these men would give Paul a run for his money.

Even though it was still almost one hundred degrees for the 6:30 P.M. program, the area was filling up fast with inmates. Some had skipped their evening meal to reserve a good seat. Our counselors were just as excited as the inmates and were also arriving early. This contest was becoming the biggest event Stateville had ever seen. I visited briefly with some of the officers about potential security problems with this large crowd, but we unanimously agreed that the program would be so exciting, there wouldn't be any problems. Everyone had gathered for one reason—to watch some great powerlifters compete.

I greeted Paul at the front gate around 5:45 P.M. and told him about the huge crowd and the excitement in the institution. Unfortunately, in his afternoon program, Paul had encountered another tough lifter and was pushed pretty hard to beat him. Having lifted weights myself through my athletic career, I knew the physical strain lifting can impose on a person's body and that Paul was already a bit worn out. However, this veteran of the powerlifting circuit had been down this road before and, although tired, he was anxious for a great competition like this. When we worked our way through the huge crowd that had gathered and listened to the applause upon our arrival, Paul got a dose of fresh enthusiasm. This was going to be fantastic!

By now the area was filled with close to a thousand inmates, which was remarkable since the entire population in Stateville at the time was about two thousand. I introduced Paul to the three challengers, and they were humble and honored to meet him. As I watched them smile and sensed their joy, all I could think of was that these men would never leave prison, and how incredibly special this was for them. As the song says, this was their "one shining moment."

222 / DOIN' TIME

Paul asked his competitors if it would be all right to just warm up with about six hundred pounds, and each of the three inmates very nonchalantly agreed that would be fine with them.

At this point, Paul looked at me and said, "I'm in trouble." Normally, he wins most prison competitions by lifting six hundred pounds. And then after watching each of these men handle six hundred pounds with ease, Paul knew for sure he'd really have to perform to win.

As the competitors continued to add weight to the bar, the crowd showed their appreciation for each lifter, and for each successful lift. As they approached eight hundred pounds, I looked around and saw faces of inmates and counselors beaming with enthusiasm and excitement. For just a moment I think everyone forgot we were on a prison yard in one of the toughest prisons in America. Everyone's focus was on these fantastic athletes and the beautiful spirit of competition and display of sportsmanship. Never mind that it was hot and we were in prison. Madison Square Garden will never come close to matching the excitement in Stateville's yard on this day. It was electric!

Probably the best part of this whole story is how the competition ended. Believe it or not, Paul and each of the inmates successfully squatted a little over eight hundred pounds, and the institution ran out of weights. There wasn't any way to go heavier, nor did time permit a longer contest. To be honest, I think each of the inmates was relieved, and I know Paul was. He was worn out; it isn't very often he has to squat over eight hundred pounds to win a competition in prison. I think everyone was satisfied. All four men had put on a brilliant exhibition of lifting in front of an enthusiastic, appreciative crowd.

I discovered later that for two of the three inmates, the final lift was a personal best for them, and they were justifiably proud of their accomplishments. In lives filled with heartache, for just a moment these three men tasted success and became heroes to their peers. As I watched them beam with pride, I choked up. I was amazed at what had just happened. These three men were all smaller than Paul, and one, in particular, weighed only about two hundred pounds. For his weight category, he would have qualified as a world-class lifter.

But instead of competing at the Olympics or other major sporting events, they simply lifted to kill time and could only revel in their own personal achievement. Unfortunately, competing against Paul in the prison was as good as it would ever get for them. Their skills would never be recognized by the rest of the sports world. That made me sad and, although I wished these men could have been released and given the opportunity to compete, I also realized they had committed crimes that required prison time. This is something that will always bother me—so much talent and ability, so much to offer to society, and it will all go to waste because of poor choices resulting in incarceration.

After the competition, Paul delivered one of the most powerful messages I've ever heard him give, and the inmates hung on every word. He had definitely earned their respect and admiration. Many responded to the invitation that evening, and our counselors were very busy following up on each decision.

It was a memorable evening—the Glass ministry at its very best. The athletic celebrity and competition got the inmates' attention and provided a platform to share the Gospel. There's no way a thousand inmates would have come out in that heat to attend a church service, but this approach allowed us to reach them and share a message that could give them the hope they were all looking for.

### Cell Too Small for Paul

An unusual experience I shared with Paul Wrenn occurred at an old building in Central Prison in Columbia, South Carolina. Although most of the facility was no longer in use, there was one old cell block that still housed inmates. I was told that the cells were built in 1867 and that they were the oldest operational cells in the United States. The doors were made of the old, wide metal bars, and the cells were very small. I entered one, and it's the only time I've ever been claustrophobic in a prison cell. I asked Ron to stop by, thinking he would enjoy taking pictures of this historic facility. He came out with Paul Wrenn prior to Paul's program, so I took them for a quick tour. I encouraged Paul to step inside to see how old and small the cells were. It was a great idea, but it didn't work. Paul couldn't fit through the door! He peeked inside, but never did get inside the cell.

### A Painful Punch

One of the highlights of Paul Wrenn's program is letting an inmate punch him in the stomach as hard as he can. The minute he mentions that he's looking for a volunteer who throws a pretty good punch, it's funny how many inmates all of a sudden believe they are the toughest dudes in the institution. Half the fun of this part of the program is watching the inmates' pecking order in progress to determine who will represent them on the platform.

I've watched a lot of inmates hit Paul over the years, and some have really pounded him pretty good, but the punch I'll never forget occurred in a facility near Montgomery, Alabama. This poor inmate got so wound up by the crowd cheering him on that he reared back and put everything he had into it. And when his fist hit Paul's flexed stomach muscles, I could hear bones crack. The inmate pulled back and grabbed his hand, grimacing in pain. I knew he had hurt himself and, sure enough, the next day he was wearing a cast. I'm surprised this hasn't happened more often, as hitting Paul in the stomach is not much different than hitting a brick wall. He is as solid as granite!

## X-Ray Reveals Gun in Surprising Place

One of the most amazing things I've ever seen in a prison was an unusual photograph hanging on the wall of the Deputy Warden's office in Draper Correctional Institution just outside Montgomery, Alabama. I saw it on my Thursday morning check-out visit and was really glad Ron was on this weekend to capture a photo for me. The photograph I'm referring to is an X-ray taken of an inmate who had inserted a loaded gun up his rectum and smuggled it inside a prison. There was also a handcuff key attached to the gun handle.

I was told that another inmate had squealed on this guy, and after repeatedly requesting an officer to X-ray the inmate, the institution finally gave in and, sure enough, discovered he was right. After the X-ray detected the weapon, the inmate was taken to a hospital where doctors surgically removed the gun. I'm sure that inmate had a little more time attached to his sentence. I never found out whether the inmate had placed the gun there himself or had help. Either way, just the thought of it sends chills up my spine. The story and picture speak volumes about how desperate some men are to escape from prison.

## Ball and Chain, Weapons Display

Ron took two other very unusual pictures in the Draper facility. One was of me wearing an old ball and chain apparatus. I remember lifting the ball and it was heavy. I certainly wouldn't want to swim laps wearing it, and it definitely served its purpose years ago in keeping an inmate from running away.

The other photo was of a display case holding a variety of weapons that were made in the prison and confiscated by officers over the years. This case was actually given as a gift to a new warden who had just assumed the job at Draper. The ingenuity of inmates to form weapons out of unusual odds and ends has always fascinated me. Seeing this weapons display served not only as a reminder of the dangerous environment in which we work, but also of the protection the Lord always provides.

## AIDS and Inmates

The AIDS epidemic sweeping the world today has certainly had an impact on the prison system as well. It has also created new problems for correctional officials as well as inmates. Many men and women involved in lifestyles that placed them at high risk to contract the disease have entered prison with the AIDS virus. Others aren't aware they've contracted AIDS until they are already incarcerated. Unfortunately, laws haven't mandated that everyone entering prison to serve a sentence automatically be tested for AIDS, so it's impossible to actually know who has or doesn't have the disease. This, of course, presents a tremendous problem for security officers, as they are often involved in breaking up fights, etc. where there is bloodshed. Battling the unknown, they tend to combat the problem by assuming every inmate could have AIDS and taking every necessary precaution to protect themselves.

Some states try to segregate all of the infected inmates from the rest of the population. This is helpful for two reasons. First, it protects the other inmates, and second, it allows an institution to place well-equipped staff with these particular offenders. They can also keep all the medications and supplies necessary to combat the disease in one location.

I've worked in many AIDS wards, and it is a unique aspect of ministry. Quite often there are certain counselors who are well suited for AIDS units as they have been specifically trained to minister to an AIDS patient, or they have a special burden to help because they've lost a family member or close friend to the disease. It isn't difficult to swing the conversation over to spiritual issues; these inmates are well aware that death is often right around the corner, and they must consider the eternal consequences. Most are grateful for our visits and many do invite Christ into their lives. He brings hope to an otherwise hopeless situation.

## An AIDS Patient Ministers to Me

Perhaps my most memorable experience with an AIDS-infected inmate was in Central Prison in Raleigh, North Carolina. Dick Hanley, the program director, had asked me to spend some time in the hospital at Central. These patients were unable to attend any of our programs, but I had the privilege of doing a little magic for them, going from room to room and bed to bed. I always enjoy working in prison hospitals because the inmates are especially grateful that someone takes the time to visit with them.

After working the entire hospital area and just before I was ready to leave, a nurse stopped Dick and me and asked a special favor. She told me about an AIDS patient in a quarantined room who was curious to know who I was and about all the activity going on in the hospital. She explained to him that I was a magician at Central for the Bill Glass Weekend of Champions and had been doing card tricks for the other patients. He told the nurse he loved card tricks and begged her to ask me if I would do a couple for him. When she asked me, I told the nurse I'd be delighted and asked her to take me to the inmate.

As we walked down the hall, she informed me that this inmate probably wouldn't live much longer. She assured me that I was perfectly safe in going into his room and thanked me again for my willingness to share with him. "Rick, this guy's pretty special," she said, "and I think you'll be glad you took the time to meet him."

I wasn't prepared at all for the sight before me in that room. Lying on the bed was a man so withered away that he looked like a skeleton with a little bit of wrinkled skin attached to bones. He was obviously in the latter stages of his illness, but despite his condition he was wearing a smile as big as the state of North Carolina. He thanked me repeatedly for stopping by to see him and asked me to do a card trick for him. I told him I saved my best one just for him.

The man was lying flat on his back in bed, so I asked if he was able to sit up in order to see the cards on the nightstand next to his bed. He told me he couldn't, but that if the nurse and I would help him, he could roll over on his side to watch. We carefully rolled him over, and I realized that without our help, he wouldn't have been able to move.

With his head buried in his pillow and now near the edge of the bed, he could at least see the table on which I was laying my cards. My concentration was tested as it was difficult to overlook the severity and grotesqueness of his condition and just entertain. His genuine joy helped me, though, and as I did a couple of tricks, he beamed in amazement. This man was truly appreciative of this little personal show, and I was sorry I had to go. By now I was enjoying every minute of our time together. Knowing I needed to be at the front gate soon to greet the platform guests for our evening program, I did one last trick, and then visited briefly with the patient. I asked him if he was a Christian, and his entire face lit up.

"Oh, yes," he said, "I trusted Christ while in prison, and even before I contracted AIDS. The Lord has been my source of strength through my time in prison, and especially as this illness has slowly taken my life away."

As this man spoke to me of his faith, I was moved to tears. The sincerity of his convictions and the strength the Lord gave him as he looked directly into the face of death overwhelmed me.

"Rick," he said, "I can feel His presence in this room. He is coming to take me home soon to a place where I will never be sick again. I'll be free from the pains of life. The work you are doing in prison ministry, Rick, is important. Were it not for people like you who come to prisons and share Christ with inmates, I would never have been able to handle this situation with the hope and strength that I have now. Thank you from the bottom of my heart for sharing a little of your time and talents with me. It meant so much, and I'm so grateful. It may not have seemed like much to you, but it was very meaningful to me. I've seen nothing but the four gray walls of this room for so long that this was an unexpected pleasure. God bless you, Rick. Keep up the good work you are doing."

By now tears were streaming down my face. My heart was so moved by this dying man's strong faith and grateful spirit. I came to minister to him; instead, he ministered to me.

"Rick, would you pray for me before you go?"

"I'd be glad to." I grabbed his trembling hands and knelt down beside his bed and prayed for him.

As I prayed, he whispered, "Thank you, Jesus. Thank you, Jesus. Yes, Lord, I'm ready to come home. Thank you, Jesus."

And as I said, "Amen," he squeezed my hands and suddenly seemed to gain a fresh, new strength.

He thanked me again, smiled, and said, "Don't worry about me. I'm in good hands."

As Dick and I left the hospital, it took me a while to gain my composure. This experience touched me. The nurse was right–this was a special man. I told Dick I wanted to be sure and go back Sunday morning to see him and visit a little longer before the conclusion of our weekend. Unfortunately, a second visit wasn't meant to be. Less than two hours later, the nurse called Dick to let him know the inmate had died. Other than the medical team, we were the last people to visit with him before he passed away.

I talked to the nurse the next morning and asked her why his family wasn't there, knowing he was close to death.

"Rick, he had no one," she said. "He never had any visitors, and what little family ties he had were gone once they discovered he had AIDS. I only wish they could have seen the change in his life since he became a Christian. He was full of the love of Christ, and it radiated from him. I will miss taking care of him. He always encouraged me."

I will never forget this man and am thankful I met him before he died. He reminded me that I need not fear death knowing Christ as my Lord and Savior. I thought of the words to that song, "Because He lives, I can face tomorrow." And I realized again the importance of this prison work. As difficult and challenging as it gets, I must "press on" and stay diligent to the task of sharing the Gospel in prisons as long as the Lord continues to provide the opportunity.

### Inmates and Divorce

I helped an inmate with another kind of pain at the Federal Medical Facility in Springfield, Missouri. This huge prison is like a maze, with tunnels going everywhere. It would be easy to get lost.

I was assigned to a very unusual part of the facility that housed four types of inmates. One wing was for suicidal inmates. A large control room with extensive surveillance equipment allowed officers to use video cameras to view the activity in each cell every eight seconds. Most of the inmates wore only a pair of boxer shorts and, other than a sink and toilet, all that was in the cell was a bare mattress with no pillow or sheets.

Another area housed inmates with AIDS, and a third wing was for psychotic inmates. Working with psychotic patients was one of the most challenging situations I've ever encountered in all my years of working in prisons. Because these men were heavily sedated, their behavior was unpredictable, which made it difficult to carry on a normal visit with them. I can recall the doctors and nurses dispensing medication and then having the inmates stick out their tongues so they could make sure the pills had been swallowed. This was an eerie place to work, and even a bit scary.

The last area of this wing of the prison was used for testing inmates to determine if they were "competent" or "incompetent" to stand trial. In the past, this issue was resolved through a long court procedure, but the system has changed so that when a trial starts, the matter of competency is already determined. The trial then proceeds under the evaluation and ruling the prison provides. As I met various inmates, it seemed that the professionals were often wasting their time with tests because from my layman's perspective, some inmates appeared either completely competent or totally incompetent within the first few minutes I was with them. But apparently there are enough signals that evidence the need for testing, so the inmates live in this area of the prison until their tests are completed . It was in this area that I had an interesting encounter with a hurting man.

I had just completed a visit with an inmate and was walking down one of the long hallways to return to the break room for a cold drink. As I passed the open door of a cell, I heard someone crying. Peeking in, I saw a large man sitting on the bed, his face buried in his hands.

"Sir, is there anything I can do to help you?" I asked. And, looking up at me and fighting back the tears, he said, "Yes, I need someone to talk to. Are you here with that Bill Glass group?"

I told him I was and sat down in a chair next to his bunk. As he slowly gained his composure, I noticed he was clutching something in his hands. He explained that minutes before I had walked by his cell, he had received his mail and had opened an envelope from his wife's attorney. She had filed for divorce. These papers were clutched in his left hand, but there was something in his right hand as well.

"This I can handle," he said as he held up the divorce papers. Then lifting his right hand, he said, "But this I can't. It's killing me." And as he opened his clenched fist, I saw a wallet-sized picture of a young boy. "I'm not sure I can handle not being with my son, or maybe even losing him. He means everything to me."

"Were you expecting this," I asked, "or did it catch you right between the eyes?"

"Unfortunately," he replied, "it's totally unexpected. I never dreamed she'd want a divorce. The thought of possibly never being able to see my little boy again may ruin me. How in the world am I ever going to make it through this?"

I felt helpless in trying to offer some hope and encouragement to this man. He was beginning a very common battle when a spouse is sent to prison. It becomes very difficult for the partner to hang on, especially if there is a lengthy sentence involved, and divorce in these scenarios is the usual result. This husband was staring into the unknown as far as a possible prison sentence. Worrying about his case, etc., was tough enough without adding this family dilemma to his problems.

What are the odds of my being there at the exact time he opened his mail? I'm convinced the Lord put me there because this man desperately needed a shoulder to cry on and a listening ear. He was able to share his pain with me. I told him that although I had never experienced this specific problem, when I encountered difficult times, I relied on my faith and the assurance that God was in total control of the situation. I didn't have much time to assess his spiritual condition, but he welcomed the opportunity for someone to pray for him. As I finished praying with this hurting man, an officer arrived at the cell to tell me it was time to vacate the blocks, and to escort me out. I gave the inmate a big hug and left some literature for him to read, and then followed the officer to the exit.

I will never forget the face of this man as he held the picture of his son and wept. Unfortunately, this same situation occurs daily in prisons all over the world. A prison sentence is frequently followed by divorce, and I often counsel inmates who are wading through all the pain that accompanies this problem. The severity of loneliness, despair, anger, and confusion seems to be multiplied when inmates face divorce while in prison. Many Bill Glass counselors have been a source of strength and encouragement to inmates struggling with marital and family problems that stem from their incarceration.

### Riot at Enfield

Obviously, not every situation Ron and I experience in prison has a happy ending. Often the outcome is tragic, as was the case when Ron was in Connecticut at the Enfield facility near Hartford. Prior to a Saturday afternoon program, an inmate named Pablo approached Ron and asked him to take a picture of Pablo's "family." However, he didn't mean his wife and kids; he meant his gang—a small group of Spanish inmates who were standing a few yards away. A little reluctant, Ron told Pablo that Paul Wrenn, a powerlifter, was going to be doing his program soon and that he always asks for volunteers, so Ron suggested that Pablo volunteer his help, and then Ron would get a snapshot. Disgusted, Pablo walked away.

At the conclusion of Paul's program, Pablo confronted Ron again. "Take a picture of my family now," he insisted.

Still a bit uneasy, Ron replied, "You'll have to wait a while because right now I've got to get some pictures of our counselors sharing with the inmates."

Ron didn't realize it at the time but later learned that Pablo had been giving the officers problems ever since he had been incarcerated. Had Ron known that, he probably would have been a little less abrupt with him.

As Ron finished shooting pictures of the counselors, he finally surrendered to Pablo's demands. He had Pablo and the seven other inmates sign a release form and then took their picture. Afterwards, Ron took the opportunity to share with them a little, but within a few minutes, Pablo, who seemed tense and uneasy, got up to leave. And, of course, as he left, so did the others.

"Where are you going?" Ron asked. "I did you a favor. The least you could do is have the courtesy to listen to me for a little while."

"I'm going to medical," Pablo snapped back.

"Why are you always running from me?" Ron questioned.

"I gotta go," Pablo just muttered. As Pablo and his family began to leave, Ron said, "You all don't have to go to medical," and with that, three of them decided to stay and visited with Ron until it was time for count and the evening meal.

After dinner, Ron noticed Pablo and his people sitting around a picnic bench near a miniature golf course located in the prison yard. Determined to try to reach Pablo, Ron headed right for the group and began sharing his faith. But, as usual, Pablo became restless and anxious to leave. This time, before he left, Ron asked him, "Pablo, if something should happen to you tonight, where would you spend eternity?"

And without any hesitation at all, Pablo replied, "Probably in hell," and then walked away. Later that evening Ron discovered why Pablo was so jumpy and tense throughout the afternoon.

The minute Ron and the counselors cleared security and left the facility, all hell broke loose and officers were racing everywhere. Something big was happening at Enfield.

Later at the hotel, we discovered rival gang members had gone to war in the yard, and the riot continued until late into the night, resulting in injuries to a number of men and the death of an inmate with the same last name as Pablo. Ron assumed it was his Pablo. Ron had spent all afternoon trying to reach him, but Pablo was restless and stubborn. We found out that Pablo and his "family" had been waiting all day for the Glass counselors to leave to attack a rival gang member. It was almost three o'clock in the morning before officers regained control of the institution.

After a restless night, Ron discovered the dead inmate was not Pablo. Rather, the victim was a rival gang member with the same last name who had been clubbed to death by one of the members of Pablo's "family" near the miniature golf course where Ron had shared earlier that day.

Ron pleaded with officials to let him visit the inmate allegedly responsible for the murder, but they wouldn't let him. The inmate was under tight security in a lockdown cell at Somers Correctional, a prison next to Enfield.

Oddly enough, the Connecticut Highway Patrol wanted a copy of the picture Ron took of Pablo's "family" because they were fairly certain one or more of the individuals in the picture were responsible for the murder. The highway patrol was involved because prison gang fights seem to transcend prison walls and spill over onto the streets to the same gangs on the outside.

Ron was discouraged that he wasn't able to convince these inmates to consider the Christian faith. He was also a little shaken that he had been so close to the murder site just before the gangs went to war.

This particular riot is the one referred to in the chapter about correctional officers. I was the coordinator at Somers when the fight broke out, and officials rushed officers from Somers over to Enfield to assist with the incident.

### "Wouldn't That Mess up the Count!"

In Lexington, Oklahoma, while he was eating breakfast at the hotel before going to the prison, an interesting thought occurred to Ron. He said, "Wouldn't it be great if the Lord would choose this day for His return while we are in the prison yard? All the inmates and counselors who have trusted Christ would suddenly be taken away."

Jack Murphy, who was eating with the group, laughed and replied, "Yeah, wouldn't that mess up the count!"

### Spider Man

In 1975 Ron met an interesting character who called himself Spider Man. Spider Man was incarcerated at Soledad in California. When Ron entered the gym to listen to Bill Glass speak, a tall, lanky, bearded inmate wearing a visor and dark sunglasses slithered up near Ron and stared at him. He nearly scared Ron half to death.

"What are you doin' here?" Spider Man asked.

Ron gave him a funny look and answered, "I'm taking pictures for the Bill Glass weekend."

"That's cool, man," the inmate replied. "Where you from?"

"Cleveland, Ohio."

"That's cool, too."

Later, after Glass had concluded his message and was introducing some of the counselors, he spotted Ron. "And we have Ron Kuntz from Cleveland, Ohio, one of the greatest photographers in the world today."

With that, Spider Man jumped to his feet and started clapping and shouting, "Yeah, Ron!"

Needless to say, this surprised Ron. At this point I think Ron was relieved the program was over and he had to leave because he wasn't sure if Spider Man was playing with a full deck.

Saturday evening Ron was back in Soledad. Three Chinese hit men prepared a special meal for Ron and invited him back to their cells. Ron had heard that the conditions at Soledad were bad, but he was surprised to see how nice their cell block and cells were. Many were decorated, and each inmate had a key to his own cell. One of the Chinese inmates even had a large aquarium and framed photos of his family. As the other inmates discovered Ron was there, they also invited him into their cells to take pictures of their artwork, paintings, crafts, and woodwork.

Just as Ron began visiting cells on the second tier, however, he felt a tap on his shoulder and turned quickly, only to be confronted again by Spider Man, who said, "I'm the boss of this tier, and nothin's gonna happen to you."

Well, up until that point, Ron really hadn't been too fearful of anything, but suddenly Spider Man's remark made him wonder if he should be afraid. It was at this moment Ron also realized he was the only Bill Glass team member in this block as all of the counselors had left to attend a program, and he thought, "What have I gotten myself into?"

Not to worry, however, as Spider Man liked Ron and began to serve as Ron's personal escort and guide throughout the entire tier, proudly introducing him to all the other inmates and bragging that Ron was the greatest photographer in the world. When they arrived at Spider Man's cell, Ron was impressed with all his motorcycle paraphernalia. Ron enjoyed taking photos of this unique cell filled with pictures of bikes and little models of motorcycles. As they visited about motorcycles, Spider Man introduced Ron to one of his buddies who had a big Harley-Davidson tattoo on his back. Ron got a great picture showing both of the inmates and their tattoos. The inmate who initially scared Ron ended up being a very interesting acquaintance, and provided Ron with some unforgettable moments and pictures in Soledad.

### "Not That Far Yet"

Another biker, who was an "ex-offender turned counselor" on one of our West Coast weekends, told Ron a great story that Ron enjoys sharing. This particular individual's name was Neal Wright. While he was incarcerated, Neal was still heavily involved with drugs and gang activity. He was a rugged inmate and not a real nice guy to be around. However, through prison ministry volunteers, he came to know the Lord and a rival gang member found out about his recent conversion.

Eager to see how legitimate Neal's profession of faith was, this gang member began to taunt Neal about being a sissy Christian and did everything possible to "get his goat," including pushing him around a little bit. Unfortunately, he carried it a bit too far, and suddenly, without warning, Neal hauled off and smacked the guy, knocking him to the ground.

The rival gang member, obviously shaken up, stared at Neal and said, "I thought you were a Christian. The Bible says you're supposed to turn the other cheek!"

Neal looked down at him with a sly smile and replied, "I haven't gotten that far in the Bible yet."

### The Road to Emmaus

Durham Stokes was a death row inmate whom Ron never met, but he left a lasting impression on Ron. A number of years ago, Ron received a Christmas card from Durham. He had made a commitment to Christ on death row. A short time later, his sentence was commuted to life and he entered the main population. It was there that Durham met an inmate by the name of David Wells, whom Ron had led to the Lord in 1974. David had given Durham Ron's address and told Durham all about Ron, his work, and all that Ron had done for David. Durham decided to write Ron, and they began corresponding. They got to know each other pretty well through the mail, despite not ever meeting.

One day Ron received a large package in the mail from Durham; it was a beautiful picture he had painted. Oddly enough, it happened to be a picture that portrayed one of Ron's favorite portions of Scripture–Luke 24:13-35, which tells the story of two men who left Jerusalem for Emmaus after Christ was crucified. The painting was of Christ breaking the loaf when he met these two individuals on the road. The picture also showed Christ with a nail-scarred hand and the two men looking up into the eyes of Jesus. Ron was touched by the painting and thought it was amazing that, although they had never met, Durham had chosen to paint a picture with a theme that was very precious and meaningful to Ron.

Over the years, Ron continued his correspondence with Durham. One day, however, one of the post cards Ron had sent to Durham was returned with a stamp across the back in big, red letters: DECEASED. Although these two men never met one another, Ron played an important role in encouraging Durham Stokes in his faith throughout the last years of his incarceration.

### Josh's Clown

Another painting Ron received from a Texas inmate is hanging in the bedroom of Joshua Kuntz, Ron's son. Ron talks about Josh quite often in the prisons and apparently mentioned to an inmate how much Josh loves clowns. It wasn't long after this visit that a beautiful painting of a clown arrived for Josh. It said, "Little brother, Jesus loves you and I do, too," and it was signed by the inmate.

### Aussie Hat

In 1976, while covering the Olympic Games in Montreal, Ron was given an Aussie hat by a photographer who lives in Sidney, Australia. Ron really loved the hat, and it became his "signature piece" whenever he covered an event. Many of our prison counselors hardly recognize Ron without his hat, and inmates have come to know Ron as "the photographer with the funny hat."

In addition to wearing it while covering major sporting events around the world, Ron always wears his hat on prison weekends. He tells inmates that if they're watching a big sporting event on television, to look for his hat because he will be under it. Ron has received letters from inmates who have spotted the hat and have seen him shooting pictures on TV. They are proud that they know someone who is associated with so many sports celebrities and that they have personally met Ron. The hat has truly become a Ron Kuntz trademark, and if Ron goes into prisons without it, inmates always ask, "Where's your hat?"

## Boring Speaker Leads to Attempted Escape

Ron loves to take pictures but also enjoys the opportunity to speak to inmates. Occasionally the platform guest schedule works out in such a way that he is given that chance. One of his most memorable speeches occurred in Raleigh, North Carolina at the Triangle Unit. While Ron was speaking, two inmates tried to escape. This unit was a minimum security facility, and the two tried to climb over a fence near the visitor area. Ron saw it all from the platform. He watched the inmates running around, looking for an opening to break out.

After Ron left the unit, the inmates were eventually caught. Ron quipped, "I've had people fall asleep while I was speaking, but this is the first time anyone has risked their life just to avoid hearing me speak!" In all honesty, Ron is an excellent speaker and inmates love hearing about his experiences shooting pictures at major events around the world.

## Nameless Headstones

Ron had a sad experience on a prison weekend at San Quentin when he was escorted to an area just outside the prison called Boot Hill—a cemetery reserved for San Quentin inmates whose bodies are unclaimed by anyone on the outside. Consequently, the cheap headstones on these graves have no names. They are identified simply by the inmate's prison system number, which is etched into the stone. Many of these graves of forgotten men overlook the San Quentin facility. Seeing this cemetery reminded Ron just how important our work is. Both of us have talked to inmates who said we were the only people from the outside with whom they have ever had any contact. Chaplain Earl Smith at San Quentin and other chaplains have expressed how difficult it is to officiate at the funeral of an inmate who will only be remembered by his number.

## "I Was Robbed!"

While Ron was talking with some young inmates in a prison dorm in Texas, one was reading a letter he received from his buddy who had just been released from prison. After reading the letter, he started laughing so hard that he was literally rolling on the floor. His curious friend asked to read the letter, and when he finished it, he started laughing hysterically too. When Ron asked what was so funny, one of them filled him in. Their ex-roommate had been released from the Walls Unit in Huntsville, Texas and had been issued the standard $200 stipend given to inmates upon their release. However, shortly after boarding a bus, he was robbed.

## ". . . The Pay Was Much Better Up North"

An inmate approached Ron at the Kansas State Penitentiary and asked, "Do you remember me?" Ron replied, "No. Why do you ask?" The inmate explained that he met Ron up at the Fox Lake Unit in Wisconsin years before when Ron was on a Glass weekend. He confessed that after he was released in Wisconsin, he got back into trouble down in Kansas and wound up serving another sentence in the Kansas State Pen. Ron asked if he liked Kansas better than Wisconsin, and the inmate replied, "It's not bad here, but the pay was much better up north."

## Cowboy's Conversion

While shooting pictures of counselors in an Alabama prison, Ron was approached by a gray-haired, older gentleman who was extremely curious about the Weekend of Champions. He was especially intrigued by the picture of Harold Thompson on the Weekend of Champions poster. He asked Ron if he knew Harold.

"Yeah, real well," Ron replied. "As a matter of fact, Harold will be speaking here tomorrow. Why? Do you know Harold?"

The inmate shrugged and laughed, "Big Tommy? Man, he and I were together on the road years ago before we both got locked up. I could tell you some unbelievable stories about Big Tom and me."

Then Earl "Cowboy" Taylor introduced himself to Ron, and they enjoyed visiting about Cowboy's life and also his relationship with Harold.

Later that night back at the hotel, Ron told Harold all about Cowboy, and learned that Harold had been praying for many years that he would someday trust Christ. Harold and Ron prayed that when Harold spoke there the next day, the message would penetrate

Cowboy's heart. And sure enough, after Harold's program and message, Cowboy gave his life to Christ. The change in his life was very dramatic and sincere.

As a matter of fact, when Cowboy met Morris Thigpen, the Alabama Commissioner of Prisons who was helping us that weekend, Cowboy said to him, "You know, Commissioner, there are some things I need to tell you that could add more time to my sentence, but I need to confess them to you. I did some horrible things against you, and I know they were wrong. I'd like to ask your forgiveness and want you to know that because of this Weekend of Champions I'm a changed man. Will you forgive me?"

And, recovering from the shock, Morris Thigpen responded, "Yes, Cowboy, I forgive you."

After Cowboy's conversion experience, there were a number of wonderful things that occurred in his life. He had a brother he hadn't seen in many years. The last he'd heard from him, he'd been sent to Vietnam, and Cowboy was certain he'd been killed over there. Then one day, Cowboy was in the yard and an officer called him over to tell him he had a phone call. He picked up the receiver and couldn't believe it–it was his brother! This really encouraged Cowboy in his faith as he had been praying regularly that the Lord would help him locate his brother.

That experience was just the turning point of a number of other amazing things that happened. And, with each one, Cowboy grew stronger in his faith. As a result of his brother's phone call, Cowboy discovered he had other relatives in New Orleans whom he hadn't seen for years. His brother and sister-in-law were living in California, so he didn't get many visits from them, but the relatives in New Orleans began to visit him regularly. Cowboy firmly believes the Lord opened these doors and many others once he gave Him a chance to guide and direct his life.

In 1995 Ron received a Christmas card from Cowboy and learned that he was released from prison, got married, and was living and working in Alabama.

### "Where the Groceries Are"

Working on over 150 prison weekends, Ron has been asked time and time again, "Why are you here? What in the world do you guys get out of this?"

And Ron's answer is always the same: "Look around at everybody here who's dressed a little bit differently from you. These people have come from all over the United States, paying their own way, including travel, hotel, and meal expenses. They do it for one simple reason–their lives have been dramatically changed through a personal relationship with Jesus Christ, and they know that if you will follow Christ and let Him direct your life, you, too, will find the same joy, hope, purpose, and direction that they have found. Because Christ loved them unconditionally, they are able to love you, despite everything you've done, as bad as it was. They simply come to tell hungry men where the groceries are."

At the conclusion of many of our weekends, Ron hears the same comment: "We have a lot of groups coming into our institution, but you guys really care about us." Ron is certain that's one thing inmates do see on a Weekend of Champions–people who really care and have answers to help those who are incarcerated.

# CHAPTER 11

# CAN YOU KEEP
# A SECRET?

*R*on and I had two objectives in writing this book. The first was to take you inside the Bill Glass Prison Ministry and give you an in-depth look at exactly what a Weekend of Champions is all about. The second was to share through stories and pictures a few of the many incredible experiences we've had during our years of involvement with this ministry. At the risk of being redundant, we are sorry we couldn't write about every person who has been special to us, but we've recognized as many faithful friends as possible. There are so many who have contributed through the years, and each has been important to the overall success of this ministry. As I write this, my prayer is that the Lord will give Ron and me more opportunities to serve together on prison ministry weekends, and that we will make many new friends as God's people continue to get involved in this exciting outreach.

In closing, I'd like to share with you the same message Ron and I share with inmates in prison. It's been said, "Bars and steel do not a prison make." Perhaps you're locked up in your own prison–the prison of alcohol and drug abuse, poor relationships, sexual abuse, greed, fear, and the list goes on and on. I've met numerous inmates who will spend the rest of their lives in prison but are more free than a lot of individuals in society today. Why? Because they're free on the inside–in their hearts. The Scriptures tell us in John 8:32 that "You shall know the truth, and the truth shall make you free." True freedom comes from knowing Jesus Christ and living a life committed to His service.

Can you keep a secret? So can I. And as a magician who's sworn to secrecy, I'm often asked after an illusion, "How did you do that?" If I disclosed the secret, the fun and the mystery would be gone. However, the one secret I'm always glad to reveal is how to experience a rewarding life. Let me share with you, like I've done with thousands of inmates, how to take the mystery out of finding true happiness.

Growing up as an athlete competing under a variety of coaches in my career, I was impressed that each coach had his own philosophy for success, so as a rookie high school coach I was committed to developing one of my own. Consequently, I studied successful teams, past and present, and discovered the following ingredients common among champions:

1. **The players loved their coach, and the coach loved them.** The team believed in, respected, admired, and followed the coach, and the coach loved the players and was personally interested in their success.

2. **The players were committed to the coach's system.** They won because they faithfully executed every aspect of the coach's game plan—no questions asked.

3. **The players and coaches kept their eyes on the rewards, not on the obstacles.** They chose to make setbacks their allies, not their enemies. Obstacles became positive vehicles toward their goals.

4. **The players and coaches developed team unity, through an unselfish attitude.** They played to their highest potential—not for personal gain, but for overall team success. They became a closely knit family.

5. **Every team member was an ENcourager, not a DIScourager.** They developed a habit of building up one another through uplifting communication. They never dwelled upon the negative.

These same common ingredients visible among successful teams parallel the keys to unlocking the secrets of experiencing a rewarding life. I know this to be true because of an event that changed my life when I was sixteen.

1. **I met a loving coach.** We all need a coach to guide and direct our lives. In 1968 I committed my life to Jesus Christ. He became an example for me to follow and pattern my life after. He was a coach I respected, admired, believed in, and trusted because I knew He cared about my success (even more than I did!).

2. **I found His system breeds success.** As a new Christian I discovered that God's system for successful living is found in the Bible. I found the answers to the tough decisions of daily living and learned that by faithfully and obediently applying His truth, I would win at the game of life.

3. **I learned to keep my eyes on the reward.** No one is immune

to life's hurts. They are inevitable. The difference between winning and losing life's battles is often found in how we choose to handle them. The winning edge depends on our focus. When my wife and I lost our son several days after he was born, we experienced tremendous sorrow. We survived the struggle by focusing on God because we trusted Him to be completely in control of our lives. With the focus on Him, we inherit the reward—a peace and assurance that comes from knowing God loves us and is constantly at work for good even through life's most difficult moments.

4. **I discovered the joy of serving others.** Jesus said, "It is more blessed to give than to receive." Applying this principle in my life has provided a tremendous source of joy. One of the most accurate measures of success in life is found in how well we use our gifts and abilities to serve others. The happiest people I know are the prison counselors I've worked with because they are true servants. They love to serve, and they give in every way on the prison weekends.

5. **I learned the value of encouragement.** I meet many men and women behind bars who grew up in environments where they were never encouraged, and the results were devastating. They remind me that it becomes difficult to climb the ladder to success without encouragement along the way. Knowing the value of encouragement in my own life, I'm trying to develop a habit of putting others up—not down. Encouragement does make a positive difference!

Now that the secret's "out of the bag," you can see there's nothing magical about living a rewarding, fulfilling life. It starts by accepting Jesus Christ as your Lord and Savior and making Him the Master Coach of your life. This relationship then provides the power source you'll need for faithfully and obediently applying God's Word in your daily life, handling your hurts, developing a desire to serve, and becoming a source of encouragement to others.

This is the message we present to thousands of men and women in prisons across America through the Weekend of Champions program. When inmates accept this invitation, they are able to live this championship lifestyle—even while they're *doin' time.*